SMU Institute of International
Banking and Finance
Dallas, Texas

Centre for Commercial Law Studies,
University of London

Institute of International
Banking, Finance and
Development Law, London

Asian Institute of
International Financial Law,
University of Hong Kong

Consumer Protection in Financial Services

Edited by

Peter Cartwright

KLUWER LAW
INTERNATIONAL

THE HAGUE – LONDON – BOSTON

Published by
Kluwer Law International Ltd
Sterling House
66 Wilton Road
London SW1V 1DE
United Kingdom

Kluwer Law International incorporates the
publishing programmes of
Graham & Trotman Ltd,
Kluwer Law & Taxation Publishers
and Martinus Nijhoff Publishers

Sold and distributed
in the USA and Canada by
Kluwer Law International
675 Massachusetts Avenue
Cambridge MA 02139
USA

In all other countries sold and distributed by
Kluwer Law International
P.O. Box 322
3300 AH Dordrecht
The Netherlands

ISBN 90-411-9717-6
© Kluwer Law International 1999
First published 1999

British Library Cataloguing in Publication Data
A catalogue record for this book is available from the British Library

Typeset in Garamond 10/12pt by On Screen, West Hanney, Oxfordshire
Printed and bound in Great Britain by Antony Rowe Limited, Chippenham, Wiltshire.

FOREWORD

In the 1960s, consumer protection was concerned essentially with the purchase of consumer goods and services, together with the need to ensure that there were adequate safety standards and protection against misleading labelling and against contractual terms that exempted suppliers from liability for defects. Financial services were considered only in so far as credit might be required to facilitate a buying transaction, typically through a hire-purchase agreement.

While in general there was some reason to be cynical about governments setting up commissions and committees to review the existing law and come up with proposals for change, there is little doubt that the Molony Committee which reported in 1962 had considerable success in that its recommendations were implemented to a very high degree by successive governments in the late 1960s and 1970s.

Concern for the rights of ordinary people buying goods, including complex appliances, in an increasingly affluent society, began to extend to people buying services of all kinds, both physical services for repairs and maintenance, as well as insurance and other kinds of financial services. For the user of credit provision, which began to emerge in a much greater variety than hire-purchase, the Crowther Committee on Consumer Credit led quite rapidly to the formidably detailed Consumer Credit Act 1974, with its novel use of real-life examples, as to how the Act operates, set out in a Schedule.

However, consumers not only borrowed and obtained goods and services and houses on credit, they increasingly used financial services to save and to invest and formed significant short-term and long-term relationships with banks, building societies, the Stock Exchange, collective investment schemes such as unit trusts and a considerable variety of advisers, brokers and institutions. The growth of occupational and personal pensions schemes and the risk of misuse of pension funds (the Maxwell scandal) and mis-selling of pensions were startling features of the new prosperity. Molony and Crowther were followed by the review of banking law and practice by the Jack Committee and the remarkable one-man review of investor protection by Professor L. C. B. Gower, and later by the Goode Committee on pension law. The relative infrequency of the purchase of financial services, as distinct from many household goods, and the more obvious imbalance in knowledge between the trader and the buyer, emphasise the special importance of protection in this field.

This collection of essays is a valuable and timely one, covering a great many of the problems of consumer and investor protection in the provision of financial services and, given growing globalisation, it appropriately surveys European Union influences and looks at some of the examples and exemplars of such protection elsewhere in the world. In the UK we are about to move to a new culture under the aegis of the Financial Services Authority by way of the Financial Services and Marketing Bill.

There was something very unstable and temporary about the profusion of regulatory and self-regulatory bodies – the 'alphabet soup' of different regulators – set up under the Financial Services Act 1986. It would be folly to imagine that the new legislative structure will be set in stone. Certainly, it will need to be flexible and adaptable to the rapidly changing national and international scene. It will also need to make use of the whole area of consumer protection – comprehensible and comprehensive information, regulatory machinery with flexible powers using both the criminal and civil law, and access to redress for consumers that adopts best practice from developing schemes of mediation, conciliation, ombudsmen and arbitration. It will have to develop over time and the legislation must not be over-prescriptive. It is vital that the law is enabled to catch up with evolving business practice without too much of a gap in time.

Gordon Borrie

CONTENTS

Introduction

Consumer Protection in Financial Services: Putting the Law in Context

Peter Cartwright

PART I   THEMES AND TRENDS IN FINANCIAL SERVICES

Chapter One

The European Union, Financial Services, and the Consumer

Anna Mörner

Table of Contents

Chapter Two

The Ombudsmen and Consumer Protection

Philip Morris and Gavin Little

PART II   BANKING

Chapter Three

Bank Confidentiality and the Consumer in the United Kingdom

Andrew Campbell

Chapter Four

Unilateral Variation in Banking Contracts: An 'Unfair Term'?

Eva Lomnicka

Chapter Five

Deposit Guarantees and the Individual Bank Customer

Peter Cartwright

PART III   FINANCIAL SERVICES AND INVESTMENTS

Chapter Six

Financial Services Regulation: Can History Teach Us Anything?

Sharon Chin

Chapter Seven

Pensions and the Consumer: Lessons from Overseas

David O. Harris and Susan P. Jones

Chapter Eight

Some Consumer Problems Relating to the Sale of Long-Term Insurance

Richard J. Bragg

PART IV   INSURANCE

Chapter Nine

Insurance Law Reform for the Benefit of the Consumer: Some Lessons from Australia

John Birds

Chapter Ten

Consumer Protection in Insurance Contracts

Chris Willett and Norma Hird

PART V   CONSUMER CREDIT

Chapter Eleven

Seeking Social Justice for Poor Consumers in Credit Markets

Geraint Howells

Chapter Twelve

Racial and Gender Equality in Markets for Financial Services

Iain Ramsay and Toni Williams

SPONSORING ORGANISATIONS

Centre for Commercial Law Studies
The Centre was established in 1980 as a distinct department within the Faculty of Laws of Queen Mary and Westfield College, University of London. The primary objectives of the Centre are to promote the systematic study and research of national and international commercial law and its social and economic implications and to develop a body of knowledge, information and skills that can be placed at the service of government, public bodies, overseas institutions, the legal profession, industry and commerce.

SMU Institute of International Banking and Finance
Established within Southern Methodist University, Dallas, Texas in 1982, the Institute serves as an interdisciplinary forum for research, publications, conferences and research seminars in the international finance area, with input from SMU's Law School, Political Science and Economic Departments, and the Edwin L. Cox School of Business. The Institute conducts several major international conferences and is actively involved in economic law reform projects in relation to emerging economies. Finally, the Institute regularly produces books and other scholarly articles and papers.

Asian Institute of International Financial Law
An Institute of the University of Hong Kong Law Faculty, in cooperation with UHK's School of Business and Management and Department of Economics, that is committed to postgraduate programmes, research publications, conferences, short courses, and seminars in the international financial law area, with emphasis on the East Asian and Greater China Areas.

London Institute of International Banking, Finance and Development Law
The London Institute is a privately incorporated, educational institution. Among other related functions, the Institute assists the International Financial Tax Law Unit at the Centre for Commercial Law Studies at Queen Mary and Westfield College, University of London, in directing research seminars, professional conferences, executive training sessions, law reform and consulting projects, and major journals and book series. This legal think-tank is also responsible for conducting research and publishing articles and essays on an array of important legal issues concerning banking, finance and development.

EDITOR'S PREFACE

I have incurred many debts of gratitude in putting this book together. First of all, I would like to thank my research assistant, Yvonne Williams, for her outstanding work on the project. Yvonne's contribution to the book cannot be overstated. Without her skills, the task of producing the work would have been considerably more arduous. Second, I would like to thank various people who, while not contributing chapters to the book, have helped and encouraged in other ways. They include Ross Cranston, Marise Cremona, Stephen Edell, Cowan Ervine, Michael James, Alan Page, Deborah Parry, Udo Reifner and Steve Weatherill. A small number of the essays in this book began life as papers delivered at a conference I organised at Queen's College Cambridge on 'Financial Services and the Consumer'. The conference was organised on behalf of the Consumer Law Section of the Society of Public Teachers of Law, and I would like to thank Francis Rose and John Tiley for all their work in making the conference a success. I would also like to thank those at Kluwer Law International, in particular Selma Hoedt, Sarah King and Lukas Claerhout for their help with the book.

Finally, I would like to thank my wife, Sue Arrowsmith, for her love and support, and our daughter, Emma Rose, for being such a welcome diversion from work.

August 1998

Peter Cartwright

LIST OF CONTRIBUTORS

Editor (and Contributor)

Peter Cartwright is a lecturer in the School of Law, Nottingham University. He was previously a lecturer in law at the University of Wales, Aberystwyth. He has published widely on consumer law and banking law, and is currently Convenor of the Consumer Law Section of the Society of Public Teachers of Law.

Contributors

John Birds is Professor of Commercial Law at the University of Sheffield where he was also Head of the Department of Law from 1987–99. He is, among other things, author of *Modern Insurance Law* (4th edn, 1997) and one of the editors of *MacGillvray on Insurance Law* (9th edn, 1997).

Richard J. Bragg is Senior Lecturer in Law at the University of Manchester and Director of the Centre for Law and Business. He is the author of two books and numerous articles on commercial and consumer law topics.

Andrew Campbell is a lecturer in law at the University of Wales, Aberystwyth where he teaches banking law and corporate insolvency law. His main research interests are insolvency law (especially in relation to banks), corporate rescue procedures, bank/customer confidentiality, depositor protection and the control of money laundering. He has written a number of articles and has presented conference papers on these topics. Prior to teaching he worked in banking, both in the UK and Canada, and he is a solicitor of the Supreme Court in England and Wales.

Sharon Chin is a graduate of the London School of Economics and Cambridge University. She currently works for Linklaters and Paines, Solicitors in London.

List of Contributors

David O. Harris has worked extensively in the regulation and evaluation of pension systems throughout the world. This experience was gained through working in the Australian Public Service and British Civil Service in the 1990s and as the 1996 AMP Churchill Fellow. He holds qualifications in business and bank management and is currently co-authoring a book on ageing populations at Watson Wyatt Worldwide in Washington DC.

Norma Hird is a lecturer in law at the University of Sheffield, and has previously worked in advertising. She is a regular contributor to the *Journal of Business Law* and specialises in insurance law.

Geraint Howells is Reader in Law at the Institute for Commercial Law Studies, University of Sheffield. He has written widely on consumer law matters and is editor of the *Consumer Law Journal*.

Susan P. Jones is a former newspaper journalist who has worked in government–press relations for the past twenty years. She is currently studying for a Masters Degree in Public Communication at Leeds University.

Gavin Little is Lecturer in Business Law at the University of Stirling. His main areas of research are Scots public law and environmental liability.

Eva Lomnicka is Professor of Law at Kings College, London University. She is a graduate and postgraduate of Cambridge University and a practising member of the English Bar. Her main research interests are securities regulation and consumer credit regulation, being editor of the *Encyclopedia of Financial Services Law* (as well as the relevant part of *Palmer's Company Law*) and the *Encyclopedia of Consumer Credit Law*. She has written extensively on those areas and is on the editorial board of a number of legal journals, including the *Journal of Business Law* and the *Company Lawyer*.

Anna Mörner is a lecturer in law in the International Financial Law Unit of Queen Mary and Westfield College, University of London. She holds LLM degrees from the universities of Lund and London. She specialises in international financial law with a particular emphasis on issues of regional integration and development.

Philip Morris is Senior Lecturer in Business Law at the University of Stirling. He is an associate member of the British and Irish Ombudsman Association and has published widely on the role of the ombudsman in the financial services industry.

Iain Ramsay is a Professor of Law at Osgoode Hall Law School, York University, Toronto, Canada. His current research interests include consumer bankruptcy, regulation of financial services and consumer protection in informational capitalism.

Chris Willett has taught at Oxford Polytechnic and Brunel University and is now a Senior Lecturer at the Unversity of Warwick. He speaks at consumer and contract law conferences around the world and his books include *Scottish Business Law*, *Aspects of Fairness in Contract* and *Public Sector Reform and the Citizen's Charter*.

Toni Williams is an Associate Professor of Law at Osgoode Hall Law School, York University, Toronto, Canada. Her research interests include administration of criminal justice, contract law, equality and the law and planning law.

TABLE OF LEGISLATION

United Kingdom Statutes

United Kingdom Statutory Instruments

Table of Legislation

Table of Legislation

TABLE OF CASES

Table of Cases

Table of Cases

United States Cases

Introduction

CONSUMER PROTECTION IN FINANCIAL SERVICES: PUTTING THE LAW IN CONTEXT

Peter Cartwright

Chapter Outline

1. Introduction

2. Consumers, Investors and Citizens

3. The Law and Theory of Consumer Protection in Financial Services

4. Consumers and Information

5. Consumers and Non-market Goals

6. Consumer Law, Regulation and Enforcement

7. The Scope and Content of this Book

Consumer Protection in Financial Services (P. Cartwright, ed.: 90-411-9717-6: © Kluwer Law International: pub. Kluwer Law International, 1999: printed in Great Britain)

1. INTRODUCTION

Consumers have been protected by the law for centuries. Implied warranties existed in Roman law against latent defects in the sale of goods,[1] the Magna Carta refers to uniformity of measures of wine, ale, corn and cloth, and it has long been seen as the law's business to protect the health and the economic interests of consumers.[2] Financial transactions, even complex ones, have a longer history[3] and the provision of finance is now an essential part of modern society. In the words of Galbraith: 'The process of persuading people to incur debt, and the arrangements for them to do so, are as much a part of modern production as the making of goods and the nurturing of wants.'[4]

That consumers of financial services are in need of the protection of the law in some form or other is not in doubt. Consumers of these services are particularly vulnerable for a variety of reasons that are discussed later. How such consumers should best be protected is, however, open to question. Financial services take a variety of different forms, from overdrafts to pensions. Consumers are equally varied, from the wealthy and sophisticated investor to the impecunious and unsophisticated holder of a current account. Legal mechanisms for protecting consumers are numerous, from disclosure requirements and self-regulation to prior approval of traders and the use of criminal sanctions for supplying misleading information. It is the task of government to decide which mechanism should be used to protect which type of consumer in which field of financial services. Such a task is far from easy.

This book examines the role of the law in the protection of the consumer of financial services. It is not intended to be an exhaustive examination of the area. Such a work could be written, although the task of producing anything of that type which was not superficial would be extremely difficult. Instead, this book aims to examine the ways in which the law is and could be used to protect consumers when purchasing financial services.

The book, as explained below, interprets the terms 'consumer' and 'financial services' in a broad way, but a way which reflects the way these terms are generally understood.

---

1. See G. Hadfield, R. Howse and M. Trebilcock, 'Information-Based Principles for Rethinking Consumer Protection Policy' (1998) 22 JCP 131.
2. See B. W. Harvey and D. L. Parry, *The Law of Consumer Protection and Fair Trading*, 5th edn (Butterworths, 1996), p. 6.
3. Swan has found evidence of futures contracts dating back to about 1700 BC. See E. J. Swan, 'The Legal Regulation of Derivative Instruments in Ancient Greece and Rome', in B. Rider (ed.), *The Corporate Dimension* (Jordans, 1998).
4. J. K. Galbraith, *The Affluent Society*, 4th edn (Andre Deutsch, 1984), p. 148.

2. CONSUMERS, INVESTORS AND CITIZENS

It is important, from the outset, to consider some definitions. First, when is someone to be described as a 'consumer' for the purposes of this book? One problem we face is that there is no single agreed definition of the term, although a number of statutes attempt to define it for their own purposes.[5] One approach is to say that a consumer is someone who purchases goods and services. This definition would include traders who make purchases and it is clear that, for most purposes, traders will not be treated as consumers.[6] Another possibility is to say that a consumer is a private individual who contracts with a commercial enterprise, but even this definition is too narrow in some ways. It would also exclude the users of goods and services who have not purchased them, such as the ultimate consumer who is given a product by a friend.[7] Furthermore, a private individual who receives services from a non-commercial state authority might be aptly described as a consumer, such as the user of National Health Service facilities.[8] As Kennedy has stated, 'consumerism is just as concerned with the supply of services as with goods. The consumer merely becomes the client, or patient, or whatever rather than the shopper.'[9]

In seeking an appropriate definition, we could even go as far as quoting Ralph Nader, the American consumer rights activist, and equate the word 'consumer' with that of 'citizen'.[10] There is no doubt that the concept of consumerism has been broadened since the days of the Molony Report, upon which much of the UK's consumer protection legislation is based.[11] As

---

5. See, for example, s. 12 of the Unfair Contract Terms Act 1977 which defines when someone 'deals as a consumer', and s. 20(6) of the Consumer Protection Act 1987 which defines 'consumer'.
6. See, for example, s. 20(6) of the Consumer Protection Act 1987 which emphasises the need for goods to be supplied 'for private use or consumption', services to be provided 'otherwise than for the purposes of any business' and accommodation to be occupied 'otherwise than for the purposes of any business' in order for the pricing provisions to apply. By contrast, some so-called 'consumer protection' statutes apply to transactions between traders, for example the Trade Descriptions Act 1968.
7. The Germans refer to such a consumer as the *endverbraucher*.
8. See I. Ramsay, *Consumer Protection: Text and Materials* (Weidenfeld & Nicolson, 1989), p. 11.
9. I. Kennedy, *The Unmasking of Medicine* (the 1980 Reith Lectures) (Allen & Unwin, 1981), p. 117.
10. See R. Cranston, *Consumers and the Law*, 2nd edn (Weidenfeld & Nicolson, 1984), pp. 7–8.
11. The Molony Committee was set up in 1959 to consider and report 'what changes if any in the law and what other measures, if any, are desirable for the further protection of the consuming public'. The Committee described the consumer as someone who purchases or hire purchases goods for private use or consumption, although they did admit that the private consumer of services could also be described as a

long ago as 1979–80, the Consumers Association in its *Annual Report* suggested that consumerism reflected the idea of 'the relationship between the individual and society'. Definitions of such width raise their own difficulties, but also illustrate the numerous contexts in which an individual could properly be regarded as a consumer. It is necessary to form a practical, if imperfect, definition, and for our purposes the term 'consumers' will mean citizens who enter into transactions to obtain goods and services from traders. Although this excludes certain individuals who could be described as consumers, it is submitted that it represents the people usually thought of as consumers, and covers the individuals addressed in this book.

When we refer to consumers of financial services we face additional problems of definition. First, we may find some difficulty in saying that anyone can 'consume' a service. Individuals are perhaps better regarded as the users or recipients of services, and the consumers of goods. It is submitted, however, that it is common to refer to the 'consumers' of services in everyday speech, and it is well accepted that provisions that protect individuals in purchasing services are aptly described as 'consumer protection' measures.[12] Second, we face difficulties when we examine the precise role of the individual in the transaction in question. We may have little difficulty in describing the person who deposits money in a bank, or enters into a contract with an insurance company to insure his house, as a consumer. More difficulties arise when we consider the role of investors as consumers. For a start, it is difficult to find an agreed definition of 'investor'. It was said in *Inland Revenue Commissioners v Rolls Royce Ltd* that 'the meaning of the verb "to invest" is to lay out money in the acquisition of some species of property'.[13]

In subsequent cases, the courts have been concerned to keep the meaning of 'investments' very general. In *Inland Revenue Commissioners v Desoutter Bros* Lord Greene said that investment 'is not a term of art, but has to be interpreted in a popular sense'.[14]

This is helpful by including within the meaning of the term those things which are commonly referred to as investments. It is possible, however, to regard this approach as too lax. For example, in *Re Price*, Farwell J said

---

(continued)

consumer (Board of Trade, *Final Report of the Committee on Consumer Protection* (Molony Committee) Cmnd 1781/1962 para. 2). It also went as far, at one point, as saying that 'the consumer . . . is everybody all of the time', although it did not suggest this as a working definition of consumer (para. 16).

12. Note, for example, s. 14 of the Trade Descriptions Act 1968 which deals with false statements about services, and part III of the Consumer Protection Act 1987 which covers misleading price indications about goods and services.
13. [1944] 2 All ER 340 *per* Macnaghten J.
14. [1946] 1 All ER 58.

that a bank deposit is not an investment, but 'money that awaits invest-ment'.[15] Many would regard such a definition of investment as too restric-tive. Perhaps the best approach is to regard the process of investing as 'employing money from which interest or profit is expected'. This is favoured by Fisher and Bewsey, and is appropriate for our purposes.[16]

This brings us back to the question of whether or not an investor is a consumer. It could be argued that an investor plays a different role in the economic process from a consumer, and that investment involves differ-ent legal relationships from consumption.[17] Harvey and Parry, for example, argue that although there are similarities between investors and consumers, investors are 'part of the apparatus of producers rather than consumers'.[18] However, it is submitted that the argument that an investor is not a consumer requires us to adopt too narrow an interpretation of the concept of consumer. The analogies between investor and consumer have long been recognised. In its 1992 Report, Justice commented that 'the small investor in the contemporary financial world is not unlike a consumer in the domestic appliance market'.[19]

Page and Ferguson go even further by directly equating consumers and investors. They state:

Given that investment represents deferred consumption, it is tempting to see investor protection as the other side of the coin from consumer protection. Any attempt to draw a distinction along these lines, however, would be misconceived. The investors with whom we are concerned . . . are also consumers – of financial services, namely the services of advisors, brokers, dealers, managers etc.[20]

It is submitted that for our purposes, investors are aptly described as con-sumers.

A second point to address, albeit briefly, is that of our definition of 'financial services'. The term is used here in a wider sense than it is in the Financial Services Act 1986.[21] The book deals with financial services in the broad sense. It therefore includes, *inter alia*, bank and building society

---

15. [1905] 2 Ch. 55.
16. J. Fisher and J. Bewsey, *The Law of Investor Protection* (Sweet & Maxwell, 1997), p. 5.
17. See A. C. Page and R. B. Ferguson, *Investor Protection* (Weidenfeld & Nicolson, 1992), p. 11. They point out that the concept of investor covers a wide variety of legal relationships, including creditor–debtor, beneficiary–trustee, shareholder––corporation and member–corporation. As will be seen later, however, they regard it as possible to equate investors and consumers.
18. Harvey and Parry, op. cit., n. 2, p. 57.
19. Justice, *The Protection of the Small Investor* (Justice, 1992), p. 9.
20. Page and Ferguson, op. cit., n. 17, p. 14.
21. The Act is concerned with 'investments', which it defines in Sch. 1, part 1.

accounts, pensions, insurance policies and loans. The definition used here reflects the general understanding of 'financial services' and it should be noted that the Office of Fair Trading adopts a similarly wide interpretation of the term. There is, therefore, a precedent for this broad approach.[22]

3. THE LAW AND THEORY OF CONSUMER PROTECTION IN FINANCIAL SERVICES

Much has been written about the role of the law in consumer protection. In order to understand the role of the law in protecting the consumer of financial services, it is necessary to say a little about why and how the law intervenes in the market place to protect the consumer. First, it should be noted that there is general agreement that the law has, in some form, a role to play in protecting consumers. Even the most passionate supporter of the free market accepts the need for the civil law to play a part in underpinning that which is agreed by the parties, one of whom will often be a consumer. Milton Friedman saw the law as having important roles in maintaining open markets, establishing property rights, protecting third parties from what he called 'neighbourhood effects' and ensuring that 'the rules of the game' are adhered to.[23] In Friedman's words: 'government is essential both as a forum for determining the "rules of the game" and as an umpire to interpret and enforce the rules decided on'.[24]

Friedman accepted that regulation could be justified. However, the economic freedom that he advocated required governments to justify regulation; the presumption would be in favour of free markets.[25] This thinking has been influential in the formulation of regulatory policy in the UK, although all governments since the 1960s have initiated consumer protection legislation. Even the avowedly pro-free market Conservative administrations of 1979–97 initiated pro-consumer legislation at a time when they

---

22. In its inquiry into vulnerable consumers and financial services, the Office includes banking, credit, insurance and saving as being within the broad subject of 'financial services'. See OFT Press Release 60/97, 16.12.97.
23. M. Friedman, *Capitalism and Freedom* (University of Chicago Press, 1962). Friedman also emphasised the law's roles of providing public order and defence.
24. Ibid.
25. For a criticism of Friedman see Galbraith, op. cit., n. 4. Some consumer lawyers have also been highly critical of the ways in which free market ideas have been applied to consumer law. See R. Cranston, 'Consumer Protection and Economic Theory', in A. J. Duggan and L. W. Darvall (eds), *Consumer Protection Law and Theory* (Law Book, 1980). Cranston likens the free market economist to 'the foolish man who built his house upon the sand' (p. 243).

were also espousing and engaging in widespread deregulation.[26] Free market ideals, it seems, will often be tempered by political expediency and palatability.

Support for free markets has underpinned much consumer protection policy. Indeed, a considerable body of literature tells of the panacea of the perfect market.[27] Many academic commentators, when examining the rationales for intervening in the market to protect consumers, take the so-called perfect market as their starting point, even if they are often dubious about its existence in practice.[28] One major piece of work to examine the reasons for intervening to protect consumers is Ramsay's *Rationales for Intervention in the Consumer Market Place*.[29] Ramsay sees market failure as the central economic rationale for government regulation of the market place. The perfect market is one where certain characteristics are present. Ramsay identifies them as follows:

(i) there are numerous buyers and sellers in the market, such that the activities of any one economic actor will have only a minimal impact on the output or price in the market;

(ii) there is free entry into and exit from the market;

(iii) the commodity sold in the market is homogeneous; that is, essentially the same product is sold by each seller in the particular market;

(iv) all economic actors in the market have perfect information about the nature and value of the commodities traded;

(v) all the costs of producing the commodity are borne by the producer and all the benefits of a commodity accrue to the consumer – that is, there are no externalities.[30]

Although it might be argued that perfect markets exist only in economic textbooks, this does not mean that it is futile to discuss them. It may be that one role of the law is to try to create, as far as possible, the conditions of a perfect market. For example, private law could be developed so that third party costs are 'internalised'.[31] This approach is consistent with the market system.[32] However, it is widely accepted that the private law

---

26. See for example, part II of the Consumer Protection Act 1987 which introduced a general safety requirement for goods, backed up with the force of the criminal law, and the Property Misdescriptions Act 1991 which introduced what appeared to be draconian measures to deal with estate agents and property developers.

27. This is generally associated with the Chicago School.

28. Howells and Weatherill describe it as being 'as alluring as it is unrealistic': G. G. Howells and S. Weatherill, *Consumer Protection Law* (Dartmouth, 1995), p. 1.

29. I. Ramsay, *Rationales for Intervention in the Consumer Market Place* (Office of Fair Trading, 1984).

30. Ibid., para. 3.3.

31. See A. Ogus, *Regulation: Legal Form and Economic Theory* (Clarendon Press, 1994), pp. 18–22.

32. Ibid.

cannot, in reality, form an adequate foundation for consumer protection. Both the market and the private law are subject to inherent limitations. In the words of Ogus: 'When . . . "market failure" is accompanied by "private law failure" . . . there is a prima facie case for regulatory intervention in the public interest.'[33]

There are numerous ways in which the perfect market fails in reality. Instead of having numerous buyers and sellers there may be a monopoly. Instead of free entry to and exit from the market there may be licensing requirements for traders. Instead of homogeneous products there may be artificial product differentiation. There will seldom be perfect information about products, and the parties to a transaction will often not bear all the benefits and burdens of that transaction. It is here that regulation may have to step in.

It is one thing to identify a justification for regulation, but another to decide on what form of regulation should be used. There are many different regulatory techniques. For example, there are traditional 'command and control' forms of regulation, which provide a sanction (usually criminal) for failure to comply with a requirement.[34] To some extent, this is found in the financial services field. For example, section 47(1) of the Financial Services Act 1986 states:

(1) Any person who
  (a) makes a statement, promise or forecast which he knows to be misleading, false or deceptive or dishonestly conceals material facts: or
    recklessly makes (dishonestly or otherwise) a statement, promise or forecast which is misleading false or deceptive,
  is guilty of an offence if he makes the statement, promise or forecast or conceals the facts for the purpose of inducing, or is reckless as to whether it may induce, another person (whether or not the person to whom the statement, promise or forecast is made or from whom the facts are concealed) to enter or offer to enter into, or refrain from entering into, an investment agreement or to exercise, or refrain from exercising any rights conferred by an investment.[35]

Other forms of regulation include everything from prior approval to self-regulation. An examination of consumer protection in financial services reveals that a variety of regulatory techniques are used to ensure protection. In some cases a mixture of techniques will be used within the same statute. The Consumer Credit Act 1974 illustrates this. For example,

---

33. Ibid., p. 30.
34. Much of the UK's consumer protection legislation uses this approach, for example, the Trade Descriptions Act 1968, the Consumer Protection Act 1987 (parts II and III), the Food Safety Act 1990 and the Property Misdescriptions Act 1991.
35. S. 47(2) contains a related offence of creating a false or misleading impression.

section 21 requires that all businesses which carry on a consumer credit business where the agreements are regulated require a licence; section 137(1) allows the courts to reopen extortionate credit bargains so as to do justice between the parties, and section 49(1) makes it an offence to canvass debtor–creditor agreements off trade premises. Provisions for the protection of debtors are also found in a number of self-regulatory codes of practice. It should be remembered that consumer protection in financial services is achieved by a diverse variety of legal mechanisms.

4.   CONSUMERS AND INFORMATION

It was mentioned above that one of the characteristics of the perfect market is that economic actors, including consumers, have 'perfect information' about the nature and value of commodities traded. One of the problems that consumers face is in relation to obtaining and using information about products, and a major element of consumer protection policy has been trying to remedy these information deficits.[36] Indeed, it has been said that the emphasis on the importance of information 'formed the key analytical basis for early consumer protection law'.[37] Informational problems in financial services are particularly great for a number of reasons.[38] First, it is extremely difficult for a consumer of financial services to identify the characteristics of a product prior to purchase. Second, financial products tend to be technically complex, and so even if the consumer received accurate and detailed information prior to purchase, it would be very difficult for that consumer to understand the information. Third, the effects of financial products are often not known until the future (a pension being a good example). Some of these difficulties are present in other services, but they are particularly acute where financial services are concerned. Consumers are said to suffer from 'bounded rationality'. This means that 'the capacity of individuals to receive store, and process information is limited'.[39] This is particularly so where financial services are concerned for the reasons mentioned above. It is also particularly so where

---

36. This has occurred at national and European level. See S. Weatherill, 'The Role of the Informed Consumer in European Community Law and Policy' (1994) 2 *Consumer Law Journal* 49. See also W. Whitford, 'The Functions of Disclosure Regulation in Consumer Transactions' (1973) *Wisconsin Law Review* 400, who examines the efficacy of forcing businesses to divulge information about their products.
37. Hadfield *et al.*, op. cit., n. 1, p. 134.
38. See Office of Fair Trading, *Consumer Detriment under Conditions of Imperfect Information*, Research Paper 11, August 1997.
39. Ogus, op. cit., n. 31, p. 41. See also H. Simon, *Models of Bounded Rationality* (MIT Press, 1982).

vulnerable consumers are concerned. The Director General of Fair Trading recently described 'vulnerable consumers' as 'those who through age, infirmity or another disadvantage, have difficulty in obtaining and understanding the information they need'.[40] This demonstrates the view of the Director General that the key to vulnerable consumers' problems is their difficulty in dealing with information.

The limitation of informational remedies causes difficulties for policy makers. An obvious solution to consumer problems is to require traders to supply them with information, thus enabling them to make rational choices about products. Under such an approach, the consumer carries out an analysis of the product, its advantages and disadvantages, and makes a choice. The consumer's choice is then respected.[41] Information flows have advantages in giving producers an incentive to cut costs or improve quality in the knowledge that these advances will be communicated to the consumer. Disclosure regulation is also favoured by those who fear the dangers of over-regulation through more traditional forms of control.[42]

Disclosure regulation has been important in the financial services sphere. For example, the Consumer Credit Act 1974 requires that the price of credit be disclosed at a number of different stages. There is an economic justification for this. In the words of Ramsay, it 'attempts to harness market incentives to police the price of credit, obviating the need to rely on government regulation of interest rates'.[43]

The Crowther Committee thought that the disclosure of the cost of credit in terms of rate per cent per annum would have a number of benefits. It would enable comparisons to be made, both with other credit providers and with the return the consumer would receive on savings, it would make creditors conscious of how their charges related to other providers,[44] and it would ensure that consumers do not 'over-extend their financial resources by ill-informed and rash use of credit facilities'.[45]

Some writers have been sceptical of the value of laws that require business to disclose information to consumers. Cranston argues that:

---

40. J. Bridgeman, 'A Speech to the Year Ahead Symposium', 28 January 1998.
41. Although there is some doubt about the extent to which consumers, in reality, use information to make rational decisions. See R. L. Jordan and W. D. Warren, 'Disclosure of Finance Charges: A Rationale' (1966) 64 *Michigan Law Review* 1285, 1320–2. The Molony Committee recognised that consumers frequently made decisions 'on instinctive but not always rational thought processes'. Op. cit., n. 11, para. 891.
42. See, *eg*, S. Breyer, *Regulation and its Reform* (Harvard University Press, 1982), p. 184.
43. Ramsay, op. cit., note 8, p. 329. *Report of the Committee on Consumer Credit* (Crowther Committee), Cmnd 4596/1971.
44. Ibid., para. 3.8.3.
45. Ibid., para. 3.8.13.

The major problem with disclosure regulation is not in securing business compliance, but rather that consumers are unaware of the information disclosed, do not appreciate its significance or simply do not employ the information provided in the market place.[46]

Furthermore, the difficulties faced by, for example, low income consumers, may not be addressed by information. Trebilcock, for example, has cited research on the psychological characteristics of the poor which indicates that they may be less able to protect themselves than others when information is supplied.[47] Recent economic research has also shown the wide range of ways in which information affects markets; in particular, it emphasises the costs faced by consumers in becoming informed about transactions.[48] It may be that information can only go so far in providing consumer protection.

Despite these concerns, there is little doubt that information plays an important role in consumer protection, and that disclosure regulation is an important method of ensuring that information is provided. In a major study of disclosure regulation, Whitford argues that although the supporters of such regulation, in particular advocates of truth in lending, have over-stated their case, there is much to be said for disclosure regulation. This is particularly so when it is compared with more interventionist techniques of regulation. In the words of Leff: 'For a Government to try to design high quality information is much cheaper than its trying to design high quality goods, and much better than its trying to design high quality people'.[49]

5. CONSUMERS AND NON-MARKET GOALS

It should be remembered that market failure is not the only reason for regulation. There are non-market goals that can be used to justify intervention. Ogus identifies these as distributive justice, paternalism and community values.[50] Distributive justice is of particular interest, as it has often been part of the UK's consumer protection policy to ensure that those who are most vulnerable in society are given particular protection. Resources will be distributed on the basis of what is just, rather than what is economically efficient. Ogus argues that the question of how the bal-

---

46. Cranston, op. cit., n. 10, p. 304.
47. M. J. Trebilcock, 'Consumer Protection in the Affluent Society' (1970) 16 *McGill Law Journal* 263.
48. Hadfield *et al.*, op. cit., n. 1, pp. 141–5.
49. A. A. Leff, 'The Pontiac Prospectus' (1974) 25 *Consumer Journal* 35.
50. Ogus, op. cit., n. 31, pp. 46–54.

ance between distributive justice and market efficiency should be drawn can only be answered on the basis of ideology.[51] He emphasises the different bases of libertarian, liberal and socialist thought, and explains how these relate to distributive questions. It is clear that distributive matters have been of concern to consumer policy makers in the UK. The Crowther Committee, whose report gave rise to the Consumer Credit Act 1974, emphasised a variety of factors that justified intervention in the credit market. Some of these related to market failure, such as inadequate or misleading information, whereas others showed the Committee's concern about the social context in which credit is frequently sought. They made reference to the difficulties for consumers in obtaining redress through 'lack of energy and initiative' and the problems for those who 'lack the ability to budget or to manage their income'. They also recognised that the poorest consumers are peculiarly vulnerable to 'harsh and oppressive terms'.[52] The Consumer Credit Act 1974, in trying to remedy some of the problems faced by debtors has some regard to questions of distributive justice. For example, section 137(1) of the Act allows the court to reopen a credit agreement so as to do justice to the parties, where it finds a credit bargain to be extortionate. The current Director General of Fair Trading has also indicated that distributive justice is a factor in the Office of Fair Trading's (OFT's) policy. He recently explained the difficulty that the OFT faces in deciding where to deploy resources, and described its approach as 'cost benefit analysis with a social distribution element'.[53] Distributive justice, it seems, is an important element in the OFT's policy.

Paternalism is another example of non-economic grounds for intervention. Dworkin describes paternalism as 'the interference with a person's liberty of action justified by reasons referring exclusively to the welfare, good, happiness, needs, interests or values of the person being coerced'.[54]

The law is therefore being invoked regardless of the desires of the individual, and it is this that places paternalism at odds with market mechanisms, where the choice of the individual is central. Ramsay argues that paternalism underlies many of the legislative measures that the UK saw in the 1960s and 1970s. In particular, he quotes from Hart, criticising J. S. Mill's views on paternalism:

51. Ibid.
52. Crowther Committee, op. cit., n. 43.
53. Bridgeman, op. cit., n. 40.
54. R. Dworkin, 'Paternalism', in R. Wasserstrom (ed.), *Morality and the Law* (Wadsworth, 1971), p. 108.

Choices may be made or consent given without adequate reflection or appreciation of the consequences; or in pursuit of merely transitory desires; or in various predicaments when the judgment is likely to be clouded; or under inner psychological compulsion; or under pressure by others of a kind too subtle to be susceptible of proof in a law court.[55]

The literature on paternalism is perhaps complicated by attempts to reconcile it with ideas of free choice by arguing consumers consent to the state overruling their immediate wishes in order to protect them from themselves.[56] Whatever the justification, it is clear that paternalism has, in some form, influenced consumer protection legislation. This has been particularly so in the financial field, largely because of the difficulties which financial transactions present, particularly for poorer consumers. It is interesting to consider paternalism in the light of the Consumer Credit Act 1974. The Act contains some measures that might be viewed as paternalistic. For example, it provides a consumer with the right to cancel a regulated consumer credit agreement where the agreement has been signed off trade premises following oral representations. This 'cooling off period' is designed to protect consumers from high-pressure sales techniques, and to give them time to reflect upon the agreement they have signed. These provisions are paternalistic in that they apply regardless of the agreement formed between the consumer and the trader, and regardless of the intention of the consumer at the time of the agreement. There are other ways in which the Act is not as paternalistic as it might have been. It does not, for example, go as far as to employ fixed interest rate ceilings, which the Crowther Committee regarded as inflexible and difficult to administer.[57] The Act did, however, as already mentioned, allow the courts to reopen extortionate credit bargains under section 137(1). Although the provisions have been criticised, they do illustrate the concern that unconscionable conduct should be unenforceable, regardless of whether the conduct was, in the loose sense, consented to. In the words of Kennedy, 'there is real value as well as an element of real nobility in the judicial decision to throw out, every time the opportunity arises, consumer contracts designed to perpetuate the exploitation of the poorest class of buyers on credit'.[58]

55. H. L. A. Hart, *Law Liberty and Morality* (Stanford University Press, 1963), pp. 32–3.
56. B. Barry, *Political Argument* (New York Humanities Press, 1965), pp. 226–7.
57. See G. Howells, 'Seeking Social Justice for Poor Consumers in Credit Markets', in this volume.
58. D. Kennedy, 'Form and Substance in Private Law Adjudication' (1976) 89 *Harvard Law Review* 1685, 1777.

It is interesting to consider briefly the indicators that the OFT in the UK uses to identify markets and practices that require close examination. The indicators are:

- where products or services are complex;
- where goods or services are purchased infrequently;
- where the purchases are by individual consumers who have little or no knowledge of the product or service, and;
- where purchases are by groups in the population who have particular difficulty in obtaining and interpreting information.[59]

This list reveals two matters of interest to us. First, it shows why consumer protection in financial services is an important area for investigation. As the Director General of Fair Trading stated 'it is not difficult to see how we decided upon our inquiry into vulnerable consumers of financial services'.[60] Second, the list shows the central importance of information in protecting the consumer. It is clear that the OFT is concerned to redress market imperfections, for example by addressing information deficits. It also appears that the OFT recognises that certain groups will face particular difficulties, not just in obtaining information with which they can make informed choices, but also in processing that information. It may be that encouraging the supply of information will not be enough, and that issues of distribution need to be assessed.

The results of the inquiry are not known at the time of writing, and will be viewed with interest. It seems likely that the inquiry's report will form the basis of the OFT's action in consumer protection in financial services in the near future.

6. CONSUMER LAW, REGULATION AND ENFORCEMENT

One final point to note here relates to enforcement. Consumer law will not be effective if its enforcement is not effective. One of the main criticisms of the private law as a means of consumer protection is that it relies upon the individual for its enforcement. There are a number of reasons for this being of concern. First, the consumer may be ignorant of his or her rights. The complexity of financial products means that it is particularly difficult for consumers to know if they have causes of action. Second, the consumer may lack the resources to be able to take action, or feel that it is

---

59. J. Bridgeman, 'Giving the Consumer a Fair Deal' (http://www.oft.gov.uk).
60. Ibid. The OFT's Report is expected in late summer 1998.

not worth the trouble. Litigation is expensive, and it may not be worth the consumer pursuing a claim, particularly one for a relatively small amount of money. It has been commented that consumers often need 'superspite' to take action. This is an important issue. The transaction costs of enforcing a claim under the private law frequently prevent consumers from enforcing the rights to which they are entitled.[61]

An obvious approach to the problems of transaction costs and resulting private law failure is to provide that consumers' rights are enforced by someone else. To some extent, public regulation under the criminal law ensures this. Trading standards officers can prosecute errant traders under the Consumer Credit Act for false advertising, for example, and the victim may be awarded a compensation order by the court. But there has been concern that criminal sanctions may not be the most efficient method of ensuring consumer protection. They are, it is argued, over-inclusive,[62] enforced inconsistently, and enforced by agencies who are liable to be 'captured'.[63] The fear of over-regulation has, however, led to a number of forms of self-regulation emerging, Where it comes to ensuring redress of consumers' grievances in the financial services field, some of the most important developments have come in the areas of self-regulation.[64] The most conspicuous of these have been the financial services ombudsmen, who are examined in the essay by Morris and Little in this book, but self-regulation is important in other ways too. The Financial Services Act was founded upon the concept of self-regulation in a statutory framework,[65] and codes of practice have become common in a number of areas of financial services.[66] It is interesting to note that this is an area that is undergoing considerable change. The Financial Services Authority is taking over responsibility for the supervision of financial services and this is leading to a re-organisation of the existing financial services ombudsmen.[67] It seems

61. See Cranston, op. cit., n. 10, p. 25.
62. See Ogus, op. cit., n. 31, p. 96.
63. See M. A. Bernstein, *Regulating Business by Independent Commission* (Princeton University Press, 1955).
64. There are difficulties with the concept of 'self-regulation' as there are 'a multitude of institutional arrangements which can properly be described as 'self-regulation and . . . it is wrong to tar them all with the same brush' (Ogus, 'Rethinking Self Regulation' (1995) 15 OJLS 97, 99).
65. See S. Chin, 'Financial Services Regulation: Can History Teach Us Anything?', in this volume.
66. See for example The Code of Banking Practice discussed by Campbell (A. Campbell, 'Bank Confidentiality and the Consumer in the United Kingdom', in this volume).
67. The new system has been outlined in *Consumer Complaints: The New Financial Services Ombudsman Scheme* (FSA, August 1998). Membership of the scheme will be compulsory for firms authorised by the FSA, and a single Financial Services Ombudsman Scheme will replace the eight existing schemes which cover the financial services area.

16

likely that the new authority will lead to more effective control of the financial services industry, and it is hoped, better redress for the consumer.[68] The OFT is reviewing the role of codes of practice and has suggested that approved codes be replaced by standards. It may be that self-regulation, for which the UK has been described as 'something of a haven',[69] is, at the very least, undergoing a re-examination.

7.   THE SCOPE AND CONTENT OF THIS BOOK

This book begins by examining two topics that have implications for the whole area of consumer protection in financial services. First, Anna Mörner looks at the role of the European Union in improving consumer protection through its work in the financial services area. The author concludes that the rational and well-informed consumer will enjoy a wide range of financial products and services under the single market, and will protected by some timely measures. However, she also expresses some concerns, particularly about the absence of efforts to take account of the needs of vulnerable consumers. Second, Philip Morris and Gavin Little examine the role of ombudsmen in ensuring consumer protection in the financial services sector in the UK. Ombudsmen have been central in providing redress mechanisms to consumers of financial services and, as the authors note, there are nine ombudsmen schemes within the financial services industry. Although the schemes will soon be replaced by one overall ombudsman for the financial services industry, it is likely that the expertise which the various ombudsmen and their staff have developed will be put to good use in the new arrangement.[70]

The second part of the book considers consumer protection in the banking industry. It is well known that banking has undergone a revolution in recent years. With building societies demutualising, and around 83 per cent of the UK adult population now holding current accounts, banks play a bigger role in consumers' lives than perhaps ever before.[71] Despite

---

68. There are, however, concerns that the new Authority may not be able adequately to deal with questions of systemic risk. See C. Goodhart and D. Llewellyn, 'A Blurred Outlook', *Financial Times*, 30 May 1997.

69. R. Baggott, 'Regulatory Reform in Britain: The Changing Face of Self-Regulation' (1989) 67 *Public Administration* 435, 438.

70. See *Consumer Complaints*, op. cit., n. 67. The Chief Ombudsman and Panel of Ombudsmen will be appointed in March 1999. As the new scheme will be compulsory for FSA authorised firms, the role of ombudsmen will become increasingly important.

71. See Bridgeman, op. cit., n. 40, quoting figures from the Association of Payment Clearing Services.

this, there is relatively little literature that deals with the role of the law in the protection of bank customers. Even the Jack Committee Report, which had as its ambit 'to examine the statute and common law relating to the provision of banking services within the United Kingdom to personal and business customers' received little comment from academics.[72] The three essays in this part of the book consider issues of considerable topical importance to bank customers. First, Andrew Campbell's essay examines the duty of confidentiality, which was described by the Jack Committee Report as being 'at the heart of the banker–customer relationship'.[73] Campbell concludes that the present state of the law is unsatisfactory, and echoes the concerns of Jack in asking if the duty of confidentiality may effectively have been replaced by a duty to disclose. The second essay in this part, written by Eva Lomnicka, examines banking law in relation to the Unfair Terms in Consumer Contracts Regulations. More specifically, the author examines terms which enable banks to make unilateral changes to loan contracts with retail customers. She concludes that there is a lack of consensus among banks' advisers about when a term is likely to be regarded as unfair, and that the provisions in the regulations have not helped the devising of a fair unilateral variation clause. The final essay in this part is concerned with the issue of what happens to bank customers when their bank becomes insolvent. Depositor guarantee schemes have become a central part of the banking scene throughout the EU and beyond. Such schemes have an important role in ensuring the stability of the banking system and the avoidance of systemic risk, but in many ways their 'direct rationale' is that of consumer protection. The essay on this topic looks at the concept of 'moral hazard' which has been important in the thinking behind deposit guarantee schemes, and concludes that the system in the UK fails to take account of the difficulties depositors face when trying to assess the risks posed by banks. It is argued that reform of the system is necessary if depositors, particularly the most vulnerable depositors, are to be adequately protected.

Investments in the narrow sense are dealt with the next part of the book. Three essays are presented, which are concerned with important issues from the point of view of the consumer. First, Sharon Chin looks at the overall picture of investment regulation in the UK. She considers the historical regulation of the financial services industry, and discusses the lessons that can be learned from the past. In particular, the author emphasises the difficulties which regulators face in an increasingly global market. The decision by the UK government to transfer the regulation of financial

---

72. *Banking Services: Law and Practice. Report by the Review Committee* (Jack Committee Report) Cm 622 (HMSO, 1969).
73. Ibid., para. 5.26.

services to the newly established Financial Services Authority makes this essay particularly topical. The author's conclusion, that 'the law can never hope to evolve as rapidly as market and practices' illustrates the challenges that the new authority will face. The second essay in this part is 'Pensions and the Consumer: Lessons from Overseas' by David O. Harris and Susan P. Jones. Pensions provision is of particular concern to consumers for a number of reasons. First, it is an area in which they have an enormous financial stake. After a house purchase, a pension is the typical consumer's largest financial commitment. Second, the area is of concern because it has traditionally been the subject of relatively little regulation. A report by Justice[74] noted Gower's observations on the lack of regulation in this field, and although there have been important developments since those observations, concerns remain.   Finally in this section, Richard J. Bragg writes on 'Some Consumer Problems Relating to the Sale of Long-Term Insurance'. This piece examines some of the difficulties faced by consumers when dealing with the sellers of life insurance products. The author concludes that while consumers are becoming more aware of the need to become informed about financial products, there is still widespread ignorance in society. In the author's view, only legislation backed by criminal sanctions will be effective in controlling what he calls 'the inevitably over-enthusiastic salesman'.

The next part of the book is concerned with consumer protection in the insurance industry. This is an area of particular interest because of a number of important recent developments. The National Consumer Council's Report *Insurance Law Reform* was published in 1997. Also, cases such as *Pan Atlantic Insurance Co. Ltd v Pine Top Insurance Co. Ltd*[75] have clarified important areas of confusion. Insurance law is still, however, racked with uncertainty, and there is widespread feeling that significant reform is necessary. In the first essay, John Birds examines the experience of insurance law reform in Australia which took place with the Insurance Contracts Act 1984 and the Insurance (Agents and Brokers) Act 1984. Although he does not advocate a wholesale adoption of the Australian approach, the author does support taking some ideas from the Australian legislation. He concludes that the Australian experience demonstrates that a thorough reform can work to the reasonable satisfaction of all the parties involved and that the Australian model can 'show us the way to go'. Next, in their essay 'Consumer Protection in Insurance Contracts', Chris Willett and Norma Hird investigate aspects of unfairness in the contractual relationship between insurers and consumers. They argue that developments in case law, changes in the field

74.   Ibid., para. 4.30.
75.   [1995] 1 AC 501.

19

of self-regulation, and the Europeanisation of contract law, have all had important ramifications for the insurer–customer relationship. They conclude that the most appropriate method for ensuring the adequate protection of consumers would be to put the regulation of warranties and disclosure on a sound legal footing. The model they favour is that found in Australia, and advocated by John Birds in the previous essay.

The final part of the book examines consumer credit. This is the topic within this book upon which the most ink has been spilled in the past, particularly by consumer lawyers. The Consumer Credit Act, one of the most ambitious pieces of consumer protection legislation ever, generated considerable comment at its inception, and has continued to provoke attention from academic commentators. However, it should not be thought that all this attention has left little to say. The two essays on the topic in this book illustrate this amply. First, Geraint Howells writes on 'Seeking Social Justice for Poor Consumers in Credit Markets'. In this essay, the author examines the particular difficulties faced by low-income consumers in obtaining credit. He argues that one of the key roles for consumer lawyers to play is that of demonstrating the feasibility of having a competitive free market 'underpinned by principles of social justice which require creditors to be sensitive to the concerns of the disadvantaged'. Finally, Iain Ramsay and Toni Williams examine a topic of enormous importance and topicality: racial and gender equality in markets for financial services. Arguing that the market mechanism will be, at best, limited in its ability to deal with issues of discrimination, the authors look at techniques for tackling discriminatory practices, such as human rights legislation, community reinvestment strategies and institutional changes in access to credit and capital. They conclude that where financial services are concerned, there is a need for much greater experimentation in the provision of services if the needs of all consumers are to be met.

The question of how we should regulate financial services in the interests of the consumer has never been more topical. As mentioned above, the UK government is in the process of revolutionising the way in which the financial services industry is regulated, and the OFT is examining the protection of vulnerable consumers in markets for financial services. At the same time, the structure of the financial services industry is changing, and the need for the law to keep pace with change has never been greater. This book aims to make a contribution to some of these issues. It is certainly not the last word, but will, it is hoped, provide some food for thought.

PART ONE

THEMES AND TRENDS IN
FINANCIAL SERVICES

Chapter One

THE EUROPEAN UNION, FINANCIAL SERVICES AND THE CONSUMER*

Anna Mörner

Chapter Outline

1. Introduction

2. The Consumer in the European Union
    2.1   The early years
    2.2   The New Approach

3. Financial Services
    3.1   Creating an internal market in financial services
          3.1.1   Freedom to provide services across borders
          3.1.2   Residual regulatory powers
          3.1.3   The 'freedom to buy'
    3.2   Measures specifically aimed at consumers
          3.2.1   Cross-border credit transfers
          3.2.2   Consumer credit
          3.2.3   Distant selling

4. Conclusion

Consumer Protection in Financial Services (P. Cartwright, ed.: 90-411-9717-6:
© Kluwer Law International: pub. Kluwer Law International, 1999: printed in
Great Britain)

1.   INTRODUCTION

Underlying the European Community project was the fundamental notion that its inception would improve the lot of the consumer: more efficient markets would lead to more competition and a wider choice of products and services at lower prices. Yet the consumer is explicitly mentioned only in four instances in the original version of the Treaty of Rome,[1] without any apparent attempt to formulate a definitive consumer policy. This illustrates what might be seen as Community ambivalence in this area since, on the one hand, the success of the Community itself depends on the creation of a society conducive to consumer satisfaction and inclusive of all people, a 'people's Europe'. On the other hand, however, the view of consumer protection and national consumer legislation tends to differ between states, thereby causing difficulties to providers of services and goods wishing to engage in cross-border trade.

The Community, in particular through the jurisprudence of the European Court of Justice, striving to create a single market through the removal of barriers to trade such as national consumer legislation, for many years lacked specific allocation of competencies to enact measures replacing national legislation in the field of consumer policy. Although the importance of the consumer was always recognised, creating a coherent consumer policy through legislative measures at Community level was a task fraught with difficulties. It would be futile, however, to reduce a discussion on this complex area to a conflict between the desire to create a level playing field, in the Community context often a de-regulatory process, and the necessity to reregulate to ensure consumer protection. As one commentator puts it, 'In judging the appropriate intensity of regulation required in the evolving European market, it is perilously simplistic to reduce the argument to "competition between regulators" versus "the level playing field".'[2] Nevertheless, this elemental tension constitutes a fundamental component in the understanding of the attitude of the Community towards the consumer and forms the backdrop against which the discussion in this chapter will take place.

The dilemma is perhaps particularly evident in the case of financial services. The removal of barriers to the single market in financial services[3] is

---

*   I am grateful to Marise Cremona for comments on an earlier version of this chapter. Remaining errors are mine alone.

1.   Arts 39 and 40 refer to the position of the consumer in relation to the Common Agricultural Policy and Arts. 86 and 86 list instances where the consumer is to be taken into account in applying EC competition law.

2.   S. Weatherill, *EC Consumer Law and Policy* (Longman, 1997), p. 4.

3.   As noted by one commentator it is appropriate to talk in this context of 'removal of barriers' rather than 'the creation of a single market' since the adoption of legal measures by itself does not achieve anything other than possibly influencing behaviour:

nearly complete, and services may be provided across borders relatively freely. Also, Community measures have been enacted, the sole purpose of which is to protect the consumer, either directly[4] or for example through enhanced provision of information.[5] Yet it is by no means clear that the single market in financial services is meeting consumers' expectations. To 'stimulate a wide-ranging debate with all interested parties' the Commission recently published a Green Paper[6] containing an overview of the consumer's situation in the area of financial services. This chapter constitutes an attempt to outline Community efforts in relation to consumer protection in the area of financial services. The discussion will be illustrated by snapshots of the relevant legislative measures and will be informed, wherever pertinent, by the points raised in the Commission's Green Paper.

2. THE CONSUMER IN THE EUROPEAN UNION

2.1 The early years

A Council resolution containing a preliminary programme for a consumer protection and information policy[7]published in 1975 illustrates the importance accorded to consumer policy in principle for many years. Listing five basic consumer rights,[8] the programme constituted the genesis of a Community consumer policy. The document also recognised, however, that consumer policy would be amplified by action under specific Community policies, such as social and environment policies, as well as by the approximation of laws, all of which affect the consumers' position.[9] Harmonisation, then, would be one of the cornerstones of the policy aimed at improving the consumer's situation.

(continued)
> E. Lomnicka, 'The Internal Financial Market and Investment Services', in M. Andenas and S. Kenyon-Slade (eds), *EC Financial Market Regulations and Company Law* (Sweet & Maxwell, 1993), p. 81.

4. A good example of this is the deposit protection directive; see P. Cartwright, 'Deposit Guarantees and the Individual Bank Customer', in this volume.
5. Thus, provision of information is an important feature of, for example, the Consumer Credit Directive: *infra*, Section 3.
6. COM (96) 209 final of 22 May 1996, Financial Services: Meeting Consumers' Expectations.
7. [1975] OJ C92/1.
8. The right to protection of health and safety; the right to protection of economic interests; the right of redress; the right to information and education; and the right of representation (the right to be heard).
9. Cf. Weatherill, op. cit., n. 2, p. 11.

For many years, the legal basis for harmonisation was Article 100 of the EEC Treaty of 1957 which empowers the Council to enact directives for the approximation of national laws directly affecting the establishment or functioning of the common market. This provision requires unanimity in the Council something which often proved difficult, if not impossible, to achieve. Instead, the jurisprudence of the European Court of Justice came to be instrumental in removing barriers to trade. What took place was what might be termed negative harmonisation, in the sense that it consisted of removal of national legislation which, although it might well pursue a perfectly justifiable goal or protect a worthwhile interest, was found to hamper inter-Community trade. Given the difficulties associated with achieving unanimity in the Council it often proved difficult to provide the same level of protection, if any protection at all, at Community level. This dilemma affected consumer policy, too, and although laudable principles were set out, these often failed to materialise.

In a second programme for consumer protection and information policy[10] the Commission advocated soft law measures, suggesting that in some areas voluntary solutions could be adopted instead of legislation. Addressing what was seen as lack of progress in the area, the Commission issued an internal communication to the Council in 1981 entitled 'A New Impetus for Consumer Protection Policy', in which the need for measures to be adopted unanimously was blamed, along with other factors, for the lack of success.[11]

2.2   The New Approach

It was clear that a new impetus was essential not only to ensure efficient consumer policy but to safeguard the original idea of a common market. In this vein, the New Approach was conceived. Based in no small measure on the jurisprudence of the Court of Justice, one of the fundamental principles of the New Approach is mutual recognition. Obstacles to movement in the Community resulting from disparities between national laws must be accepted only in so far as they may be recognised as being necessary in order to satisfy certain mandatory requirements. Where this is not the case, mutual recognition prevails. A further aspect of the New Approach is adoption at Community level of standardised rules laying down essential health and safety requirements, so-called minimum harmonisation.

10.   [1981] OJ C133/1.
11.   Cf. G. Howells and T. Wilhelmsson, *EC Consumer Law* (Ashgate, 1997), p. 10.

Furthermore, the Single European Act of 1986 introduced an alternative legal basis for adoption of measures which have as their object the establishment and functioning of the internal market, Article 100a, which requires not unanimity but qualified majority in the Council. In summary, negative harmonisation was to be complemented by positive legal measures, laying down minimum Community-wide standards.

During this period, in the area of consumer policy, specific legislative measures[12] were complemented by soft law.[13] A pattern emerged, indicating that where appropriate, in so far as possible, the Community would enact legislative measures to protect the consumers, and the measures would be complemented by soft law such as recommendations and Council resolutions. Frequently, the emphasis was on transparency and information, features seen as enabling the consumer to make a well-informed choice between services and products, thereby reaping the benefits of the common market. Thus, the two three-year action plans published by the Commission Consumer Policy Service in 1990[14] and 1993[15] stressed the need for consumer information: product labelling as well as education measures, together with initiatives such as consumer representation and the need to integrate consumer policies with other policies.

The consumer policy emerging during this era seems to convey the message that the emphasis is on consumers being reasonably capable of looking after their own interests. In a sense, the Community sees its role as ensuring maximum transparency, relying thereafter on the consumer to make rational decisions. It has been observed that 'From the emphasis on transparency strategy, at least in the form it is perceived in the Community today, it seems to follow that the dominating consumer image in Community law is of the rational information seeking consumer.'[16]

A further concept of importance in the area of consumer policy is subsidiarity.[17] Inserted in the Maastricht Treaty[18] the essence of the principle is that:

In areas which do not fall within its exclusive competence, the Community shall take action, in accordance with the principle of subsidiarity, only if and in so far as

---

12. Such as for example directives on product liability, product safety and unfair contract terms.
13. Such as the Council resolution on future priorities for relaunching consumer protection policy, cf. Howells and Wilhelmsson, op. cit., n. 11, p. 11.
14. COM (90) 98.
15. COM (93) 378.
16. Howells and Wilhelmsson, op. cit., n. 11, p. 18.
17. For a thorough account of the principle of subsidiarity see N. Emiliou, 'Subsidiarity: an Effective Barrier against the "Enterprises of Ambition"' (1992) 17 *English Law Review* 383.
18. Art. 3b.

the objectives of the proposed action cannot be sufficiently achieved by the Member States and can therefore, by reason of the scale or effects of the proposed action, be better achieved by the Community.

As outlined above, the Community legislative process has continuously been affected by the ongoing debate about whether action should be taken by Member States or at Community level. It should be appreciated, in this context, that the effect of subsidiarity is not to reduce Community competencies but to establish efficient administration. It is important that it should not be seen as a reason for lack of activity in the area of consumer policy, but as a way to ensure democratic involvement in policy making, implementation and enforcement, as has been stressed by the European Parliament.[19] In its resolution, the European Parliament further stressed that formulation of consumer policy at Member State level coupled with weakening of minimum harmonised Community-wide standards would directly undermine the Single Market.

Although the principle of subsidiarity may be of importance in the area of consumer policy, the most important addition of the Maastricht Treaty is no doubt the provision of a specific legal basis for measures relating to consumer protection, the new Article 129a:

1. The Community shall contribute to the attainment of a high level of consumer protection through: (a) Measures adopted pursuant to Article 100a in the context of completion of the internal market; (b) specific action which supports and supplements the policy pursued by the Member States to protect the health, safety and economic interests of consumers and to provide adequate information to consumers. 2. The Council, acting in accordance with the procedure referred to in Art 189b and after consulting the Economic and Social Committee, shall adopt the specific action referred to in paragraph 1(b). 3. Action pursuant to paragraph 2 shall not prevent any Member State from maintaining or introducing more stringent protective measures. Such measures must be compatible with this Treaty. The Commission shall be notified of them.

While the provision confirms that consumer policy shall be seen as an element of internal market policy, it also establishes an independent competence to act in the field of consumer protection. At face value, this provision seems to greatly enhance the position of consumer policy in the Community. It has been observed, however, that difficulties may occur in trying to establish the correct legal basis in the choice between Article 100a(4) and Article 129a(3). The matter is of importance since the latter,

---

19. Resolution on the application of the principle of subsidiarity to environment and consumer protection policies, [1993] OJ C42/40.

following the minimum harmonisation formula, is more permissive of national action than the former.[20]

Although the issue of legal basis renders the application of the new provision on consumer policy more difficult, it does illustrate the fact that consumer policy remains firmly on the Community agenda, and that it informs actions taken in the course of completing the internal market. Thus, in its latest Communication on Priorities for Consumer Policy[21] the Commission points out that 'consumer policy was directed over the last six years towards contributing to the success of the major European Community goal of completing the Internal Market'.[22] This, as we shall see, is of importance not least in the area of financial services.

3. FINANCIAL SERVICES

The objective of creating an internal market in financial services, set out in the Commission's White Paper on the Completion of the Internal Market,[23] has been achieved through adoption of numerous legislative measures, aimed primarily at the financial sector but inevitably also affecting the rights and interests of the consumer. The Commission, convinced that the establishment of a single market serves the consumers' interest, recently stated that

the providers are gaining access to a much wider market and at the same time are being subjected to fiercer competition at home. The buyers of financial services are benefiting from greater competition in terms both of price and a wider choice of financial products.[24]

This familiar assumption underlies Community activities in the area of financial services, and efforts to complete the internal market focused to a great extent on the activities of financial institutions. While it is impossible, within the constraints of this chapter, to explore those measures in detail, it is pertinent to provide an overview of the effect they have had on the situation of the consumer.[25] True to its overall approach to consumer policy, the Community has also adopted measures more specifically

20. Weatherill, op. cit., n. 2, p. 27.
21. COM (95) 519 final.
22. At p. 3.
23. COM (85) 310 final, Completing the Internal Market.
24. Financial Services: Meeting Consumers' Expectations, op. cit., n. 6, p. 1.
25. The issue has been explored in greater detail by Marise Cremona in 'Freedom of Movement of Financial Services', in A. Caiger and M. A. Floudas (eds.), *1996 Onwards: Lowering the Barriers Further* (Wiley, 1996), p. 65, and in R. Cranston and C. Hadjiemmanuil, "Banking Integration in the European Community: The European

designed to improve the situation of the consumer, in certain cases through protection but, more importantly, through measures designed to ensure transparency and information. Following the initial overview of consumer aspects of directives aimed primarily at the financial services sector, measures directed more specifically at the consumer will then be examined in somewhat greater detail.

3.1 Creating an internal market in financial services

3.1.1 Freedom to provide services across borders

With the impetus created by the White Paper came what has been termed an explosion of Community legislation in the financial services sector.[26] In the insurance, banking and investment services sectors, directives essentially following the same approach were adopted.[27] Based on the by now familiar approach of mutual recognition combined with minimum harmonisation, the directives in the area rely heavily on a division between 'home state' and 'host state' responsibilities. The idea is to make possible the granting of a single licence recognised throughout the Community, and to ensure the application of the principle of home Member State prudential supervision.[28] Authorisation is granted by the competent authorities of the home state[29] subject to minimum conditions set by the directives. Having been granted the licence the firm may then, through cross-border provision of services or through the establishment of a branch, offer services in other Member States. The purpose is to eliminate the need for separate licences in each Member State, thereby removing barriers to trade. To discourage regulatory arbitrage, Member States must confer with each other before granting authorisation to subsidiaries of institutions authorised in other Member States.[30] Authorisation conditions

---

(continued)

Community's Unfinished Agenda", in J. J. Norton, M. Andenas and M. Footer (eds), *The Changing World of International Law in the Twenty-first Century: A Tribute to the Late Kenneth R. Simmonds* (Kluwer Law International, 1998), p. 341.

26. J. A. Usher, 'The Implications of the Single European Market for Banking and Finance: an Overview', in R. Cranston (ed.), *The Single Market and the Law of Banking* (LLP, 1995), p. 1.

27. Second Banking Directive 89/646 [1989] OJ L386/1; Third Directive on Direct Life Insurance 92/96 [1992] OJ L360/1; and Investment Services Directive 93/22 [1993] OJ L141/27. The three directives operate in a similar manner. For reasons of brevity, reference is made in the following only to the Second Banking Directive, 2BCD, and to the Investment Services Directive, ISD.

28. 2BCD, op. cit., n. 27, rec. 4.

29. ISD Art. 3, 2BCD Art. 4.

30. ISD Art. 6, 2BCD Art. 7, cf. 2BCD rec. 8.

relate to capital,[31] identity of shareholders or members or, in the case of investment firms, the persons who effectively direct the business, and are of an ongoing nature.[32] Detailed rules on the capital of an institution are set out in separate directives.[33] It is the responsibility of the home state to supervise on an on-going basis and ensure that these conditions are met, as well as to ensure compliance with prudential rules.

Once authorisation has been granted, institutions will be permitted to carry out in any Member State activities covered by the licence, even though locally licensed institutions in other Member States may not be allowed by their own domestic regulations to carry out certain of these services.[34] In the long term it is unlikely, however, that Member States would wish to impose more stringent requirements on institutions located within their territory since this might have the adverse effect of driving business elsewhere.

There are certain areas where Member States retain a measure of regulatory powers, not only over institutions licensed within their territory but also over businesses licensed in other Member States. The question of the extent to which a Member State is permitted to protect the interests of, for example, its consumers has generated much debate since, in relation to consumer matters, for a Member State to be able to do this effectively it is necessary to be able to regulate all business taking place within its territory, not only the business of locally licensed institutions. This flies in the face of the aim of the principle of mutual recognition to remove barriers to trade: an inevitable consequence of permitting each Member State to lay down separate rules to protect consumers is distortions in the playing field.

3.1.2 Residual regulatory powers

The problem is compounded by what has become known as the 'general-good' provision. Providing that host Member States may 'take appropriate measures to prevent or to punish irregularities committed within their territories which are contrary to the legal rules they have adopted in the interest of the general good',[35] it does not clarify the extent to which Member States may undertake regulatory action, nor interests which may

31. ISD Art. 3:3, 2BCD Art. 4.
32. ISD Art. 8, 2BCD Art. 10.
33. Solvency Ratio Directive [1989] OJ L386/14, 89/647/EEC, Own Funds Directive [1989] OJ L1224/16, 89/299/EEC, Capital Adequacy Directive, OJ 1993 L141/1, 93/6/EC.
34. Reverse discrimination is possible also in so far as the initial authorisation requirements are concerned, cf. 2BCD Art. 4:1 *e contrario*.
35. 2BCD Art. 21:5. The corresponding provision of the ISD goes further, detailing the principles those rules must implement: ISD Art. 11.

be protected by such action. The Court of Justice has recognised professional rules intended to protect the recipient of services,[36] and consumers[37] as well as preservation of the good reputation of the national financial services sector[38] among other areas as being covered by the concept of the general good. Furthermore, the Court, in its case law on the general good, has established certain principles which must be respected by the Member State:

- restrictions must be justified by imperative reasons relating to the public interest, such as the need to ensure compliance with professional rules of conduct or to safeguard interests of others;
- this interest is not already protected adequately by controls in their home state;
- the same result cannot be achieved by less restrictive means; and
- host state rules must be applied in a non-discriminatory way to all operators in the host state.[39]

It should be noted in this context that the assessment of proportionality may differ depending on the mode of operation. Thus, as noted by the Commission,[40] a restriction could be more easily regarded as proportionate when an operator carries out his activities permanently within the territory of a Member State than when he does so temporarily.

As pointed out by one commentator, provisions of national consumer credit laws for example, may offer higher protection than the EC directives and are unlikely to be found to be in breach of the principle of free movement.[41] This area is problematic, however, since it is closely connected to the question of the law applicable to banking contracts. The Second Banking Directive contains no specific rules for determining the law applicable to contractual obligations, and reference must therefore be made to the Rome Convention on the law applicable to contractual obligations. If application of the provisions of the Convention results in the law of the host country applying to a contract concluded with a consumer then, argues the Commission, this law should be applied only if either it does not conflict with the principle of mutual recognition or it is in the interest of the general good.[42] An alternative approach has been suggested by Howells and Wilhelmsson, distinguishing between the public law supervi-

---

36. Joined Cases 110/78 and 11/78 *Van Wesemael* [1979] ECR 35.
37. Case 205/84 *Commission v Germany* [1986] ECR 35.
38. Case C-384/93 *Alpine Investments BV* [1995] ECR.
39. *Commission v Germany*, loc. cit., n. 37.
40. [1995] OJ C291/7, p. 18.
41. Howells and Wilhelmsson, op. cit., n. 11, p. 192.
42. C291/7, loc. cit., n. 40 at 19.

sory powers which are the main concern of the Second Banking Directive, and the laws governing the resulting contracts which are the province of the Consumer Credit Directives, arguing that the latter should be a matter for host state regulation. This would result, it is argued, in ensuring that all consumers contracting in the same state receive the same protection, whether using a domestic credit institution or one from another state.[43]

Altogether, according to a study carried out by the Commission, the directives adopted in this area have resulted in increased competition in the banking retail market, and consumers now have a wider range of products and services to choose from.[44] In the Commission's view 'open competition . . . is the consumer's best friend'. In its evaluation of consumer satisfaction, the Commission notes that all measures directed at the financial services sector contribute to the goal of creating a trustworthy industry. In this respect, the importance of provisions laying down minimum standards for senior staff and major shareholders is emphasised.

3.1.3   The 'freedom to buy'

The image, then, is of a near complete single market in financial services. In its European Consumer Guide to the Single Market[45] the Commission boldly states that 'In principle you can: keep your money where you want to; transfer your money wherever you want to and borrow money wherever it suits you best.'[46] This is in stark contrast to the findings of the Green Paper:

Some consumers have been refused financial services in another Member State on the grounds that they are not resident in or nationals of that state . . . in another Member State, certain credit institutions, allegedly for tax reasons, refuse to offer some banking services (current account, credit card etc) to non-residents.[47]

It is indeed clear, as observed initially,[48] that legislative measures cannot create a single market in financial services but only remove barriers to trade and, at best, influence behaviour. It was observed several years ago that, in focusing on the freedom of the financial institution to provide services across borders, the Community neglected the other side of the coin,

43. Howells and Wilhelmsson, op. cit., n. 11, p. 193.
44. The Impact of the Single Market in Banking and Insurance, Annex to COM (97) 309 final.
45. European Commission (Office for Official Publications of the European Communities, 1995).
46. Ibid., p. 171
47. Green Paper, op. cit., n. 6, p. 8.
48. Lomnicka, op. cit., n. 3.

the consumers' 'freedom to buy'.[49] While it is easy to sympathise with the view that 'it is time that the Commission took steps to build a fourth freedom into its strategy – the freedom of the consumer to buy financial services without national or residential discrimination',[50] it is difficult to see what could be done in reality – contractual freedom is an essential principle of contract law, and Community law cannot oblige financial institutions to accept clients, be they national or foreign.[51]

3.2   Measures specifically aimed at consumers

As discussed in Section 1, Community consumer policy seems to be aimed largely at providing the active and well-equipped consumer with information and ensuring transparency, thereby making well-informed decisions possible. Although the removal of barriers to a single market in financial services is now more or less complete, information provision is one of the areas seen by consumers as deficient. Complaints by consumers in the area of banking, for example, frequently concern lack of information on prices and conditions, lack of professional advice and the difficulties in comparing various services and products.[52] Lack of information hampers competition and this is an area where the Commission is particularly concerned to address consumer misgivings. Considering that the parties involved should be given an opportunity to agree on voluntary measures to improve the situation, the Commission recently called for a 'constructive dialogue' between financial industry associations and consumer representatives.[53] It is hoped that such a dialogue will promote solutions such as codes of conduct.

3.2.1   Cross-border credit transfers

As mentioned in Section 2, the Commission in areas of consumer protection frequently favours an approach whereby, initially, soft law measures are published, setting out objectives and encouraging Member States or affected parties to take action to achieve those. Where this is seen as failing to deliver the desired results, hard law measures may follow. In

---

49. J. Mitchell, *Banker's Racket or Consumer Benefit? A Consumer's View of the Single European Market for Financial Services* (Policy Studies Institute, 1991).
50. Ibid., p. 148.
51. Green Paper, op. cit., n. 6, p. 8.
52. Ibid., p. 10.
53. COM (97) 309 final, Financial Services: Enhancing Consumer Confidence, p. 7.

addition to stimulating national debate, it may be assumed that by spurring Member States to action in the area, soft law measures promote a degree of harmonisation, thereby paving the way for hard law, should the desired results fail to materialise. In this context, it is interesting to note that the Commission seems to be using this as a 'carrot-and-stick' method, for example in addressing lack of information, in the following terms:

The Commission, therefore calls for clear commitment from the industry and consumers to agree voluntarily improvements in the provision of information . . . If sufficient progress is not voluntarily made . . . the Commission will propose further initiative, including legislation.[54]

The sequence of events in the area of cross-border credit transfers well illustrates this approach. Following a Commission recommendation[55] in which six principles aimed at improving transparency were set out, the Commission published several reports on this subject. This self-regulatory approach was seen as inadequate and eventually a directive was proposed. Finally adopted in January 1997, the Directive on Cross-Border Credit Transfers[56] sets out mainly to improve provision of information to consumers wishing to effect transactions across borders. To ensure transparency, the consumer should be provided with adequate information before as well as after the execution of the transfer.[57]

The information requirements include indication of the complaints and redress procedures.[58] Whereas pre-contractual information, such as indication of the time needed to complete the transaction and manner of calculation of fees and charges, *shall* be provided, information subsequent to the transfer, such as a reference enabling the customer to identify the transfer, the original amount of the transfer and the amount of charges and fees payable, shall be supplied *unless the consumer expressly forgoes this.*[59] Again, it seems the Community favours the active and well-equipped consumer likely at least not to forgo information of this kind.

In addition to the information requirements, obligations relating to the time taken for transfers are imposed on the institutions. Thus, where the agreed time limit is not complied with, or where no time limit has been agreed, at the end of the fifth banking business day following the transfer

---

54. Ibid., p. 7, addressing the perceived lack of information in the area of financial service.
55. Commission Recommendation 90/109/EEC on the transparency of banking conditions relating to cross-border financial transactions, [1990] OJ L67/39.
56. [1997] OJ L43/25, 97/5/EC.
57. Arts 3 and 4.
58. Art. 3, p. 5.
59. Art. 4.

order, if the funds have not been credited to the account of the beneficiary's institution, the originator's institution shall compensate the originator.[60] Also, the beneficiary's institution may become liable if failing to
execute the transaction.[61] Where it can be established that the delay was
attributable to the originator or the beneficiary, no compensation is
payable.[62]

Clearly, the minimum obligations laid down in relation to cross-border
transfers will serve to harmonise information requirements in this area.
The decision to adopt 'hard law' should not, however, lead to the conclusion that soft law measures are always insufficient. Self-regulatory measures have an important role to play and it is hoped that industry as well as
consumers will heed the Commission's call for action,[63] thereby limiting
the need for further Community legislation.

3.2.2   Consumer credit

In keeping with the Community penchant for transparency as outlined
above, action in the area of consumer credit has focused mainly on provision
of information. The Consumer Credit Directive[64] thus aims to ensure that the
consumer is aware of the cost of the credit. The application of the directive is
limited to contracts with a value of ECU200–20,000, thereby excluding contracts for small value as well as for larger amounts.[65] Also, agreements
intended primarily for the purpose of acquiring or retaining property rights
in land or in an existing or projected building are excluded.[66] There is thus
no Community legislation in the area of mortgage credit, a matter which has
caused some concern among consumer groups.[67] Lack of information leads
to difficulties in making meaningful comparisons and the problem is exacer-
bated by widely differing national laws in the area. Although the Commission
is aware of the problem, Community action seems distant.[68]

---

60. Art. 6, p. 1.
61. Art. 6, p. 2.
62. Art. 6, p. 3.
63. COM (97) 309 final.
64. 87/102/EEC [1987] OJ L42/48, as amended by 90/88/EEC [1990] OJ L61/14.
65. The rationale behind this is that 'credit agreements for very large financial amounts
     tend to differ from the usual consumer credit agreements' and 'the application of pro-
     visions of this Directive to agreements for very small amounts could create unneces-
     sary administrative burdens both for consumers and grantors of credit', ibid., rec. 4.
66. Art. 2(1)(a).
67. COM (97) 309 final, p. 10.
68. Ibid., p. 10.

In relation to consumer credit in general, the instrument widely acknowledged to enable the consumer to make informed choices is known as annual percentage rate (APR) and the directive goes a long way towards laying down a common formula for calculation thereof. Member States which already use a different formula are permitted to retain this, as long as only one formula is used within their territory.[69] It is easy to see that a completely harmonised system would empower the consumer further, and new legislation has recently been adopted in the area.[70]

While aiming to protect consumers against unfair contract terms[71] the main purpose of the directive is to enable well-informed consumers to choose the best available credit. Community efforts in this area fall well short of addressing the problem of over-indebtedness, an issue of concern to consumer groups. In this respect, the Commission has agreed only to implement 'certain pilot projects' aiming at improving consumer information and education. The problem is perceived, then, not as a matter of 'irresponsible over-promotion of credit'[72] but as one of lacking information and inadequate education.

3.2.3   Distant selling

Distant selling may take place by traditional means, such as mail-order catalogues and personalised direct mail, as well as by modern audio-visual techniques: telephone selling and, with the further spread of personal computers, virtual banking. While allowing customers to shop from the comfort of their own home across borders, thereby participating actively in the single market with relative ease, distant selling also gives rise to concern. Lack of knowledge of the seller and the risks of impulse buying, perhaps as a consequence of high-pressure selling, all constitute rationales for consumer protection in this area.

Financial services are increasingly commonly sold at a distance, and may involve important decisions for the consumer in relation to matters such as insurance as well as more complex financial services.[73] The exclusion of financial services from the Distance Contracts Directive[74] is there-

---

69.   Art. 1(a)(5).
70.   Directive 98/7/EC, OJ 1998 L101/17.
71.   Rec. 5.
72.   Cf. Howells and Wilhelmsson, op. cit., n. 11, p. 194.
73.   See *Alpine Investments*, loc. cit., n. 38.
74.   Directive 97/7/EC on the protection of consumers in respect of distance contracts, [1997] OJ L144/19.

fore a matter of great concern to consumers. In particular, the absence of a cooling-off period in relation to contracts for non-life insurance has been lamented.[75] The Commission has therefore agreed to put forward a proposal to address this gap in consumer protection. Stating that 'this proposal confirms the difference between distance contracts in financial services and other types of distance contracts' the Commission proposes the right, for example, to withdraw a contract which is not appropriate if the price of the financial product depends on market fluctuations or if the contract has already come into force (which may be the case in relation to motor insurance).[76]

4.   CONCLUSION

From the overview contained in the previous sections it is possible to conclude that the removal of barriers to an internal market is well underway. It is reasonable to assume that, in this market, the well-informed and rational consumer will enjoy a wider choice of products and services, and will be protected in many instances by timely measures. Furthermore, a limited right has been preserved for national governments to retain measures aimed at protecting consumers. However, it is slightly disturbing that there is no concerted effort to take into account the needs of the more vulnerable consumers, for example in relation to refusal to sell.

Although the Commission recognises that 'a bank account is one of the primary needs of life like electricity or a telephone'[77] it is prepared to do no more than support efforts at a national level. While it may be argued that this is consistent with the principle of subsidiarity it should be recalled that subsidiarity should not be seen as a reason for lack of activity in the area of consumer policy.[78] If, however, it is accepted that this is an area where action at national level is indeed more appropriate, this should at least be a conscious and well-informed decision.

---

75.   Commission Communication Priorities for Consumer Policy 1996–1998 COM (95) 519 final.
76.   COM (97) 309 final, p. 6.
77.   Ibid., p. 8.
78.   Ibid., s. 2(b).

Chapter Two

THE OMBUDSMEN AND CONSUMER PROTECTION

Philip Morris and Gavin Little

Chapter Outline

1. Background: the Proliferation of Ombudsmen and Problems Posed by Growth of the Ombudsman Technique

2. The Banking Ombudsman Scheme

3. The Building Societies Ombudsman Scheme

4. The IMRO Investment Ombudsman Scheme

5. Conclusions

6. Addendum

Consumer Protection in Financial Services (P. Cartwright, ed.: 90-411-9717-6: © Kluwer Law International: pub. Kluwer Law International, 1999: printed in Great Britain)

1. BACKGROUND: THE PROLIFERATION OF OMBUDSMEN AND PROBLEMS POSED BY GROWTH OF THE OMBUDSMAN TECHNIQUE

Writing in 1989, Sir Gordon Borrie, the then Director General of Fair Trading, observed that Ombudsmen were 'the flavour of the decade' and that there appeared to be 'no stopping the onward march of the Ombudsman concept'.[1] The spectacular growth of the ombudsman technique has resulted in some twenty-two recognised ombudsman schemes in the UK and Ireland, with nine of them located in the financial services industry.[2] While some commentators may regard this 'staggering development'[3] as no more than further evidence of the growing influence of the alternative dispute resolution movement,[4] others, correctly in our opinion, view it in more fundamental terms: as the creative adaptation of a traditional public law concept in order to subject the exercise of *private* power to a measure of accountability.[5] Such an adaptation is entirely proper given the blurring of the public–private sector divide in the modern state, coupled with the fact that the immense commercial power (and its corresponding impact on consumers) wielded by many financial sector institutions (such as banks, building societies and insurance companies) can be equated with the administrative power exercised by state agencies. This commercial power has characteristically been exercised free of effective legal restraint, largely due to the fact that litigation for most individual consumers is not a realistic option due to expense, delay, undue formalism and deficiencies in substantive consumer law. The relative inaccessibility of the courts as a consumer redress mechanism means that ombudsmen are *de facto* not so much an *alternative* form of redress as the *only viable* means of redress for consumers, particularly in financial services where the monetary value of many consumers' claims renders litigation an option simply not worth pursuing.[6]

---

1. G. Borrie, 'The Regulation of Public and Private Power' (1989) *Public Law* 552, 564.
2. British and Irish Ombudsman Association, *Directory of Ombudsmen* (March, 1995).
3. P. Birkinshaw, *Grievances, Remedies and the State*, 2nd edn (Sweet & Maxwell, 1994), p. 242.
4. See, *eg*, C. M. Schmitthoff, 'Extra-judicial Dispute Settlement', *Forum Internationale* (May 1985); and C. Harlow, 'The Issues', in R. Gregory *et al.* (eds), *Practice and Prospects of the Ombudsmen in the United Kingdom* (The Edwin Mellin Press, 1995).
5. Birkinshaw op. cit., n. 3, p. 243; and A. R. Mowbray, 'Ombudsmen: the Private Sector Dimension', in W. Finnie, C. M. G. Himsworth, and N. Walker (eds), *Edinburgh Essays in Public Law* (Edinburgh University Press, 1991).
6. P. Rawlings and C. Willett, 'Ombudsman Schemes in the United Kingdom's Financial Sector: the Insurance Ombudsman, the Banking Ombudsman, and the Building Societies Ombudsman' (1994) 17 *Journal of Consumer Policy* 307, 325.

While the emergence of ombudsmen as a mechanism of consumer redress is, therefore, both theoretically valid and sorely needed, there are two problems, in particular, posed by the development which are worth noting. The first is the glaring lack of legal controls on use of the 'ombudsman' template. Given this fact and in view of the rapid expansion of the ombudsman technique in the private sector there is:

a danger that the concept and the dignity of the office will be diluted by inappropriate and random attribution. The Ombudsman on present trends is in danger of being seen as little more than a provider of information, a sorter our of petty annoyances, an extension of the customer relation function of business or as a means of deflecting rather than satisfying the complaints of irate consumers.[7]

As we endeavour to show in our three case studies below, these fears, at least in the context of the financial services industry, are probably exaggerated. The fact remains, however, that the lack of legal regulation means there is a very real risk of devaluation of the ombudsman title. Recognising this, the existing ombudsmen have formed the British and Irish Ombudsman Association which, on a self-regulatory basis, confers recognition on ombudsman schemes meeting the benchmarks of independence, effectiveness, fairness and public accountability.[8] A second problem is that the *ad hoc*, unsystematic growth of ombudsman arrangements in the financial services industry has generated jurisdictional overlaps, so that 'rather than a beneficial choice of available machinery, the consumer may end up confused and bewildered by a multiplicity of different schemes'.[9] The response so far has been a pragmatic and rather unsatisfactory one: individual ombudsmen have struck pacts with each other, where there is a lack of clarity as to which ombudsman enjoys jurisdiction, allocating jurisdiction on particular issues to a specified ombudsman. On both this and the devaluation problem though, the only acceptable long-term solution, we feel, lies in the establishment of a permanent, statutory Ombudsman Commission[10] charged with rationalisation of the current untidy 'system' by strictly regulating

---

7. M. Hayes, 'Emerging Issues for Ombudsmen', in United Kingdom Ombudsman Conference, 17–18 October 1991, *Conference Report*, p. 8.
8. British and Irish Ombudsman Association, *Rules and Criteria* (June 1997).
9. R. Thomas, 'Alternative Dispute Resolution: Consumer Disputes' (1988) 7 *Civil Justice Quarterly* 206, 213.
10. P. Birkinshaw, 'The Ombudsman: What Next?' (British and Irish Ombudsman Association Annual Lecture, 9 May 1995), p. 9; and J. Farrand, 'Ombudsmen and the Consumer', in Gregory *et al.*, op. cit., n. 4. Such a reform is not, however, apparently supported by the Ombudsmen themselves, see British and Irish Ombudsman Association, *Memorandum* (11 April 1995), rejecting the creation of a Council on Tribunals type body for ombudsmen – a rejection which would probably also apply to a proposed Ombudsman Commission.

award of the ombudsman title, specifying definitive rules on the allocation of jurisdiction and arrangements for speedy re-routeing of complaints to the correct ombudsman scheme.

We now turn to the utility of the ombudsman technique in the financial services industry. Rather than giving (necessarily brief) accounts of all such ombudsman schemes currently operating in the industry,[11] we have decided instead to carry out a critical evaluation of three distinct schemes (namely the banking, building societies and investment ombudsmen) having different legal bases, institutional frameworks and operational experiences. Our discussion will draw upon public law style principles of independence, openness, accessibility, fairness and effectiveness which have been posited as appropriate measures of the utility of complaints-handling arrangements.[12] A selective but reasonably in-depth study along these lines will, we feel, provide readers with a useful starting point for understanding the contribution ombudsmen can make to improving levels of consumer protection in the financial services industry. After the three case studies we conclude by reflecting on the extent to which the three ombudsmen have raised standards of consumer protection in their respective sectors and identify future matters for concern.

2. THE BANKING OMBUDSMAN SCHEME[13]

In this section we briefly consider reasons for creation of the scheme and provide a thumbnail sketch of its key substantive features. It is now generally acknowledged that the High Street banks launched their own self-regulatory ombudsman scheme in 1986 for two reasons: (i) to pre-empt the prospect of an unwelcome statutory complaints procedure and (ii) to gain a 'marketing edge' over their rivals – most notably building societies – in the fiercely competitive market for personal financial services.[14]

---

11. Which in any event can be found elsewhere. See, *eg,* A. McGee, *The Financial Services Ombudsmen* (Fourmat Publishing, 1992); R. W. Hodgin, 'Ombudsman and Other Complaints Procedures in the Financial Services Sector in the United Kingdom' (1992) 21 *Anglo-American Law Review* 1; and R. James, *Private Ombudsmen and Public Law* (Dartmouth, 1997).

12. See J. Birds and C. Graham, 'Complaints Mechanisms in the Financial Services Industry' (1988) 7 *Civil Justice Quarterly* 312; and J. Birds and C. Graham, 'Alternative Dispute Resolution: Financial Services', in K. J. Mackie (ed.), *A Handbook of Dispute Resolution: ADR in Action* (Croom Helm, 1991), chapter 9.

13. On which see generally the now rather dated accounts in P. E. Morris, 'The Banking Ombudsman: I and II' (1987) *Journal of Business Law* 131, 199; P. E. Morris, 'The Banking Ombudsman: Five Years On' (1992) *Lloyd's Maritime and Commercial Law Quarterly* 227; and McGee, op. cit., n. 11, chapter 3.

14. Morris, op. cit., n. 13 (1987), 131, 134, and (1992) 227, 228–9.

In terms of its legal basis and institutional structure, the scheme uses the legal vehicle of a company limited by guarantee, funding is provided by the sponsoring banks and its institutional set up is consciously modelled on the tripartite constitutional arrangements pioneered by the Insurance Ombudsman Bureau in 1981. Thus the Board is composed entirely of representatives from the banking industry and has three principal functions: (i) to raise the funding necessary for the operation of the scheme; (ii) to approve the Ombudsman's annual budget; and (iii) to approve changes to the scheme's terms of reference. In contrast, the Council is composed of five independent and three banking representatives.[15] Its key role is to act as a 'buffer', protecting the Ombudsman against improper pressure brought to bear by the architects and financiers of the scheme.[16] More specifically, the Council appoints (and renews the appointment of) the Ombudsman, proposes changes to his terms of reference to the Board, receives the Ombudsman's Annual Report and liaises closely with the Ombudsman on a regular basis. Finally, the Ombudsman's dual mission is to receive, investigate and resolve complaints falling within his jurisdiction, and to stimulate the adoption of (and adherence to) good practices in the retail banking industry.

Despite the recommendation in the Jack Report[17] and the recent statement by the Labour Party[18] that ideals of fairness and perceived independence require the scheme to be placed on a statutory footing, there are in fact compelling reasons for retention of the scheme's self-regulatory character.[19] First, a statutory-based scheme would inevitably involve loss of the Ombudsman's executive remedial power (because of the so-called 'constitutional principle' that legislation should not oust an individual's right of access to court for a determination as to his legal rights), which is crucial in persuading banks to respond positively to the Ombudsman's suggestions during the conciliation process. Second, a self-regulatory scheme brings with it the vital advantage of flexibility, in terms of capacity for

---

15. The Office of the Banking Ombudsman, *The Banking Ombudsman Scheme: Terms of Reference* (May 1995), (hereafter TR), p. 1.
16. The Office of the Banking Ombudsman, *The Banking Ombudsman Scheme: Annual Report 1985–86* (Chair of the Council, Dame Mary Donaldson), p. 13.
17. *Banking Services: Law and Practice*, Report by the Review Committee (Chairman: Professor R. B. Jack) (February 1989), Cm 622, chapter 15. This proposal was rejected by the government though it conceded that the decision was a 'fine one': *Banking Services: Law and Practice* (March 1990), Cm 1026, annex 3, paras 16, 17 and 37.
18. Gordon Brown MP, Speech delivered to the Labour Finance and Industry Group (1 May 1995), p. 7.
19. See: *Banking Services: Law and Practice* (1990), op. cit., n. 17, annex 3; and The Office of the Banking Ombudsman, *The Banking Ombudsman Scheme: Annual Report 1988–89* (Chair of the Council, Dame Mary Donaldson), pp. 3–4.

prompt changes to the Ombudsman's remit, which is an important quality in the fast changing world of modern retail banking. Third, a scheme enshrined in legislation creates the risk of banks abandoning their current supportive stance toward the Ombudsman and instead reacting to his determinations in a legalistic manner by frequent recourse to rights of appeal and applications for judicial review.

The reach and coverage of the scheme is perhaps one of its most impressive features. It embraces some fifty sponsor banks and their designated associates and is estimated to cover 99 per cent of individual personal accounts.[20] Complaints can be entertained in relation to 'banking services', which are expansively defined as 'all banking services provided by banks in the ordinary course of their business to individuals and the provision by banks of credit card services, executors and trustee services and advice and services relating to taxation, insurance and investments'.[21] Individuals embrace not simply private persons but also partnerships, unincorporated associations and 'small companies', which are defined as companies having a turnover not exceeding £1 million during the previous financial year.[22] Extension of the scheme to small companies in 1993 was initially opposed by both the Ombudsman[23] and the government[24] on the basis that the essence of an ombudsman service is to provide a quasi-judicial means of resolving disputes for individuals, a facility which should be denied to an organisation which has gained the benefit of limited liability. However, both relented in the face of a campaign from the small business community unhappy with alleged unfair treatment by banks during the severe economic recession of the early 1990s.

A plethora of exclusions make inroads into this prima facie enormous jurisdiction. The most important are, first, that the Ombudsman is precluded from questioning a bank's judgement on lending or security decisions unless the decision is tainted by maladministration,[25] and secondly, complaints cannot be entertained in relation to banks' general interest rate policies.[26] The former is a perfectly valid exclusion: it is no part of an ombudsman's function to question the substantive merits of commercial lending decisions. The latter exclusion underlines the point that interest

20. The Office of the Banking Ombudsman, *Banks and Companies in the Scheme* (April 1996); and The Office of the Banking Ombudsman, *The Banking Ombudsman Scheme: Annual Report 1991–92* (Chair of the Council, Dame Mary Donaldson), p. 2.
21. TR, para. 29(a)(ii).
22. TR, para. 29(a)(iii).
23. L. Shurman, 'Remit and Process: a Private Sector View', in Gregory *et al.*, op. cit., n. 4, p. 108, a stance supported by his Council: *Annual Report 1988–89*, op. cit., n. 19, p. 43.
24. *Banking Services: Law and Practice* (1990), op. cit., n. 17, annex 3, para. 38.
25. TR, paras 16(a), 29(a)(iv).
26. TR, para. 16(b).

rate policies are a 'matter of commercial judgement where the only real restraint is that of market forces'[27] and may well generate frustration among 'small company' complainants, who have persistently criticised banks for charging, in their view, penal interest rates on loan and overdraft facilities.

Turning to the Ombudsman's procedural *modus operandi*, it is essentially a document-based, inquisitorial investigation with a powerful accent on the promotion of conciliated settlements.[28] Before this process even begins, however, the complaint must have reached 'deadlock', that is to say it has been considered at senior management level in the bank without settlement proving possible.[29] This requirement, coupled with the obligation in the Code of Banking Practice[30] for banks to establish and properly publicise internal complaints procedures, has evidently produced a formalisation and sharpening of banks' internal grievance resolution procedures so that a growing quantity of customer complaints are settled locally and informally. Another procedural point worth noting is the so-called 'test cases procedure'.[31] Under this procedure a bank may, with the Ombudsman's consent, refer a dispute to court for determination upon agreeing to pay the erstwhile complainant's legal costs, if it feels the complaint may have important consequences for the business of the bank or banks generally or raises a novel or important point of law. Thus far the procedure has only been invoked on a single occasion[32] during the decade in which the scheme has been operational, suggesting that its value is as a symbolic affirmation of the independence of the scheme rather than a potentially fruitful mechanism for the development of substantive banking law.

27. McGee, op. cit., n. 11, p. 22.
28. See generally Shurman, op. cit., n. 23, and *Annual Report 1988-89*, op. cit., n. 19, pp. 9–10.
29. TR, para. 19(c) and (d).
30. BBA, BSA and APACS, *The Banking Code* (3rd edn, 1997), paras. 5.5–5.6. For useful commentaries on the Code generally and its utility as a consumer protection instrument, see further A Campbell, 'Banking and the Consumer in the United Kingdom: An Examination of Some Recent Developments in Consumer Protection' (1993) *Consumer Law Journal*, 81; P. E. Morris, 'Banking Practices Revised: the Code of Banking Practice' (1992) *Lloyd's Maritime and Commercial Law Quarterly* 474; and L. Shurman, 'A Fair Banking Code?' (Chartered Institute of Bankers, Ernest Sykes Memorial Lecture, 1991).
31. TR, paras 20 and 21.
32. *Sutherland v The Royal Bank of Scotland* (Scottish Court of Session, 4 December 1995, unreported) where the pursuer succeeded in persuading the court to take a different view to that of the Ombudsman on the substantive banking law point of when a cheque is paid into an account. For a full discussion of the test cases procedure and the ruling in *Sutherland*, see further P. E. Morris and G. F. M. Little, 'Banks, the Ombudsman and the Courts' (1997) *Journal of Business Law* 80.

Once engaged in conciliation the Ombudsman is not concerned to simply identify and ratify the lowest common denominator of agreement between the parties; rather *he* has to be satisfied that any proposed settlement is objectively fair. When the Ombudsman promotes an informal settlement or is minded to make a recommendation, either of which involves the payment of compensation by a bank, the proposal is only open for acceptance by the complainant 'if he accepts it in full and final settlement of the subject matter of the complaint'.[33] In formal terms the Ombudsman possesses an executive remedial power to compel sponsor banks to pay up to £100,000 compensation.[34] In practice the power is never used since banks have consistently accepted the Ombudsman's suggested informal settlements or formal recommendations.

A crucial issue, of course, is the principles applied by the Ombudsman during the dispute resolution process. His overarching obligation is to do what is 'fair in the circumstances'.[35] In particular he is enjoined to: (i) observe any applicable legal rule or relevant judicial authority; (ii) have regard to general principles of good banking practice and any relevant code of practice; and (iii) deem maladministration or inequitable treatment as being in breach of a duty owed by the bank.[36] Fairness is regarded by the Ombudsman as having two distinct facets: a highly subjective extra-legal character which permits the conduct of *both* disputants to be evaluated, and a legal foundation via the recently enacted Unfair Terms in Consumer Contracts Regulations.[37] The notion of good banking practice has in the past proved an elusive and controversial one; in particular, doubt existed as to whether such practices were a matter for the exclusive prerogative of the banks or were open to innovative development by the Ombudsman. To a large extent the heat has been taken out of this debate by the emergence of the Code of Banking Practice, which sets forth a raft of principles on bank–customer relations in the context of general banking facilities and the use of cards. Moreover, it now seems that where there are gaps not covered by the Code, the Ombudsman enjoys a power to formulate standards of practice which may not necessarily meet with the universal approval of the banking community. In specific terms, the Code has considerably assisted the Ombudsman by taking

33. TR, para. 11.
34. TR, paras 12 and 13.
35. TR, para. 20.
36. TR, para. 21.
37. SI 1994/3159, on which see generally G. Howells, *Consumer Contract Legislation* (Blackstone Press, 1995), chapter 4. The Ombudsman's views on the effect of the regulations on his case work can be found in The Office of the Banking Ombudsman, *The Banking Ombudsman Scheme: Annual Report 1993–94*, p. 14.

the sting out of 'phantom withdrawal' disputes (*ie*, apparently inexplicable withdrawals from the customer's account at an automated teller machine ('ATM')). The customer's liability for loss in such cases is now limited to £50 unless the bank can prove he or she has acted fraudulently or with gross negligence.[38] The Ombudsman has been provided with guidelines in assessing whether the customer was grossly negligent, though he has been keen to retain his discretion on this by stressing the matter is a question of fact in every case.[39] Not surprisingly the effect has been that ATM disputes, which previously regularly topped the annual 'league table' of complaints to the Ombudsman, are now in significant decline and slipping down the 'league table'.

Another important aspect of the Code are the obligations cast on banks to create effective and properly publicised internal complaints' procedures, and give appropriate publicity to the scheme by such means as leaflets, notices in branches and literature displaying the Ombudsman's address and telephone number.[40] The track record of the banks in publicising the scheme is a patchy one,[41] and regular monitoring of their publicity efforts will be crucial if this aspect of the Code is to be a substantial obligation rather than a mere aspiration. If the banks' record does not improve drastic action should be contemplated, such as detailed specification of minimum publicity requirements or even, in the case of banks consistently failing in their publicity responsibilities, the threat of expulsion from the scheme.

Despite these fears on proper publicity levels for the scheme, there is at least some evidence that adoption of the Code, especially the requirement for banks to operate internal complaints' procedures, and clarification of the previously opaque and incrementally developing notion of good banking practice, is having the desired effect of reducing the Ombudsman's workload.

As a concluding note it is worthwhile reflecting on the basic functions of the Ombudsman. Perusal of his *Annual Reports* indicates quite clearly that the Ombudsman is not simply a 'grievance man' concerned to obtain a remedy for the individual on the receiving end of unlawful, unfair or incompetent conduct by a bank. In addition the Ombudsman performs a strategic 'quality control' function which uses the individual complaint as

38. *The Banking Code*, op. cit., n. 30, paras 20.4 and 20.5.
39. Above para. 18.2; *Annual Report 1991–92*, op. cit., n. 20, p. 25; and The Office of the Banking Ombudsman, *The Banking Ombudsman Scheme: Annual Report 1994–95*, p. 32.
40. Ibid., para. 7.4
41. See further on this, the valuable empirical research by C. Graham, M. Seneviratne and R. James, 'Publicising the Bank and Building Societies Ombudsman Schemes' (1993) 3 *Consumer Policy Review* 85.

50

Table 2.1

Banking Ombudsman scheme: complaints statistics

Year	Total complaints received
1985–86	782
1986–87	1,748
1987–88	2,089
1988–89	2,706
1989–90	3,915
1990–91	6,327
1991–92	10,109
1992–93	10,231
1993–94	8,691
1994–95	7,424
1995–96	8,044
1996–97	8,818

Sources: The Office of the Banking Ombudsman, *Annual Reports*

a vehicle for the identification and rectification of systemic defects in the delivery of banking services. He has, to take just a few examples, suggested:

- a series of measures to improve the security of cards and their PINS;[42]
- better steps to inform customers about new accounts and the consequent downgrading of their existing accounts;[43]
- regular reviews to prevent the underfunding of mortgages;[44]
- that advice given by banks in the context of a business loan application is reasonably competent;[45]
- that banks, in the context of loan protection assurance, should provide customers with an overview and highlight exclusions of particular significance;[46]
- that better and clearer information should be provided to customers when loss insurance is effected;[47]

42. *Annual Report 1988–89*, op. cit., n. 19, pp. 21–5; *Annual Report 1993–94*, op. cit., n. 37, p. 26; and The Office of the Banking Ombudsman, *The Banking Ombudsman Scheme: Annual Report 1989–90*, pp. 17–19.
43. The Office of the Banking Ombudsman, *The Banking Ombudsman Scheme: Annual Report 1992–93*, p. 25.
44. *Annual Report 1994–95*, op. cit., n. 39, p. 15.
45. Ibid., p. 18.
46. Ibid., p. 19.
47. *Annual Report 1992–93*, op. cit., n. 43, p. 23.

- greater transparency *vis-à-vis* the level, methods of calculating and types of service subject to bank charges;[48]
- transparency in relation to interest rates as well as indicating a willingness to scrutinise whether the bank's published interest rates have been correctly applied.[49]

Even with the advent of the Code, it is probable that these quality control activities will continue, if only because the Code cannot hope to cover every conceivable customer grievance which may occur in relation to their dealings with banks.

Perhaps the most disappointing feature of the scheme is the failure of the Code and successive Ombudsmen to tackle substantive policy issues which may result in unfairness to bank customers. Instead the focus has been firmly on fair process – encouraging transparency in bank–customer relations and checking bank observance of its published standards but, ultimately, eschewing any responsibility to scrutinise and criticise bank policies causing hardship or distress to consumers. Two outstanding illustrations are bank charges and interest rates: these have to be clearly communicated to the customer and correct application of them in individual cases will be carefully checked, but their levels are regarded by the Ombudsman (to be fair, in accordance with the Code and Scheme's terms of reference) as commercial matters beyond his supervision. It may be that these matters are best left to the interplay between market forces and free competition (though the existence of substantial competition *in practice* in the retail banking sector is by no means clear) or, alternatively, as issues for a regulatory agency rather than an extra-judicial dispute institution such as the Ombudsman. Until such regulatory machinery emerges and provides consumers with a measure of protection against banks' unfair commercial policies, the Ombudsman is the only hope for bank customers. Judging from the Ombudsman's track record to date – and despite some recent promising hints[50] – it may be a considerable time yet, if at all, before this hope is fulfilled.

Despite this (possibly harsh) criticism it should be acknowledged that the scheme scores highly on our criteria for judging the utility of complaints-handling arrangements. The scheme's constitutional structure, strong sup-

48. *Annual Report 1991–92*, op. cit., n. 20, p. 16; and *Annual Report 1994–95*, op. cit., n. 39, p. 22.
49. See for example *Annual Report 1993–94,* op. cit., n. 37, p. 16.
50. Ibid., p. 9, where the Ombudsman observes that, in his opinion at least, banks' terms of service should not only be expressed in plain and fair language but should also be substantively fair. This observation, however, is made in the context of criticism of the Code and does not yet appear to be a standard applied by the Ombudsman during his case work.

port from the banks and a high level of consumer usage are all indicative of few grounds for concern in regard to the Ombudsman's actual and perceived independence. Openness is unproblematic given the easy availability of the scheme's terms of reference and the publicly declared standards of good banking practice embodied in the Code. The Ombudsman appears to be easily accessible provided the significant hurdle of 'deadlock' has been overcome, though worries about adequate levels of publicity (an essential means in practice of promoting accessibility) still remain.

In terms of procedural methods, a fair hearing for both disputants is attained and, in terms of outcomes, it is clear that the Ombudsman has successfully resisted the temptation to assume the mantles of either 'consumer champion' or 'bank defender'; rather he is clearly an impartial arbiter of disputes between banks and their customers. Finally, the Ombudsman has, on the whole, been effective not simply in dispensing justice to aggrieved bank customers, but has also made a valuable contribution towards improved levels of banking services via his quality control work and his input into the creation and continuing development of the Code.

3. THE BUILDING SOCIETIES OMBUDSMAN SCHEME

The Building Societies Ombudsman scheme has been in operation since 1987.[51] It established 'arrangements for an independent adjudicator ("the Ombudsman") to investigate and resolve certain types of complaints from individuals' made as a result of action taken by their building society, or an associated body.[52] From its inception, the scheme has had to face indifference, and at times outright hostility, from the building societies sector. Indeed, primary legislation in the form of the Building Societies Act 1986 (the '1986 Act') was required to make provision for a Building Societies Ombudsman scheme, as it became apparent that building societies, unlike banks, were unenthusiastic self-regulators.[53] The provisions of the 1986 Act concerning the Ombudsman scheme have, however, been amended by the Building Societies Act 1997 (the '1997 Act').[54] As will be seen below, this has

---

51. The scheme was recognised by the Building Societies Commission on 5 June 1987.
52. See Building Societies Ombudsman Scheme, *Ombudsman Scheme under Part IX of the Building Societies Act 1986* (July 1994), p. 4. The scheme was revised as *The Building Societies Ombudsman Scheme* (December 1997), and all further references are to the 1997 scheme unless stated otherwise.
53. Rawlings and Willett, op. cit., n. 6, pp. 321–2.
54. The Ombudsman scheme is provided for under Part IX of the Building Societies Act 1986, as amended by the Building Societies Act 1997, ss. 34–5. See James, op. cit., n. 11 *supra*, chapter 4 for a recent comprehensive evaluation of the scheme.

53

inter alia widened the matters of complaint to be considered by the Ombudsman, and extended the range of persons to whom the scheme is available.

As is clear from our discussion of the Banking Ombudsman and the IMRO Investment Ombudsman, the interrelated issues of independence from the industry and fairness and impartiality in decision taking are central factors in assessing private sector ombudsmen. An independent decision taker can be more easily accepted as being impartial, and the fair and impartial exercise of discretion in decision taking advertises and bolsters the reality and perception of independence. If the judiciary, or the parliamentary and local government ombudsmen, are taken as representing an ideal which requires not only that decision takers strive to be independent, fair and impartial, but that they are perceived to be so, the Building Societies Ombudsman faces real difficulties.

In the Building Societies Ombudsman scheme *Annual Reports*, the Building Societies Council Chairman has had, perhaps tellingly, to stress the independence of the Ombudsman on more than one occasion. Indeed, in the 1996–97 *Annual Report*, the Ombudsman himself chose to emphasise his independence in trenchant terms.[55] None the less, a 1993 National Consumer Council (NCC) report into private sector ombudsmen services had found that, rather alarmingly, 49 per cent of complainants rated the Ombudsman's decisions as not very or not at all fair. Only 49 per cent of complainants felt that the Ombudsman's decisions were very or fairly independent.[56] To adopt the view that these findings should be viewed with caution because those who had lost were less likely to consider the decisions of the Ombudsman to be fair or independent is, it is submitted, to miss the point.[57] The independence and impartiality of the judiciary and the parliamentary and local government ombudsmen can be accepted without question by litigants and complainants, notwithstanding that they may not obtain the remedy sought.

It should be appreciated at the outset that it is not thought that the Ombudsman or his staff are responsible for the failure to attain a high standard of perceived independence: it is clear that as individuals they are independent, fair, well qualified and competent. It is, however, contended that the constitution of the building societies scheme, whilst in some respects satisfactory, has, in part, created the impression amongst an unac-

---

55. See *Building Societies Ombudsman: Annual Report 1992–93*, p. 4; *Annual Report 1993–94*, p. 4; *Annual Report 1994–95*, p. 4; and *Annual Report 1996-97*, pp. 7–8.
56. National Consumer Council, *Ombudsman Services* (1993), para. 3.6.
57. Ibid., and see Lord Barnett's comments in *Building Societies Ombudsman: Annual Report 1993–94*, p. 4.

ceptably large proportion of complainants that the Ombudsman's decisions are insufficiently independent and fair. There have also been a number of serious criticisms of, *inter alia*, the range of the Ombudsman's jurisdiction, the industry's tendency to create barriers which restrict access to the Ombudsman, and delay in the dispute resolution process. Although since 1993 the Ombudsman has taken firm action to deal with these and other difficulties, and the provisions of the 1997 Act will bolster his efforts, it is likely that they too have influenced consumers' perceptions of the scheme. These issues are discussed below.

Under the amended 1986 Act, the Building Societies Commission, as the statutory regulator, has the power to recognise and authorise independent bodies to administer complaint resolution schemes which will satisfy the relevant sections of the Act.[58] The Building Societies Ombudsman scheme, which was established by directors of the Building Societies Ombudsman Company Limited ('the company'), is the only scheme to have been so recognised. The board of the company is comprised of representatives from the industry. The original scheme made provision for the Ombudsman, as an independent adjudicator, to conduct investigations into specific categories of complaints made by private individuals against building societies and their associated bodies, and to resolve the complaints. As indicated above, however, the 1997 Act has extended the availability of the scheme: any partnership, club, other unincorporated body, or body corporate, can now make a complaint to the Ombudsman, provided that its turnover for the last financial year did not exceed £1 million. Ironically, given the unwillingness of building societies to initiate self-regulation, all societies are required to participate in the scheme. They are also required to pay for it.[59]

In order to ensure that the Ombudsman (currently Brian Murphy) is perceived by complainers to be impartial and independent of the company and the industry, the scheme established the Building Societies Council. As with its counterpart in the Banking Ombudsman scheme, the Council serves as a 'buffer' between the company and the Ombudsman and is, *inter alia*, responsible for administering the scheme, and the appointment of the Ombudsman. It is made up of eight members, of whom four are 'independent' members representing consumer or public interests and three are appointed from the industry – there is also a Council Chairman (formerly Lord Barnett and now Lord Brooke), who cannot be an industry representative.

58. See generally, Building Societies Act 1986, ss. 83, 83A, 84, and 85 and Schs 12, 13 and 14.
59. See Building Societies Act 1986, ss. 83 and 83A; *Building Societies Ombudsman Scheme*, op. cit., n. 52, clauses 14–15 and 35–40; and for useful discussion, Rawlings and Willett, op. cit., n. 6, pp. 319–22.

Council members are appointed and remunerated by the directors of the company for terms of up to four years and are eligible for reappointment. Independent members cannot be employed or hold office or a place of profit with the company, a building society, connected undertaking (*ie*, an undertaking which is associated or subsidiary to a building society), or, where the member's independence may be 'materially compromised', a person providing goods and services to any of the aforementioned entities. For obvious reasons, there are no such constraints on the building society members. It should be noted that the scheme enables the company to determine remuneration and terms and conditions of Council members, and to decline to reappoint members (including independent members) of the Council.[60]

None the less, the non-industry members *ex facie* possess a reasonable degree of constitutional independence. Moreover, the constitution of the Council is such that it is reasonable to perceive them as independent, able to exercise an effective influence over the Council's business, and able to protect the independence of the Ombudsman from industry interference.

The Ombudsman is appointed by the Council, subject to the approval of the directors, for a fixed term.[61] He or she is eligible for reappointment. Since 1987 there have been three Ombudsmen.[62] The Ombudsman is supported by a staff of approximately twelve legally qualified assistants.[63] In order to safeguard his independence and impartiality, he cannot be a Council member, or a director of the company, and he cannot be an employee of, or hold any office or place of profit under, a building society, a connected undertaking, or a person providing goods and services to the aforementioned bodies. The Ombudsman is also prohibited from acting (either by himself or by his firm) in a professional capacity for the company, a building society or connected undertaking.[64] He can be dismissed if the directors, with the consent of the Council, move to have him removed from office under the strict terms of the scheme (*eg*, where, *inter alia*, he has been hospitalised under the terms of the Mental Health Acts, or declared bankrupt). The Ombudsman can also be dismissed by the directors at the request of the Council.[65]

Viewed from this perspective, it is clear that the Ombudsman *ex facie* possesses a high degree of independence and security of tenure. None the

---

60. See generally *The Building Societies Ombudsman Scheme*, op. cit., n. 52, clauses 1–10.
61. See generally ibid., at clause 11(A).
62. Stephen Edell (latterly PIA Ombudsman), the late Jane Woodhead and Brian Murphy.
63. See *Building Societies Ombudsman: Annual Report 1996–97*, Appendix D.
64. See *The Building Societies Ombudsman Scheme*, op. cit., n. 52, clause 11 (B). The Council can make an exception under clause 11(B)(iv).
65. Ibid., clause 11(C).

less, as indicated above, the Ombudsman's decisions have not been perceived to be particularly independent or fair. What, in the context of the constitution of the scheme, may have given rise to this perception? A number of possibilities can be mooted. First, the limitation of the Ombudsman's tenure of office to fixed terms, which are subject to renewal at the discretion of the directors of the company, is, in constitutional terms, unsatisfactory. It is submitted that it may be preferable for the Ombudsman to either serve for one fixed term only, or to hold office *ad vitam aut culpam,* to be determined under the existing provisions of the scheme, or under the auspices of a statutory Ombudsman Commission of the sort mentioned above.

Second, the provision that the terms and conditions of engagement (including remuneration) are subject to the approval of the directors may – notwithstanding its *de facto* operation – again be seen as detracting from the Ombudsman's constitutional independence and impartiality. This aspect of the directors' role is, it is argued, unsatisfactory, and should also be subject to the authority of a statutory Ombudsman Commission.

As indicated above, all building societies are required to participate in the Building Societies Ombudsman scheme.[66] Under the 1986 Act as amended, any entitled person is able to make a complaint to the Ombudsman with regard to an action taken by a building society in the United Kingdom, or a connected undertaking, if:

- the action was taken by the building society or its connected undertaking in relation to a relevant service provided by it;
- the grounds of the complaint fall within the specified grounds; and
- the complainant alleges that the action has caused him pecuniary loss, expense or inconvenience.[67]

'Relevant service' is defined under section 83(12) as a service of a kind which is provided by building societies for individuals in the ordinary course of business. This is a welcome development, as prior to the 1997 Act the Ombudsman had been limited to complaints arising out of specific activities set out at part II of Schedule 12 to the 1986 Act. The specified grounds are relatively broad, and have also been revised by the 1997 Act: a breach of obligation by the building society under the 1986 Act, its rules or a contractual agreement; or a corresponding breach by a 'participating undertaking' (*ie*, connected undertaking); unfair treatment; maladministration, or a decision in connection with the provision of a relevant service

---

66. See n. 59.
67. See the Building Societies Act 1986, s. 83; and *The Building Societies Ombudsman Scheme*, op. cit., n. 52, clause 14.

'which is made otherwise than in the legitimate exercise of commercial judgement, or action consequential on such a decision'.[68] The last ground was introduced by the 1997 Act, and is presumably intended to complement and widen the Ombudsman's existing powers to investigate unfairness and maladministration; it is not, however, defined in statute.

The other grounds of complaint focus on the *legal* obligations of the society, although the remit of the Ombudsman to make his determination 'by reference to what is, in his opinion, fair in all the circumstances',[69] and the grounds of unfair treatment and maladministration have required the development of more general standards and (potentially) the exercise of a wide discretion in decision taking. For example, in contractual disputes the Ombudsman will have regard to the Unfair Contract Terms Act 1977, the Unfair Terms in Consumer Contracts Regulations 1994, and relevant case law: compensation may, however, be awarded to the complainant on the grounds of fairness, notwithstanding the legal merits of the complaint. Similarly, an award may be made for maladministration, although the building society may not have breached a contractual or other legal obligation. In fact, the development of general standards of fairness and maladministration has been conservative, although the present Ombudsman has adopted a forthright approach to both tests in his published decisions.[70] It will be interesting to see how the new additional ground of complaint will be construed.

The Ombudsman will not investigate a complaint or continue an investigation if the complaint is frivolous or fictitious, or the building society's action is the subject of court proceedings, or was the subject of a judgment on the merits. The 1997 Act has, sensibly, enabled the Ombudsman to 'close' files which have not been pursued by claimants for six months or longer.[71] He is able to direct the building society to 'take, or desist from taking, such steps which he may specify . . . and/or . . . order the participant to pay the complainant a sum (not exceeding £100,000) by way of compensation'. Building societies can, however, opt to accept publicity 'in such a manner as the Ombudsman requires', as an alternative sanction. Clearly, in an increasingly competitive market, adverse publicity can be extremely damaging, and building societies have not made any significant use of this provision.[72]

68. See the Building Societies Act 1986, s. 83(1),(2); and *The Building Societies Ombudsman Scheme*, ibid., clause 18.
69. See *Building Societies Ombudsman Scheme*, op. cit., n. 52, clause 29(A).
70. See for example, *Building Societies Ombudsman: Annual Report 1995–96*, pp. 16–32, and Rawlings and Willett, op. cit., n. 6, pp. 322–4 for an interesting discussion of the standards utilised by the Ombudsman.
71. See *Building Societies Ombudsman Scheme*, op. cit., n. 52, clauses 16–17; and the Building Societies Act 1986, s. 83(3)(b).
72. Ibid., clauses 30 and 33; and see R. James, C. Graham and M. Senerviratne, 'Building Societies, Customer Complaints, and the Ombudsman' (1994) 23 *Anglo–American Law Review* 214, 237.

While the scheme does present real advantages to complainants by comparison with litigation – it is free and the complaint is dealt with by individuals of comparable expertise and qualifications – a number of serious deficiencies have become apparent. It may be that these have, in part, given rise to the relatively high levels of public dissatisfaction noted by the NCC survey: consideration should therefore be given to the main areas of concern.

A major area of concern has been the restricted range of the Ombudsman's jurisdiction, although the recent redefinition of the matters of complaint referred to above should resolve this difficulty to a considerable extent. One feature of the jurisdiction which had attracted particular adverse comment was the Ombudsman's inability to investigate the actions of building societies or associated bodies before a mortgage or insurance contract was completed.[73] Particular problems arose with regard to complaints made in connection with pre-completion property valuations carried out by building society surveyors or valuers.[74] In practical terms, the pre-completion valuation is a crucial stage in a mortgage application. Not only does it determine whether or not the value of the property is sufficient to provide security for the lender, it is also of great significance to the borrower. Clearly, if it transpires subsequently that the value of the property is materially less than the sum borrowed on the basis of the valuation, the borrower may pay a heavy price for the defective survey: in addition to excessive mortgage repayments, any personal capital paid into the property is lost on resale or repossession, as is the balance of the sum borrowed and the 'real' value of the property.

The extent of the Ombudsman's jurisdiction was clarified in *Halifax Building Society and Others v Edell and Others*,[75] in which it was held that the Ombudsman could only investigate a pre-completion complaint regarding a mortgage valuation if the complainant was an established client and the surveyor was in house. It was clear that this was an unsatisfactory decision, as first time buyers and those who had redeemed an existing mortgage and taken their business to a different lender for their next purchase were unable to approach the Ombudsman. Eventually, as of 30 June 1994, the Ombudsman's jurisdiction was extended to enable him to investigate pre-completion complaints about in-house valuations, even when the complainant was not an established client of the building society

---

73. See for example Rawlings and Willett, op. cit., n. 6, pp. 321–2.
74. *Building Societies Ombudsman: Annual Report 1992–93*, para. 5.2.
75. [1992] 1 All ER 389.

concerned (provided the transaction was completed subsequently).[76] Rather unsatisfactorily, for those affected by negligent in-house valuations during the ill-fated 1980s property boom, inspections carried out prior to 30 June 1994 could not be investigated.

The pre-completion issue has been similarly resolved in relation to home income plans, equity release schemes, and mortgage protection plans, although once again the cut off date of 30 June 1994 has meant that the Ombudsman is unable to provide a remedy for those who were most adversely affected by the economic recession of the early 1990s.

It is worth noting that extensions to the Ombudsman's jurisdiction of this sort have tended to be implemented against the backdrop of industry hostility. This became apparent when the Alliance and Leicester Building Society raised an action against the Ombudsman in order to prevent 'test case' investigations into complaints relating to investment interest rates.[77] In the event, the society withdrew the action before the matter came before the court, but a subsequent internal report of the Building Societies Association contemplated a reduction in the Ombudsman's jurisdiction.[78]

The second area of concern is the *de facto* requirement for the complainant to exhaust the building society's internal complaint procedures before the Ombudsman initiates his investigation. The NCC survey indicated that there was very strong consumer dissatisfaction with building societies' internal complaints procedures: 56 per cent of complainants felt that the procedures had been 'a complete waste of time'; 61 per cent strongly disagreed that the procedures were fair and impartial; and 54 per cent strongly disagreed that their complaints had been taken seriously.[79]

Without being unduly cynical, it is not difficult to appreciate that it must be tempting for building societies to delay and obfuscate in order to encourage the complainant to give up. The fact that internal complaints procedures are not generally well publicised tends to support the view that this may well be a tactic which has been adopted by at least some building societies.[80] The NCC survey indicated that 50 per cent of complainants felt that their complaint had been passed around too many people in the building society's office, and that it had taken an inordinate

---

76. See *Ombudsman Scheme under Part IX of the Building Societies Act 1986*, op. cit., n. 52, clause IV, 17(B). This has since been superseded. See n. 67 *supra*.
77. *Building Societies Ombudsman: Annual Report 1992–93*, para. 5.1.
78. *The Observer*, 13 February 1994; and Rawlings and Willett, op. cit., n. 6, pp. 322 and 329.
79. See n. 56 *supra*, para. 2.7.
80. See James *et al.*, n. 72, pp. 223–32. The authors note differences in approach to customer complaints between large and small building societies, and between main offices and branch offices.

amount of time to exhaust the internal complaints procedure.[81] It can therefore be appreciated that arriving at the stage where it is possible to present a complaint to the Ombudsman is not necessarily a simple matter.[82] Indeed, the NCC recommended that the internal complaints procedures should be upgraded and publicised more effectively, and that the Ombudsman should be responsible for setting general standards.[83] The Ombudsman has since taken steps to encourage building societies to participate in a voluntary scheme which will set clear time limits on the internal complaints procedure.[84]

The third related cause for concern is the building societies' reluctance to advertise the existence of the Building Societies Ombudsman scheme to their customers. Some societies have admitted that it is their policy not to advertise the scheme.[85] It is something of an indictment that only 33 per cent of the complainants in the NCC survey were given a contact address for the Ombudsman by their building society.[86] It is not possible to gauge how many dissatisfied customers have exhausted their society's internal complaints procedure but have failed to take their complaint to the Ombudsman because they were unaware of his existence. Clearly, however, any procedure for grievance resolution is seriously flawed if its existence is not communicated to those who may have cause to use it. In this context, it is worth noting that building societies are required to comply with the new codes for banking and mortgage lending practice, which require building societies to publicise the Ombudsman scheme.[87] The Ombudsman has made an open statement of his dissatisfaction with the conduct of the building societies in this regard: it remains to be seen what action, if any, has been taken.[88]

The final areas of concern are the interrelated issues of procedure and delay. The NCC report commented adversely on the complicated and

81. See n. 56 *supra*.
82. See n. 72 *supra*, pp. 235–6. Note that the Ombudsman has a discretionary power to take up a complaint prior to the completion of the ICP: it is now being exercised. See *Building Societies Ombudsman Scheme*, op. cit., n. 52, clause 17 and *Building Societies Ombudsman: Annual Report 1996–97*, p. 11.
83. See n. 56 *supra*, para. 6.3.
84. *Building Societies Ombudsman: Annual Report 1993–94*, para. 5.4 and see *Building Societies Ombudsman: Annual Report 1996–97*, op. cit., n. 82.
85. See n. 72 *supra*, p. 236, and further for an interesting discussion, Graham *et al.*, op. cit., n. 41.
86. See n. 56 *supra*, para. 2.8.
87. See *The Banking Code*, op. cit., n. 30, para. 5.10; and The Council of Mortgage Lenders, *The Mortgage Code* (March 1997), para. 9.5.
88. *Building Societies Ombudsman: Annual Report 1993–94*, para. 5.3; and *Annual Report 1996–97*, p. 38.

Table 2.2

*The Building Societies Ombudsman: initial complaints
and cases disposed of*

	1	2	3	4	5	6	7	8	9	Total
1987–88	114	192	57	19	–	–	–	–	38	420
1988–89	241	694	78	36	–	–	–	–	168	1,217
1989–90	586	1,044	111	42	–	–	–	–	238	2,021
1990–91	375	1,351	114	81	–	–	–	–	361	2,282
1991–92	1,426	5,208	317	–	148	98	–	–	392	7,589
1992–93	1,572	6,190	260	–	217	386	–	–	630	9,255
1993–94	1,601	6,526	280	–	354	434	–	26	589	9,810
1994–95	1,958	6,286	692	–	355	16	–	303	705	10,315
1995–96	1,168	7,147	1,116	–	–	–	532	742	670	11,375
1996–97	1,951	9,277	941	–	–	–	530	390	486	13,575

Sources: The Building Societies Ombudsman Scheme, *Annual Reports* 1987–97

KEY
1. Initial complaints outside terms of reference
2. Complainant did not proceed with initial complaint
3. Resolved through internal complaints procedure (ICP) or conciliation
4. Resolved after completion of ICP but before decision made
5. Resolved after completion of ICP but before provisional assessment or decision
6. Disposed of/resolved by provisional assessment
7. Resolved after completion of ICP but before preliminary conclusion
8. Resolved by preliminary conclusion
9. Decision

lengthy procedure utilised by the Ombudsman.[89] Substantial improvements have, however, been made since 1993, and a new streamlined procedure is continuing to cut the time taken by the Ombudsman to reach a decision, whilst dealing with an ever larger number of complaints. Under the new procedure, each complaint is allocated to an individual member of the Ombudsman's legal staff. The legal officer investigates the complaint with a view to encouraging a settlement between the parties. If settlement at this stage is not possible, the Ombudsman circulates his preliminary conclusion (with full reasons) to both parties in order to encourage settlement. If the preliminary conclusion is not accepted, the Ombudsman considers further submissions from the parties before presenting his final decision. It is clear from recent *Annual Reports* that this

89. See n. 56 *supra*, paras 2.6 and 5.1.

procedure has much to commend it.[90] The figures set out opposite in Table 2.2 detailing complaints received, complaints proceeding to preliminary conclusion (and formerly to provisional assessment), and complaints resolved by final decision for the period 1987–96 illustrate the Ombudsman's heavy and increasing workload clearly.

To conclude, the Building Societies Ombudsman would, in all probability, not exist had it not been for government determination to ensure that the consumer has an informal, free alternative to the court process in the event of a grievance arising from the actions of building societies and associated bodies: the industry's enthusiasm for the Ombudsman scheme has always been muted.

The scheme itself, which was established by representatives of the building societies under statute, has been fortunate in that the independent members of its Council, the Ombudsmen and their support staff have proved to be both able and independent. There have, however, been a number of serious deficiencies in the constitution and operation of the scheme – for example, a perception amongst complainants that the Ombudsman is not sufficiently fair or independent, that his jurisdiction is unduly restrictive, that building societies are failing to provide adequate internal complaints procedures and to publicise the existence of the scheme, and that the Ombudsman's decision-taking procedures are too complicated and slow. As indicated above, many of these problems have been identified by the Ombudsman and – in recent years in particular – robust action taken to deal with them. The changes brought about by the 1997 Act are, without doubt, also welcome, and will enable the Ombudsman to continue to develop his role as an impartial adjudicator. It remains arguable, however, that the industry's hostility to the scheme and its influence over it has meant that reforms have tended to be 'too little and too late', and that it will not be an easy matter to put an end to the perception that the Ombudsman scheme is insufficiently fair and independent.

4.   THE IMRO INVESTMENT OMBUDSMAN SCHEME[91]

In terms of its legal basis, the Investment Ombudsman scheme is neither self-regulatory nor regulated in detail by legislation; instead it is a 'hybrid' complaints-handling arrangement created by IMRO pursuant to the

---

90. See *Building Societies Ombudsman: Annual Report 1994–95*, part 2; and *Annual Report 1995–96*, pp. 8–15.
91. On which see generally P. E. Morris, 'The Investment Ombudsman: a Critical Review' (1996) *Journal of Business Law* 1; and McGee, op. cit., n. 11, chapter 6.

63

obligation in the Financial Services Act 1986 for self-regulatory organisations to have effective procedures for the investigation of complaints.[92] The scheme therefore exists by virtue of statutory compulsion, but its key substantive features are self-regulatory in that they have been specified by IMRO free of statutory interference. These self-regulatory features are, however, underpinned by a legal basis: IMRO member firms are contractually bound to observe the terms of the scheme.[93] Furthermore, coverage achieved by the scheme in the investment management sector is comprehensive in view of the fact that membership of the scheme is compulsory for IMRO members.

As from 1 May 1995 important changes to the scheme have been made which are intended to bolster the perceived independence of the Ombudsman and take into account the emergence of the PIA, which has its own Ombudsman scheme.[94] In response to the previous glaring lack of institutional guarantees of the Ombudsman's independence, IMRO has created a committee of the main IMRO board, composed of a permanent majority of independent representatives, which is entrusted with powers of (re)appointment, revocation of appointment and fixing the remuneration of the Ombudsman.[95] IMRO has also committed itself to preservation of the Ombudsman's independence by boldly declaring it 'will maintain no power of direction or influence over the Investment Ombudsman in the exercise of any of his functions . . . in relation to the investigation or adjudication of any complaint'.[96] It is hoped that this constitutional reform and declaration of intent will allay fears concerning independence of the Ombudsman from IMRO and the industry. So far as the recently established PIA is concerned, IMRO feared that the PIA's own Ombudsman scheme would render the Investment Ombudsman's case-work 'excessively expensive'[97] given the substantial loss of 'complaints business' consequent upon the transfer of investment firms from IMRO to the PIA. Accordingly it has reacted by abolishing the IMRO Complaints Unit (and with it the requirement for complainants to

---

92. Sch. 2. For fuller discussion of the legal basis of the scheme see Morris, op. cit., n. 91, pp. 4–5.
93. The Office of the Investment Referee, *The Investment Referee: Annual Report 1989–90*, p. 1.
94. IMRO, *The Investment Ombudsman: Complaints Handling* (Consultative Document 21, January 1995) contains the initial proposals. Most of these proposals were subsequently incorporated into the Ombudsman's revised terms of reference: IMRO, *The Investment Ombudsman: The Ombudsman Memorandum* (March 1995) (hereafter *Memorandum*). See also: IMRO, *The Investment Ombudsman: Informal Guide to the Investment Ombudsman System* (March 1995).
95. *Memorandum*, paras 4.1 and 4.2.
96. Ibid., para. 4.4.
97. *The Investment Ombudsman: Complaints Handling*, op. cit., n. 94, p. 7.

Table 2.3

Summary of complaints received and dealt with by the Investment Ombudsman

	Cases referred	Cases submitted to adjudication
1989–90	63	1
1990–91	134	2
1991–92	67	–
1992–93	103	3
1993–94	73	–
1994–95	91	–
1995–96	373	1
1996–97	249	1
Totals	1155	8

Sources: The Office of the Investment Ombudsman, *The Investment Ombudsman: Annual Reports*.

exhaust their grievances within that unit prior to recourse to the Ombudsman), with the result that the number of complaints reaching the Ombudsman have more than trebled.[98] However, complainants are still not permitted to proceed direct to the Ombudsman: investment firms must have been given a 'reasonable opportunity' (*ie*, no less than two months) to resolve the grievance to the satisfaction of the complainant before the Ombudsman enjoys jurisdiction.[99]

Moving on to the grievance resolution process, the scheme is virtually unique among the financial services Ombudsmen in that the procedure is rigidly demarcated into two distinct stages, namely conciliation and adjudication. Before examining these stages in turn it is worthwhile summarising the use made so far of the Ombudsman's services.

During the conciliation stage the Ombudsman does not use the documents-based, inquisitorial investigative methods favoured by most of his counterparts in the financial services industry. Instead heavy use is made of personal interviews and hearings,[100] a method the Ombudsman defends on the basis that:[101] (i) it facilitates his exercise of human judgement and

98. The Office of the Investment Ombudsman, *The Investment Ombudsman: Annual Report 1995–96*, p. 1; and The Office of the Investment Ombudsman, *The Investment Ombudsman: Annual Report 1996–97*, p. 2.
99. *Memorandum*, para. 7.2(a).
100. For fuller discussion of this procedural methodology see further Morris, op. cit., n. 91, pp. 6–8.
101. The Office of the Investment Ombudsman, *Annual Report 1994–95*, pp. 10–11.

thus increases the prospect of a just solution being arrived at; (ii) in fact it usually works out cheaper than a 'documents only' investigation which often involves protracted exchanges of correspondence with the complainant; and (iii) it aids the less articulate complainant who is usually at a serious disadvantage relative to the (often legally advised) investment firm. For the Ombudsman therefore his 'Rolls Royce' investigative *modus operandi* is defensible and cost effective when examined in the context of the financial services sector in which he operates. Whether it will continue to be so with a trebling of the number of complaints received must be open to considerable doubt.

Turning to the nature of conciliation itself, the Ombudsman openly pursues a pro-conciliation policy on the basis that it avoids the 'winner takes all' nature of an adjudication and the inevitable lingering resentment which may be held by the losing party.[102] On the other hand he does not regard his role as simply being to identify and 'rubber stamp' the lowest common denominator of agreement between the parties. Rather he must *also* be satisfied that the proposed settlement is objectively fair:

I do not regard it as my task to promote conciliation simply in the form of a cessation of hostilities but rather to produce a settlement which is fair and proper as between the parties having regard to all the circumstances. In other words conciliation involves a solution which is not only acceptable to the parties but regarded by myself as right.[103]

During the process of conciliation the Ombudsman takes into account not only legal rules but also the demands of fairness. The law and fairness are, of course, not always in harmony, but the demanding task of the Ombudsman is to reconcile them to the best of his ability.[104] Legal representation for either or both of the parties during conciliation (and during the later adjudication stage) is now permitted subject to conditions imposed by the Ombudsman, which may include requiring one party to meet the other party's legal expenses.[105]

If the conciliation process fails to produce a settlement, the Ombudsman enjoys an unfettered discretion to offer the option of an adjudication.[106] In practice, however, the offer is one sided: if the complainant accepts the offer, the investment firm is required by IMRO rules to submit

---

102. The Office of the Investment Referee, *The Investment Referee: Annual Report 1990–91*, p. 2; and The Office of the Investment Ombudsman, *The Investment Ombudsman: Annual Report 1992–93*, p. 1.
103. *Annual Report 1989–90*, op. cit., n. 93, p. 2.
104. McGee, op. cit., n. 11, p. 56.
105. *Memorandum*, para. 36.1, discussed by Morris, op. cit., n. 91, p. 20.
106. *Memorandum*, para. 17.3.

to the adjudication.[107] The adjudication is conducted by an individual selected from a panel of experienced commercial lawyers maintained by the Ombudsman, is a legally binding arbitration and decided entirely by legal rules with no room for extra-legal standards.[108] As with all arbitrations, there is a right of appeal, on a point of law, to the High Court, but given the restrictive criteria for such appeals embodied in the Arbitration Act 1979, in practical terms the adjudication 'is the last hope of a complainant'.[109]

So far as remedies are concerned, the scheme allows for the payment of compensation up to £100,000.[110] Recommendations made during the conciliation process are not binding, though if the investment firm has accepted a recommendation it is required by IMRO rules to promptly comply with it;[111] failure to do so will almost certainly result in a disciplinary response by IMRO. The same principle applies in relation to awards made during an adjudication; and, in any event, such awards are enforceable as binding arbitrations in the court system.

The Ombudsman regards his primary role as gaining a remedy for the individual investor aggrieved by unlawful or unfair action by the investment firm rather than usurping the regulatory mission conferred on IMRO.[112] He does, however, acknowledge a secondary quality control mission which involves communicating to the industry, via his *Annual*

---

107. *Memorandum*, para 20.3; and IMRO Rules, chapter 14, 'Compliance, Reporting, Records and Complaints: section 3, Complaints', reproduced in *CCH Financial Services Reporter*, Vol. 3: *Rules*, pp. 213, 164–264.
108. *Memorandum*, para. 18.1; McGee, op. cit., n. 11, p. 55.
109. Ibid., p. 55.
110. *Memorandum*, para. 18.2 though this ceiling does not apply to complaints concerning pension transfers, pension opt-outs and non-joiners as described in SIB guidelines: SIB, *Pension Transfers and Opt-Outs: Review of Past Business*, Part I: *Statement of Policy* (October 1994), where the SIB observes, however, that it expects the PIA Ombudsman 'will be the forum for the majority of disputes in this area' (para. 49). See further on this *Annual Report of the Personal Investment Authority Ombudsman Bureau Ltd 1994–95*, where the PIA Ombudsman remarks that he expects the aftermath of the mis-selling of personal pension policies scandal to result in a substantial case load for his office (p. 26). A full account of the PIA's approach can be found in PIA, *Pension Transfers and Opt-Outs: Review of Past Business: Statement of PIA's Policy* (1995). For a critical evaluation of the PIA Ombudsman scheme and points of comparison with the Insurance Ombudsman see further P. E. Morris and J. A. Hamilton, 'The Insurance Ombudsman and PIA Ombudsman: a Critical Comparison' (1996) 47 *Northern Ireland Legal Quarterly* 119; and R. James, op. cit., n. 11, chapter 7. Evidently the PIA Ombudsman scheme has experienced considerable administrative difficulties and complainants face lengthy delays before their complaints are even investigated: *The Times*, 7 September 1996.
111. Rule 3.1 (8) IMRO Rules, op. cit., n. 107.
112. The Office of the Investment Ombudsman, *Annual Report: 1991–92*, p. 2; Morris, op. cit., n. 91, p. 15 and *Annual Report 1995–96*, op. cit., n. 98, p. 9.

Reports, the lessons to be gleaned from his casework. An accurate picture of this activity can be captured by running through a selection of these lessons:

- more rigorous 'fact finds' to discover clients' investment objectives should be conducted;[113]
- payment of *ex gratia* compensation should be regarded by firms not as a sign of weakness but as a means of securing a customer's goodwill;[114]
- advisers should take contemporaneous notes of meetings with clients, if only as a defence to later claims by clients;[115]
- investors should endeavour to make clear to advisers their investment objectives;[116]
- investors should read carefully all contractual documentation, though in this context the test is whether 'a reasonably intelligent investor with limited experience in investment' would make sense of the documentation;[117] and
- a fund manager should exercise reasonable care in making investment decisions but will not be penalised simply because the market turned against him.[118]

It is clear from this selection of principles that the Ombudsman pursues a balanced approach which strives to improve levels of service for investors but insists that investors, too, have responsibilities to protect themselves. The major drawback with these quality control activities is that there appears to be no means of guaranteeing that the Ombudsman's strictures are in fact absorbed and implemented by the industry. While it is true that patterns of complaints reaching the Ombudsman's office can provide some evidence of industry reaction (a couple of recent examples are the Ombudsman's findings that the quality of advisers' 'fact finds' and contemporaneous note taking of meetings with clients appear to have improved in response to his exhortations), there remains a pressing need for the Ombudsman, perhaps in conjunction with IMRO, to systematically monitor the impact of his quality control activities.

---

113. *Annual Report 1991–92*, op. cit., n. 112, p. 5, an instance of good practice which the Ombudsman feels is being absorbed by the industry: *Annual Report 1992–93*, op. cit., n. 102, p. 4.
114. *Annual Report 1989–90*, op. cit., n. 93, p. 6.
115. *Annual Report 1990–91*, op. cit., n. 102, p. 5.
116. Ibid., p. 6.
117. *Annual Report 1994–95*, op. cit., n. 101, p. 7. See also *Annual Report 1990–91*, op. cit., n. 102, p. 5.
118. The Office of the Investment Ombudsman, *The Investment Ombudsman: Annual Report 1993–94*, p. 3. See also *Annual Report 1990–91*, op. cit., n. 102, p. 4.

To conclude, efforts have been made to underline the independence of the Ombudsman from IMRO, but it is still too early to judge (and such judgement will probably require empirical research into complainants' experiences of the Ombudsman's services) whether this will prove successful. The Ombudsman clearly scores highly on openness and accessibility given the articulation of key principles in his *Annual Reports* and the new right to proceed directly to him after first giving the investment firm a reasonable opportunity to resolve the grievance. The Ombudsman is effective in the narrow sense that securing compliance with his recommendations or (adjudicators') awards is no problem in view of the backing provided by IMRO's disciplinary powers.

In a broader sense, however, that of stimulating improvements in industry practice for the enduring benefit of *all* investors and not simply those sufficiently knowledgeable and determined to lodge a complaint, the Ombudsman's full potential has yet to be realised, largely due to a combination of undue emphasis on his 'grievance man' function and the relatively light use so far made of the scheme.

5. CONCLUSIONS

Our three case studies have revealed that the ombudsman concept is a valuable consumer redress mechanism in the financial services industry. Ombudsmen not only secure effective remedies for consumers' grievances – many of which would otherwise go unremedied – they also make a useful contribution to the raising of service standards. The relative priority accorded to 'individual redress' versus 'quality control' functions differ from scheme to scheme, and seems to turn not so much on a scheme's legal basis and institutional framework as on the particular ombudsman's personal predilection. Those ombudsmen operating in close proximity to a regulatory agency face a difficult task in ensuring that their quality control activity does not result in them straying unwittingly into a regulatory role which is hard to square with the essentially quasi-judicial nature of an ombudsman service. It is perhaps this danger which explains why in our three case studies the ombudsman's primary focus appears to have been on *procedural* fairness rather than engineering changes in sectoral policies which have a very real impact on the price, quality and availability of financial services.

Looking into the future (which always a somewhat speculative affair), there are probably two particular issues which will dominate thinking about the future development of ombudsmen in the financial services industry. First, the issue of accountability. While there is a form of *legal* accountability to the courts, via the principles of judicial review of administrative action, for those ombudsmen whose scheme has a statutory under-pinning and satisfies the test of performing a governmental function,[119] as well as a channel of *internal* accountability to the Ombudsman's Council, there remains a worrying lack of on-going accountability in relation to policy issues arising during the course of an ombudsman's work. An Ombudsman Commission may have a role to play here or, alternatively, powerful political muscle and prestige could be provided by a parliamentary select committee on ombudsmen operating in both the public and private sectors.

Second, ombudsmen in the financial services industry are in danger of becoming victims of their own success: growing consumer awareness of their existence is leading to increasing case work and corresponding delays in dispute resolution. In view of the fact that one of the key advantages of ombudsmen, in comparison with the courts, is that they represent a *speedy* form of consumer redress, it is clear that the ombudsmen now face the challenging task of reforming their operating procedures in order 'to speed up dramatically the time they take without sacrificing the thoroughness necessary to safeguard fairness to both sides'.[120] Key themes of such reforms should be the formulation of codes setting out consumers' entitlements and responsibilities, coupled with an obligation on financial institutions to create effective, well-publicised internal grievance-resolution procedures. The recent experience of the Banking and Building Societies Ombudsmen schemes suggests that these measures can alleviate the ombudsman's case-load burden and enable him to reduce average time spans in resolution of complaints.

6. ADDENDUM

Since the above account was written, the new Financial Services Authority (FSA) has been created and entrusted with responsibility for policing a postulated revamped financial services regulatory structure. It seems fairly clear at the time of writing that, as part of a general regulatory reform package, there will be reform of ombudsman arrangements in the financial

---

119. *R v Insurance Ombudsman Bureau, ex parte Aegon Life Assurance Ltd*, *The Times*, 7 January 1994, on which see further P. E. Morris, 'The Insurance Ombudsman Bureau and Judicial Review' (1994) *Lloyd's Maritime and Commercial Law Quarterly*, 358; and James, op. cit., n. 11, pp. 4–13 and pp. 30–2.

120. Shurman, in Gregory *et al.*, op. cit., n. 4, p. 112. This need has recently been acknowledged by the new Banking Ombudsman, David Thomas, who has in response streamlined procedures within the Office of the Banking Ombudsman and placed a greater emphasis on conciliation, see The Office of the Banking Ombudsman, *The Banking Ombudsman Scheme: Annual Report 1996–97*, pp. 5 and 13.

services industry. Details of the new arrangements are far from finalised at this juncture but ministers and the FSA are evidently committed to creation of a single 'super' Financial Services Ombudsman scheme, membership of which will be compulsory for all firms authorised by the FSA.[121]

The main driving force behind this sweeping reform is that the current raft of ombudsman schemes 'present the appearance of a "patchwork quilt" and that consumers find this confusing'.[122] While this single scheme will enjoy a statutory basis flowing from inclusion in a new financial regulatory reform bill (which will probably not be operative until autumn 1999) the FSA's preference is for detailed rules on the functioning of the Ombudsman to be embodied in the rules of the scheme itself.

In terms of internal organisational structure, the FSA envisages a scheme with different departments enjoying jurisdiction over different types of business and possibly headed by the existing sectoral ombudsmen. This would both permit retention of accumulated ombudsman expertise and deliver the following consumer benefits:

The main attractions from a consumer perspective would be those of simplicity, accessibility and consistency. Consumers would deal with what was visibly a single ombudsman service, with only one entry point for all complaints, so that once the complaint had been submitted, it would be allocated to the relevant department.[123]

Consultation on the shape and substantive features of a provisional 'blue-print' scheme is currently underway, but the FSA has expressed the following preferences:

- jurisdiction of the new Ombudsman should not be restricted to matters requiring FSA authorisation but should also embrace activities relating to financial services;
- eligibility to complain should be confined to private individuals, unincorporated bodies, partnerships and small companies;
- the ceiling on awards should be set at £100,000;
- Ombudsman awards should be binding but only at the conclusion of a protracted process (which it is envisaged few cases will reach) and only then after a full 'court-like' hearing (including cross-examination of witnesses, legal representation and reasons for decisions, etc.) specified in the Ombudsman's internal procedures;

---

121. Financial Services Authority, *Customer Complaints* (Consultation Paper 4, December 1997).
122. Ibid., p. 8.
123. Ibid., p. 12.

- the Ombudsman would be appointed by a board separate from and independent of the FSA and composed of 'public interest' representatives in order to safeguard the Ombudsman's independence and ensure proper accountability;
- a link with regulatory processes will be established by requiring the Ombudsman to furnish details of serious regulatory breaches to the FSA;
- in general the new Ombudsman and compensation arrangements[124] should not be harmonised since they are conceptually distinct; and
- the scheme will be industry funded via a combination of a 'standing charge' and 'case fees' based on usage.

So far as the Ombudsman's *modus operandi* is concerned, this should be left to his subjective discretion but the FSA regards it as vital that it should be 'informal, flexible and speedy, avoiding, as far as possible, legalistic argument, lengthy oral hearings, extensive discovery of documents and delays which can sometimes occur in civil litigation'.[125] Finally, a twin-track mechanism for the enforcement of Ombudsman awards is suggested: FSA disciplinary/legal proceedings and legal action by the Ombudsman in the court system. Both are regarded as preferable to leaving the consumer to his own devices in enforcing Ombudsman awards.

These are radical proposals which will certainly simplify and, on paper at least, improve the user-friendliness of complaints-handling arrangements in the financial services industry. There must be legitimate concerns, however, that they will involve the dissipation of over a decade's expertise of dispute resolution in the various sectoral schemes and, at first glance, the creation of a bureaucratic, unwieldy organisation remote from the needs and expectations of both consumers and firms in particular sectors of the financial services industry. For these reasons the proposals may well encounter stiff opposition during the consultation process, with the result that the eventual outcome may well be not a single Financial Services Ombudsman but a rationalisation of the various schemes (in the form of a reduction in their number) and harmonisation of their legal bases and remedial powers.

---

124. Ibid., pp. 27–8. Full details of the FSA's proposed reform of compensation arrangements in the financial services industry can be found in: Financial Services Authority, *Consumer Compensation* (Consultation Paper 5, December 1997).
125. Ibid., p. 30.

PART TWO

BANKING

Chapter Three

BANK CONFIDENTIALITY AND THE CONSUMER IN THE UNITED KINGDOM

Andrew Campbell

Chapter Outline

1. Introduction

2. The Common Law Duty

3. The Review Committee's Report and the Government's Response

4. The Code of Practice

5. The Four Qualifications to the Duty
    5.1 'Under compulsion by law'
    5.2 'Duty to the public to disclose'
    5.3 'Where the interests of the bank require disclosure'
    5.4 'Where the disclosure is made by the express or implied consent of the customer'

6. What Information is Covered by the Duty of Confidentiality?

7. Black Information

8. Remedies for Breach of the Duty

9. Conclusion

Consumer Protection in Financial Services (P. Cartwright, ed.: 90-411-9717-6: © Kluwer Law International: pub. Kluwer Law International, 1999: printed in Great Britain)

The principle of confidentiality applied to a customer's private financial affairs is placed by the common law tradition at the heart of the banker–customer relationship. It is a tradition which should be respected and, when under threat, emphasised the more strongly, because its roots go deeper than the business of banking; it has to do with the kind of society we want to live in.[1]

Financial privacy is a privilege that may be extended by a bank or foreign nation's law; it is not a right.[2]

1. INTRODUCTION

The aim of this chapter is to examine the development and current state of the law in the UK relating to the confidentiality of financial, and other information, held by banks about their customers. The examination will focus on consumer issues and accordingly will concentrate on private customers, although much of what is covered will relate also to business customers. Most adults in the UK, and a significant number of younger people, have accounts with banks and/or building societies. The term 'bank' will be used throughout this chapter but what is discussed applies equally to building societies. Banks are in a position to gather a significant amount of information about their customers – where they work, where they shop, social habits, income and expenditure and so on. Indeed, someone who actively uses a bank account will provide a lifestyle profile to the bank. This information can be very valuable as it can provide marketing opportunities where, for example, there may be an opportunity to sell life assurance or investment products, or alternatively, the bank may be made aware of potential problems such as a tendency to overspend or that the customer is gambling or drinking heavily.

Until the late 1960s a bank branch in the UK (and generally elsewhere) existed as a separate unit. Customers of one branch would rarely visit another branch, and when they did it was normal for some sort of introduction to be provided. The account details would be kept in ledgers at the branch and whilst the head office of the bank would be provided with daily information including details of total deposits, loans etc., the actual details of individual accounts would not be provided. The only place where up to date and complete details about a particular customer could be obtained

---

1. *Banking Services: Law and Practice*, Report by the Review Committee (HMSO, 1989), Cmnd 622, para. 5.26.
2. G. Moscarino and M. Shumaker, 'Beating the Shell Game: Bank Secrecy Laws and Their Impact on Civil Recovery in International Fraud Actions' (1997) 1 *Journal of Money Laundering Control* 42, 47.

would be the bank branch where the account was held. Additionally the bank staff would tend to know customers well as they would have to use the bank branch and deal with a cashier. Automated teller machines (ATMs) did not exist at that time. As a result of this, it would be reasonably easy to ensure that information about customers did not leak out and, if it did, it would also be generally easy to identify the source of the leak.

In the computerised banks of the 1990s the situation has altered radically. Bank statements now tend to provide such information as where customers shop and when; withdrawals from ATMs will be shown giving the exact time and place of the transaction. Spending patterns can easily be monitored. The inexorable decline in the use of cash has been fuelled by the electronic banking revolution and the continuing growth of plastic cards and telephone banking. The traditional non-cash payment method, the cheque, is becoming less popular.

From the perspective of the consumer, or individual customer, bank confidentiality is a matter which should be of some considerable importance. However, in recent years the duty of a bank to keep the affairs of their customers confidential has come under attack from a number of sources, both from within the banking industry itself and from external sources. The concept of banking confidentiality is not new, although the legal status of the duty in the UK is relatively recent, dating back to 1924.[3] It has been suggested that confidentiality in banking may have existed in Babylon more than 5,000 years ago[4] and whether or not that is entirely accurate there is no doubting that the duty has been well established in Austria, Italy and Germany for several hundred years.[5]

Switzerland has gained a reputation for having total bank secrecy laws which provide complete protection to depositors. So seriously did the Swiss take the issue of bank secrecy that breach of the duty by a Swiss banker was made a criminal offence in 1934. The existence of total bank secrecy had the effect of making Switzerland an extremely popular place to open a bank account for those who, for whatever reason, wanted to ensure that details of the account and even the existence of the account would not be disclosed to anyone.[6] From an economic perspective Switzerland benefited enormously as a result of its bank secrecy laws. The Swiss, contrary to popular belief, do not at present actually have total bank secrecy,[7] but the public perception

---

3. See the Court of Appeal decision in *Tournier v National Provincial Bank of England* [1924] 1 KB 461, which is discussed below.
4. See D. Campbell, *International Bank Secrecy* (Sweet & Maxwell 1992), p. iv.
5. Ibid.
6. Art. 47(b) of the Federal Law relating to Banks and Savings Banks 1934.
7. See H. S. Steiner and M. D. Pfenninger, 'Switzerland', in F. Neate (ed.), *Bank Confidentiality* (Butterworths, 1997).

still remains. For those who are seeking total bank secrecy it is now necessary to look elsewhere.[8]

Why should customers of a bank wish to have their financial affairs kept private? For the purposes of this chapter it is convenient to consider the reasons under two headings: first, those reasons which can be considered to be legitimate and second, certain other reasons which may be classified as illegitimate or even illegal. Legitimate reasons include the idea that there should be a right to privacy and also that there is a legitimate expectation that one's financial affairs should not be released to anyone who does not have a legitimate right to receive the information and also, of course, to protect assets. In the UK there is no fundamental right to privacy[9] and it has been suggested[10] that in relation to financial information this is a privilege which the law of a particular country may choose to extend. It is sometimes also argued that the relationship of banker and customer is akin to that of lawyer–client, doctor–patient or priest–penitent and that this relationship provides sufficient justification for confidentiality of financial information. As will be seen below, although there is no fundamental right to privacy in the UK the common law has recognised that a duty of confidentiality does, in fact, exist in the banker–customer relationship.

The protection of assets can, in certain circumstances, be classified under the heading of a legitimate reason for bank confidentiality. For example, it is entirely understandable and surely right in view of the circumstances which existed at that time when German Jews transferred vast sums of money to Switzerland to avoid seizure of their assets by the Nazi government of the time.[11]

The second heading covers illegal, or illegitimate, reasons. The attractions of jurisdictions with virtually complete secrecy for members of organised crime syndicates, money launderers and tax evaders are considerable.

The term 'bank secrecy' describes something more than bank confidentiality and it suggests an attempt to hide information for a particular reason which may be legitimate but is often not. Bank secrecy jurisdictions are of obvious appeal to certain elements of society and many offshore financial centres, or 'tax havens', have been established around the world.[12] One of

---

8. See M. Grundy, *Offshore Business Centres: A World Survey* (Sweet & Maxwell, 1997).
9. See the House of Lords decision in *R v Khan* [1996] 3 All ER 289. For a discussion of the question of the right to privacy under English law see J. Breslin, 'Privacy: the Civil Liberties Issue' (1996) 14 *Dick. J. Int L*. 455.
10. Moscarino and Shumaker, op. cit., n. 2.
11. Such arguments are beyond the scope of the present examination. For a discussion of this see ibid.
12. See Grundy, op. cit, n. 8.

the most interesting examples is the Cayman Islands which, with a population of 32,000, has almost 600 banks with more than US$420 billion in assets. The Cayman Islands is reported to be the fifth largest banking centre in the world.[13] Prior to passing bank secrecy laws there were only two local banks. The Cayman Islands does not, however, have total bank secrecy laws and the Proceeds of Criminal Conduct Law of 1996 follows the UK legislation on money laundering. However, divulging financial information in other circumstances is a criminal offence attracting severe penalties.[14]

Many jurisdictions, including all of the Member States of the European Union and the United States, have bank confidentiality laws which do not attempt to provide complete secrecy but which, while respecting the need for privacy, accept that in certain situations this right has to be overridden to protect wider interests. Since a duty of confidentiality was first recognised at common law in the UK there has been a gradual chipping away of the extent of that duty although, as will also be seen, absolute confidentiality has never existed. It is arguable that from the consumer perspective there is no need for a high degree of secrecy in relation to financial affairs, but what is needed is an adequate level of protection which will ensure privacy where appropriate, but which will allow disclosure of information in certain situations.

2.   THE COMMON LAW DUTY

The starting point for an examination of the banker's duty of confidentiality is a case which reached the Court of Appeal in 1924. In *Tournier v National Provincial and Union Bank of England*[15] a bank manager divulged information about a customer and the state of his account to a third party. Briefly, the facts were that Tournier was a customer of the bank and that his account was overdrawn. He reached an agreement with the branch manager to repay the overdraft by weekly payments. In reaching the agreement Tournier satisfied the branch manager that he was in employment and he supplied the name and address of his employer. Tournier subsequently failed to make the agreed repayments. The bank manager contacted Tournier's employer to obtain his home address and in the course of the conversation the bank manager revealed that Tournier's account was overdrawn and that he had failed to make the agreed weekly payments. He also advised the employer that he suspected Tournier of being involved in gambling. When Tournier's period of pro-

13.   Ibid.
14.   See the Cayman Islands Confidential Relationships (Preservation) Law.
15.   [1924] 1 KB 461.

bation expired he was dismissed from his position. Tournier sued the bank for slander and additionally on the basis that the bank had breached an implied term in the contract that the bank would not release information to a third party without his consent.

At first instance Tournier failed and he appealed to the Court of Appeal where it was held unanimously that a bank does owe a duty of confidentiality to its customers, that the duty is a legal one which arises from the contract, and that the duty is not absolute but subject to certain qualifications. According to Bankes LJ: 'At the present day I think it may be asserted with confidence that the duty is a legal one arising out of contract, and that the duty is not absolute but qualified. It is not possible to frame any exhaustive definition of the duty.'[16]

The Lord Justice then set out the qualifications to the duty of confidentiality as follows:

On principle I think that the qualifications can be classified under four heads: (a) where disclosure is under compulsion by law; (b) where there is a duty to the public to disclose; (c) where the interests of the bank require disclosure; (d) where the disclosure is made by the express or implied consent of the customer.[17]

These four qualifications, or exceptions, to the duty of confidentiality are considered in detail later in this chapter.

The *Tournier* rules became the accepted common law position, not only in the UK, but in many common law jurisdictions worldwide.[18] This case, in the absence of any statutory provisions, still represents the legal status of the duty in the UK despite the fact that the banking industry has undergone major changes since 1924.

3. THE REVIEW COMMITTEE'S REPORT AND THE GOVERNMENT'S RESPONSE

In 1987, sixty-three years after the landmark decision in *Tournier*, the UK Treasury, in association with the Bank of England, set up a Committee to review the law relating to banking services. The Review Committee, under the Chairmanship of Professor R. B. Jack, completed its report in December 1988 and the issue of the banker's duty of confidentiality was considered to be sufficiently important to justify an entire chapter in the lengthy

16. Ibid., p. 471.
17. Ibid.
18. For example Australia, Bahamas, Canada, Cayman Islands, Hong Kong, Ireland, Malaysia, New Zealand, Pakistan and Singapore all have bank confidentiality laws based on *Tournier*. In certain US jurisdictions *Tournier* has been followed. See Campbell, op. cit., n. 4.

and detailed report.[19] Not surprisingly, the Review Committee started with an examination of the *Tournier* decision and concluded that 'taken simply as a framework of legal principle' it had stood the test of time.[20] It was felt that while both the duty itself and the stated qualifications were still broadly relevant there was considerable concern that due to the fact that the four qualifications lacked precise definition there was potential for abuse.

The Review Committee was concerned about a number of aspects of the law relating to the duty of confidentiality and the following were identified as the main areas of concern. First, with regard to the first of the four qualifications to the duty, disclosure under compulsion of law, there has been a massive growth in legislation which requires, or permits, banks to divulge information about customers. This has become even more relevant as a result of the anti-money laundering legislation which is dealt with later in this essay. Concern was expressed about the 'formidable burden on bankers',[21] together with the uncertainty as to the precise nature of the obligations imposed. However, perhaps the main area of concern in relation to the first of the four qualifications was that the amount of legislation when considered cumulatively constituted 'a serious inroad into the whole principle of customer confidentially as conceived at the time of *Tournier*'.[22] Second, with regard to the third and fourth qualifications, (c) where the interests of the bank require disclosure and (d) where disclosure is made by the express or implied consent of the customer, the Review Committee recognised that (c) probably offered few problems at the time of *Tournier* but by the late 1980s this was no longer the case. Concern was expressed about the perception by some banks of an entitlement to release information to other companies in the same group of companies without the express consent of the customer and the claim by the banks that this was justified on the basis of implied consent. The Review Committee also noted that many of those consulted by the Review Committee expressed concern about the use which would be made of the information.[23] Third, was the question of disclosure of information by banks to credit reference agencies. The Review Committee expressed concern about this and it was noted that in May 1988 the banks and the credit reference agencies entered into an agreement whereby information about borrowers in default could be passed on to credit reference agencies.

---

19. Above n. 1, chapter 5.
20. Above n. 1, chapter 5.05.
21. *Banking Services* (1989), op. cit., n. 1, chapter 5.08.
22. Ibid.
23. Ibid., chapter 5.14.

The Review Committee was of the opinion that the exact scope of the duty needed to be stated with some accuracy as the *Tournier* guidelines had become blurred as a result of subsequent events. The following reasons for this were identified:

First, the cause of crime prevention and detection, praiseworthy though it may be, has led to a statutory erosion of the duty on a massive, and it seems ever increasing scale. Secondly, the growing risk of debtor default in a credit-based economy, allied it seems with the commercial pressures of a highly competitive age, has led banks increasingly to seek a free flow of confidential information about customers within their own banking group. Thirdly, the same growing risk of default has increased the pressure on banks to release such information to approved credit agencies.[24]

It was proposed that the law should be strengthened and that the *Tournier* rules be put into statute with appropriate updating. It was also proposed that the 'duty to the public' exception be removed as the Review Committee could see no justification for its continued existence. The proposed statutory provisions were that the duty of confidentiality itself should be defined as in *Tournier*.[25] In relation to disclosure under compulsion of law it was proposed that all statutory exemptions should be consolidated in the proposed legislation.[26] The interests of the bank exception should be limited to (i) disclosure in court where the bank is a party to legal action, (ii) disclosure between banking companies within the same group, (iii) disclosure in relation to the sale of the bank (or a substantial part of it).[27] It was also proposed that the fourth exception be changed to require the express consent of the customer.

The response of the government was to dismiss the proposal for new legislation in relation to the duty of confidentiality.[28] According to the White Paper 'the approach favoured by the Government is to build, wherever possible, on competition for banking services, buttressing that, where necessary, with a voluntary and not a statutory code of banking practice'.[29] Instead, the government was of the opinion that the introduction of a Code of Practice, with the *Tournier* rules spelled out in 'clear and simple terms' would be desirable.[30] The government did not accept that there had been a massive erosion of the duty as a result of the statutory exceptions which existed.

24. Ibid., chapter 5.24.
25. Ibid., chapter 5.39.
26. Ibid., chapter 5.40.
27. Ibid., chapter 5.42.
28. *Banking Services: Law and Practice* (HMSO, 1990), Cmnd 1026.
29. Ibid., para. 27.
30. Ibid., para. 24.

However, the government felt it desirable that the Code should contain a statement of good practice in relation to the disclosure of information for marketing purposes and for passing information to credit reference agencies.[31] In relation to black information[32] the government was of the opinion that bankers must be allowed to pass on such information to credit reference agencies.[33] This was seen by the government as in the best interest of consumers who would have to pay higher charges to cover the costs of bad debts.

4.   THE CODE OF PRACTICE

The Code, entitled *Good Banking: Code of Practice to be Observed by Banks, Building Societies and Card Issuers in their Relations with Personal Customers* was prepared jointly by the British Bankers' Association, the Building Societies' Association and the Association for Payment Clearing Services. The first edition of the Code came into force on 16 March 1992; a second edition was published in 1994 and the third, and current, edition came into effect in July 1997. Paragraph 4(1) of the current edition has the effect of setting out the *Tournier* qualifications in the following way:

We will treat all your personal information as private and confidential (even when you are no longer a customer). Nothing about your accounts nor your name and address will be disclosed to anyone, including other companies in our group, other than in four exceptional cases permitted by law. These are:

   (i)   where we are legally compelled to do so;
   (ii)   where there is a duty to the public to disclose;
   (iii) where our interests require disclosure;
          This will not be used as a reason for disclosing information about you or your accounts (including your name and address) to anyone else including other companies in our group for marketing purposes;
   (iv)   where disclosure is made at your request or with your consent.

This is a welcome development which shows an apparent commitment to the duty of confidentiality by the banking industry. Under the common law banks would not have been in a position to release information to other companies unless one of the four qualifications to *Tournier* applied.

Banks, at least until the 1970s, provided basic banking services such as current accounts, deposit accounts, loans and overdrafts. In the last two

31. Ibid., para. 28.
32. For an explanation of this term, see Section 7, 'Black Information'.
33. *Banking Services* (1990), op. cit., n. 28, annex 2, para. 2.17.

decades banks, and companies within the same banking group, have offered a wide range of services, *eg*, estate agency, insurance products, pensions, travel agency services and others. There would be no problem in the provision of information to, for example, the insurance services division of the bank if the insurance services were actually provided by the bank itself, but for other legal reasons these services will generally be provided by other companies within a group of companies. In *Bank of Tokyo v Karoon*[34] the Court of Appeal considered whether a bank was entitled to disclose confidential information to the parent company of the bank. The Court of Appeal was of the opinion that there was an arguable case that this would amount to a breach of the duty. However, it has been suggested that this case is of limited assistance as no final determination of the issue was made.[35]

The banks, according to the first edition of the Code, were not to use the third exception for the purpose of marketing within the group of companies, and paragraph 8 provided that banks were not to supply the names and addresses of customers to other companies within the same group without the express consent of the customer. The second edition of the Code was published in February 1994 and in relation to the duty of confidentiality a change was included. Paragraph 6 of the first edition was unchanged, other than to become paragraph 8, but in relation to the marketing of services a change had been introduced. A completely new provision had been added and this read as follows:

10.1 Except in response to a customer's specific request, banks and building societies will not pass customers' names and addresses to other companies in the same group for marketing purposes, in the absence of express written consent. Banks and building societies will not make the provision of basic banking services conditional on customers giving such written consent. For this purpose, 'basic banking services' include the opening and maintenance of accounts for money transmission by means of cheques and other debit instruments.

This gives the impression, on a first reading, that the banks will actually consult customers before passing the information to another company within the same group. However, this is easily achieved by a clause on an account opening form, *ie*, by signing the opening form the customer agrees to the release of the information whenever the bank is presented with a marketing opportunity.

The current edition of the Code contains the following:

---

34. [1987] All ER 468.
35. M. Hapgood, *Paget's Law of Banking*, 11th edn (Butterworths, 1996), p. 123.

2.15. Unless you specifically request it, or give your express consent in writing, we will not pass your name and address to any company, including other companies in our group, for marketing purposes. You will not be asked to give your permission in return for basic banking services.

The term 'basic banking services' is defined in the same way as before but with the addition of 'this would normally be a current account'. This suggests the possibility that a potential customer, when requesting a service which is not a current account, may be denied that service if he or she refuses to give his or her consent to the release of information to other companies within the same group for marketing purposes. There is also a problem left unresolved in relation to the idea of a 'specific request' from a customer. Banks may not be providing customers with a real opportunity to understand what will actually be happening in this situation.

Passing information to other companies within the same group is clearly in the economic interests of the banking group as a whole and many customers will be quite happy to have their names and addresses passed on but equally there will be others who will not. An examination of actual bank practice in relation to the release of information to other companies within the same group suggests that information will normally be made available throughout the group irrespective of the customer's wishes.

The clear commitment in paragraph 2.15 of the current edition of the Code relates only to information being passed to other companies within the same group of companies for marketing purposes. Passing information to other group members for non-marketing purposes is a different matter entirely.

Account opening forms will normally contain a clause which states that the customer agrees to be bound by a set of terms and conditions which are provided to the customer, either on the account opening form, or on a separate form which is handed to the applicant at the time the account is being opened. The terms and conditions are likely to state that the person in whose name the account is being opened agrees that personal information may be stored on a computer system which can be accessed by other companies in the banking group. No opportunity will be given to refuse permission to allow the information to be made available to other companies in the group. Accordingly the customer is bound by the terms and conditions which permit disclosure on the basis of express consent. Where the customer has refused to give express consent for the release of information for marketing purposes this will not mean that information will not be shared throughout the group, as the customer will have agreed to be bound by the terms and conditions which are likely to contain an agreement to disclose the information. However, in such a situation a member company in the group will not be allowed to contact the customer about marketing opportunities. The other group members will, however, have access to the information in any event.

When the second edition of the Code was published in 1994, Sir Bryan Carsberg, who at the time was Director General of Fair Trading, stated that

the principle of confidentiality requires that details of personal accounts are not passed, without express consent, to a bank's financial services sales team or company. Some banks are side-stepping this principle, and the revised Code does nothing to stop them.[36]

The Consumers Association was also critical about this aspect of bank practice. Nothing in the latest edition of the Code or in the current practice of banks improves this situation.

5.   THE FOUR QUALIFICATIONS TO THE DUTY

5.1 'Under compulsion by law'

Disclosure under compulsion by law was a relatively straightforward concept at the time of *Tournier* but this is no longer the case in the 1990s. There are presently at least twenty statutes which provide that in appropriate circumstances information can be released to a third party. The Review Committee noted that at the time of *Tournier* there were few instances where banks could be required to release information under compulsion of law. They could only think of two: section 7 of The Bankers' Books Evidence Act 1879 and section 5 of the Extradition Act 1873. By the time the Review Committee met in the late 1980s the picture had altered dramatically and they cited nineteen statutes[37] which include a requirement for banks to disclose information. Since 1989 this number has increased. Examples of these include the Bankers' Books Evidence Act 1879, the Financial Services Act 1986, Banking Act 1987, Building Societies Act 1986 and various tax statutes. The picture presented is one of a complicated framework of exceptions to the duty of confidentiality which has become even more complicated as a result of the introduction of the Criminal Justice Act 1993, which amends part VI of the Criminal Justice Act 1988. These new provisions have had an enormous impact on banks and their customers as they form part of internationalised efforts to eradicate the serious global problem of money laundering.

---

36. Office of Fair Trading Press Release, No. 11/94, 8 February 1994.
37. *Banking Services* (1989), op. cit., n. 1, appendix Q.

Where disclosure to a particular third party is required under a statutory provision, what is the role of the bank in relation to its customer? Banks owe a number of implied common law duties to their customers and are expected to always act in the best interests of their customers.[38] Where a request for information is received through a proper channel is the bank under a duty to inform the customer that such a request has been made and that information is to be disclosed? Indeed, it can also be asked whether the correct course of action is for the bank to challenge the release of the information. The matter was considered in *Barclays Bank v Taylor*,[39] where it was unanimously held by the Court of Appeal that no implied term exists in the banker–customer relationship which requires a banker to notify its customer that confidential information has been released to a third party where the disclosure has been made in accordance with a statutory provision. Lord Donaldson referred to the public interest aspect of helping the police to investigate criminal activity and stated that it would have been both surprising and disappointing if the customer had been warned by the bank that information had been passed to the police in this case which concerned section 9 of the Police and Criminal Evidence Act 1984. As will be seen later, under the money laundering offences notification to a customer will amount to a criminal offence.

Perhaps the most important amendment to the duty of confidentiality since the Report is the introduction of tough anti-money laundering provisions which have far reaching effects. Money laundering has been defined as follows:

It is broadly the process or scheme by which both the identity of dirty money representing the proceeds of crime and the true ownership of those proceeds are changed so that the money appears to come from a legitimate or lawful source.[40]

Money laundering has become a problem of huge international dimensions and using the banking system is the most obvious channel for money launderers. Previous money laundering offences concentrated on drug trafficking and terrorism but now all indictable offences are covered.[41] One obvious source of laundered funds would be by tax evaders attempting to disguise the origins of the funds. The new legislation, together with the relevant regulations, has become of singular importance to bankers. No attempt is being made here to provide a detailed analysis of the money

---

38. Except, of course, where there is suspicion of money laundering.
39. [1989] 3 All ER 563.
40. G. Bhattacharya and E. Radmore, 'Fighting Money Laundering: a United Kingdom Perspective', in B. Rider and M. Ashe (eds.), *Money Laundering Control* (Sweet & Maxwell, 1996), p. 101.
41. Provisions contained in the Criminal Justice Act 1993 extended the scope of the anti-money laundering provisions to cover most forms of criminal activity.

laundering offences and readers are referred to other works on the topic, but as banks are specifically included in the anti-money laundering provisions some discussion is necessary.[42]

The punishments for breaching the regulations are severe with a maximum penalty of two years' imprisonment. Regulation 5 requires that 'any person carrying on relevant financial business in the UK' must have in place procedures to cover identification, record-keeping, internal reporting and internal communication procedures including staff training. The requirement for the introduction of identification procedures is the one which will have been most noticeable to consumers. When an attempt is being made to open an account the bank will require the customer to provide satisfactory evidence of identity. Regulation 11(1) provides that this is evidence which will be reasonably capable of establishing that the customer is who he or she claims to be, and also that the person who receives the evidence is satisfied that it does actually establish the person's identity.

This requirement applies not only to account opening but also to single financial transactions. Normal bank practice is to ask for two pieces of identification – one, such as a passport or driving licence which will show the identity of the individual and one which will verify the address of the applicant, *eg*, recent gas, electricity or phone bill. Potential customers are often confused by this, especially when, after perhaps having been in a lengthy queue, they are sent away without having been able to open an account and often without an explanation as to why such identification is necessary.[43]

Apart from account opening problems the major potential difficulty for a customer is the requirement for an internal reporting procedure for 'suspicious' transactions. Each bank must establish a money laundering reporting officer and reports of suspicious activity must be made to that person. All members of bank staff must now receive training to ensure that they are aware of the required procedures. It is now an offence for anyone who suspects, as a result of something discovered in the course of his or her employment, that a customer may be involved in money laundering, to fail to make a report of this to the relevant authorities.[44] The provisions also prevent the bank from notifying the customer that such a report has been made.[45]

---

42. For detailed information on the anti-money laundering provisions see generally Rider and Ashe, op. cit., n. 40. See Money Laundering Regulations 1993, SI 1993/1933.
43. The position in relation to identification requirements for other types of customer, *eg*, companies or partnerships is beyond the scope of this chapter.
44. The failure to disclose knowledge or suspicion of money laundering applies to drug trafficking and terrorist related activity: s. 52 of the Drug Trafficking Act 1994 and s. 18A of the Prevention of Terrorism (Temporary Provisions) Act 1989.
45. S. 93D Criminal Justice Act 1988, s. 53 of Drug Trafficking Act 1994 and s. 17(2) of Prevention of Terrorism (Temporary Provisions) Act 1989. This applies to criminal offences generally.

These provisions are a potential problem for both bank staff and cus-tomers. Bank staff will have to be trained to be vigilant and will be on the lookout for unusual account activity. Kate Main, of the Building Societies Association, has stated that 'the existing, known customers with a one-off transaction probably won't raise any suspicions at all and certainly won't be asked lots of questions'.[46] A Midland Bank spokesperson has stated that where a customer has maintained a fairly low balance for a number of years and then suddenly deposits a large sum of cash this would be con-sidered to be suspicious.[47] It is therefore quite possible that because of activity on an account which is perceived as unusual by a member of staff at the bank, a report will be made to the National Criminal Intelligence Service (NCIS). Customers are generally unaware of these requirements and bank staff seem uncertain about how far they can go in questioning customers in circumstances where the account activity does not conform to the normal pattern for that customer. The fear of possibly 'tipping off' the customer may mean that a perfectly innocent transaction is reported. It is difficult to criticise bank staff in this situation and this is an area which requires some degree of clarification.

5.2 'Duty to the public to disclose'

Bankes LJ did not elaborate on the extent of this exception to the duty and ever since *Tournier* there has been uncertainty as to what exactly comes within this heading. The only example he provided was where there was danger to the state. The Review Committee recommended the abolition of this exception but this was not accepted by the government.

5.3 'Where the interests of the bank require disclosure'

It is often suggested that this will cover situations where a bank has to take action against one of its customers. Information relating to the dispute will have to be provided on court forms and pleadings. Bankes LJ specifi-cally referred to the situation where a bank would have to issue a writ for failure to repay a loan. But what about releasing information to other com-panies within the same banking group? This will obviously be in the eco-nomic interests of the bank but would clearly seem to be beyond the

46. *The Guardian*, 28 August 1993.
47. Ibid.

narrow confines under which Bankes LJ appeared to be operating. This is a subject which has been considered by the Review Committee and the courts and will be returned to later.

5.4 'Where the disclosure is made by the express or implied consent of the customer'

Lord Atkin in *Tournier* was of the opinion that express consent should not present any difficulties.[48] However, it seems that at present express consent is not without its difficulties and the concept of implied consent carries with it even more difficult questions. Express consent is where the customer has instructed the bank to divulge information. This is most likely to be the case where the customer wishes the bank to provide a reference to a third party. Paragraph 4.5 of the Code provides: 'We will tell you if we provide bankers' references. If a banker's reference about you is requested, we will require your written consent before it is given.'

In practice, banks will usually provide this service and have done so for a considerable length of time, although it is also their practice to provide such references only to other banks and not to other individuals or organisations. Bankers have always been very careful about what is contained in a reference. Such references are written in a language of apparent vagueness but to those on the inside clear messages are provided.[49] The Code defines a banker's reference as 'an opinion about a particular customer's ability to enter into or repay a financial commitment'.[50]

As has been noted, it has traditionally been the case that banks would only reply to enquiries from other bankers but, as Cranston points out, where the express consent of the customer is provided there is no reason why opinions should not be provided direct to an enquirer.[51] The Review Committee noted that banks would only give status opinions 'in the ordinary course of business' and that to give opinions direct to non-bankers would not be in the ordinary course of business.

Bankers have traditionally relied on the concept of implied consent as the justification for providing such references. Now the Code makes it clear that the express written consent of the customer will be required before a reference is provided. This is a welcome development which

---

48. [1924] 1 KB at 486.
49. A discussion of the question of the bank's potential liability for references is beyond the scope of this chapter. For a detailed discussion see Hapgood, op. cit., n. 35, pp. 125–9.
50. S. 6.
51. R. Cranston, *Principles of Banking Law* (Oxford University Press, 1997), p. 194.

benefits customers and banks. This reflects the proposals of the Review Committee that implied consent should not be relied upon but that consent should be in writing and should state the purpose for which it has been given.[52] The Review Committee felt that few customers were aware that when they opened an account they would be assumed by the bank to have given implied consent for the bank to reply to enquiries about their financial status.[53]

6.   WHAT INFORMATION IS COVERED BY THE DUTY OF CONFIDENTIALITY?

Lord Atkin considered the extent of the duty in the following terms:

> It clearly goes beyond the state of the account, that is, whether there is a debit or credit balance, and the amount of the balance. It must extend to all the transactions that go through the account, and to the securities, if any, given in respect of the account; it must, I think, extend beyond the period when the account is closed or ceases to be an active account. It seems to me inconceivable that either party would contemplate that once the customer has closed his account the bank was to be at liberty to divulge as it pleased the particular transactions which it had conducted for the customer when he was such. I further think that the obligation extends to information obtained from other sources than the customer's actual account.[54]

Even the fact that a person has an account with a bank would appear to come within the scope of the duty. Therefore if someone contacts a bank branch to ask if a particular individual has an account there the bank will be in breach of its duty if it discloses that there is an account. The safest, and proper, course of action for the bank would be to advise the inquirer that it does not comment on such matters.

However, it will often be the case that an individual, by using a cheque, plastic card or other means, divulges the fact that he or she has an account with that bank. But this is a matter of choice for the customer not the bank. One potential problem is the situation where, for example, a husband and wife have a joint account with a particular branch of a bank and either or both also have individual accounts. Here the bank must be careful not to divulge even the existence of the individual account to the non-account holder.

52.   Para. 5.43.
53.   Para. 6.27.
54.   [1924] 1 KB at 485.

The duty will cover virtually all information which the bank has in its possession, unless that information is in the public domain, and this will cover information obtained from sources other than the customer.

7. BLACK INFORMATION

'Black information' is information relating to a customer who has borrowed funds from a bank and who has failed to keep up to date with repayments. The attitude of the banks towards the disclosure of this type of information is contained in paragraph 4.2 of the Code which provides:

Information about your personal debts owed to us may be disclosed to credit reference agencies where:

- you have fallen behind with your payments; and
- the amount owed is not in dispute; and
- you have not made proposals satisfactory to us for repayment of your debt following formal demand; and
- you have been given at least 28 days' notice of our intention to disclose.[55]

The banks have stated in the Code that they will not provide any other information to credit reference agencies without the consent of the customer.[56]

What is the legal justification for the release of such information? There is no doubt that banking practice, prior to the introduction of the Code, had been to release 'black information', but it is difficult to understand what legal justification existed for what appears to be a breach of the duty of confidentiality. This continues to be the case. It can only be assumed that the banks have been relying on either exception (b), public interest, or on (c) that the interests of the bank require disclosure. It is arguable that they have no entitlement to divulge such information under the common law. The safest, and proper, course of action for the banks to adopt would be to ensure that loan documentation specifically gives permission for such information to be released to registered credit reference agencies.

The provisions of the Code merely reflect existing bank practice prior to the introduction of the first edition of the Code in 1992, but from a consumer perspective the position has been strengthened as a result of the

---

55. A Credit Reference Agency is defined in the Code as an organisation, licensed under the Consumer Credit Act 1974, which holds information about individuals which is of relevance to lenders.
56. Code, para. 4.3.

requirement that a minimum of 28 days' notice must be given to a customer where there is an intention by the bank to disclose. Additionally there is a requirement that the amount owing must not be in dispute, but this is an area which could cause some problems. For example, what if bank charges have been added, as is common with unauthorised overdrafts, and these are disputed by customers? Clearly the threat of notification will often lead to further proposals by the customer, or at least may have the effect of forcing the customer to actually make contact with the bank.

8.   REMEDIES FOR BREACH OF THE DUTY

The remedy for a breach of the duty will lie in contract. It would also be possible to seek an injunction where the disclosure is ongoing or where it has not yet taken place but where the customer is aware that it is about to happen. Injunctive relief will, however, rarely be sought as the breach will already have taken place and, therefore, the normal claim will be for damages. Where the plaintiff is a private individual the likely course of action will be to use the Banking Ombudsman scheme rather than resorting to the civil courts. Complaints about breaches of the duty are a regular feature of the Banking Ombudsman's *Annual Report*. There were 127 complaints to the Banking Ombudsman concerning confidentiality in 1995–96 and 132 in 1996–97. Twenty-eight of these complaints led to full investigations.[57]

9.   CONCLUSION

The Review Committee[58] noted that a customer of a bank could be forgiven for wondering if the banker's duty of confidentiality had been replaced by a duty to disclose. There are now even more situations where a bank is not only able to disclose information about customers, but where the bank is under a positive duty to disclose. Indeed, as has already been seen, the anti-money laundering provisions create a situation whereby a customer behaving in a manner which is not perceived to be normal for that individual may well lead to a report being made to the NCIS.

The present state of the law is unsatisfactory for the protection of individual customers, although the introduction of a Code of Practice has been an improvement on the previous situation. The clear statements in the

57. *The Banking Ombudsman Scheme: Annual Report 1996–97.*
58. *Banking Services* (1989), op. cit., n. 1, chapter 5.26.

latest edition of the Code, coupled with the availability of the Banking Ombudsman Scheme, should provide a higher level of protection for customers. However, concerns still remain. For example, there is still some doubt about whether the banks are as committed to the Code as they claim to be and the question of whether consent, express or implied, has really been given is an area ripe for abuse.

A balance has to be struck between the release of information and the protection of private financial information. Total bank secrecy as offered by certain jurisdictions cannot be justified in the UK. It would not be in the interests of society at large nor, it is suggested, can it be in the interests of individual consumers. It is understandable that bank customers expect their financial affairs to be a matter between themselves and their banks. As the law stands in the UK there is no such thing as bank secrecy but there does exist a common law duty of confidentiality owed by a bank to its customers. The *Tournier* rules provide a fair balance between the need for confidentiality and the public interest in ensuring that customers cannot hide behind bank secrecy laws. Stringent secrecy laws are not needed in the UK.

What is still of concern, however, is that customers, banks and bank staff are faced with a legal regime which is overly and, arguably, unnecessarily complicated, and this is not in anyone's interest. The Review Committee recommended that the *Tournier* rules and the exceptions to the duty of confidentiality be consolidated into a new statute. This was, of course, rejected by the government of the time and there is little likelihood of any such legislation from the present government. Since the Review Committee made its recommendations the framework has become even more complicated as a result of the anti-money laundering provisions.

One positive feature for consumers is the existence of the Code of Practice coupled with the Banking Ombudsman scheme. When the second edition of the Code was introduced in 1994 there was concern expressed by this writer, and others, about the level of commitment shown by the banks to the Code.[59] All of the major banks now display an awareness, not only of the existence of the Code, but also of its provisions and copies of the Code are now generally available at branches of the clearing banks. However, it still appears to be the case that despite the public commitment to the duty of confidentiality displayed in the Code, one is left with the feeling that the banks are putting their own interests first when it suits them, regardless of the Code's provisions. It is the practice of the major banks to use terms and conditions upon account opening which allow for information to be

---

59. See A. Campbell, 'Banks and Customer Confidentiality' (1994) 4 *Consumer Policy Review* 80.

passed to other companies within the same group on the basis of having received the express consent of the customer. From a legal perspective the banks are acting in a way which does not infringe any legal rules but it cannot be said that they are acting within the spirit of the Code of Practice. From the consumer protection perspective a significant opportunity was lost when the government, in 1990, refused to support the Review Committee's proposals for new legislation.

Chapter Four

UNILATERAL VARIATION IN BANKING CONTRACTS: AN 'UNFAIR TERM'?

Eva Lomnicka

Chapter Outline

1. Introduction

2. Unilateral Variation in General

3. The Unfair Terms in Consumer Contracts Regulations
    3.1   Keeping outside the grey list
           3.1.1   General
           3.1.2   Schedule 3, paras 1(j) and (k)
           3.1.3   'Valid reason'
           3.1.4   'Specified in the contract'
    3.2   The derogations
           3.2.1   General
           3.2.2   Schedule 3, para. 2(b): the first derogation
                   3.2.2.1   Scope
                   3.2.2.2   The proviso
           3.2.3   Schedule 3, para. 2(b): the second derogation

4. Present Practice

Consumer Protection in Financial Services (P. Cartwright, ed.: 90-411-9717-6: © Kluwer Law International: pub. Kluwer Law International, 1999: printed in Great Britain)

1. INTRODUCTION

The need to implement the Unfair Terms in Consumer Contracts Direc-tive[1] has been hailed as an opportunity to rethink the English law's atti-tude to consumer protection.[2] Whatever the long-term effect on our jurisprudence, it is clear that the implementation of that directive by the Unfair Terms in Consumer Contracts Regulations ('the Regulations')[3] has had the salutary effect of causing sellers and suppliers of services – or at least those who keep an eye on the legal environment within which they operate – to re-examine their standard term contracts.

Much has already been written about the impact the Regulations might have, in particular, how our jurisprudence will cope with the 'good faith' concept.[4] This chapter has a narrower focus in concentrating on one important type of term in banking contracts which has had to be reconsid-ered in the light of the Regulations: a term enabling the banks to make unilateral changes to their loan contracts with their retail customers.

2. UNILATERAL VARIATION IN GENERAL

In the banking context there are at least two varieties of such terms. First, there is the term which enables banks to alter the interest rate at will. Such terms are, of course, often a feature of variable rate loans and savings accounts, if the rate is not directly linked to a base or other rate and so varies automatically with that rate.[5] Second, and more controversially,

---

1. Council Directive 93/13/EEC ([1993] OJ L95, 21.4.93, p. 29), which came into effect on 1 January 1995. For discussions see Duffy, 'Unfair Contract Terms and the Draft EC Directive', [1993] JBL 67; Dean, 'Unfair Contract Terms: the European Approach' (1993) 56 MLR 581; Willett, 'Directive on Unfair Terms in Consumer Contracts' (1994) *Consumer Law Journal* 114; Dean, 'Consolidation or Confusion?' (1995) 145 NLJ 28; (on the Scottish position) MacNeil, 'Good Faith and the Control of Contract Terms: the EC Directive on Unfair Terms in Consumer Contracts' (1995) *Juridical Review* 147. For a brief history, see Bright and Bright, 'Unfair Terms in Land Contracts: Copy Out or Cop Out?' (1995) 111 LQR 655, 656–9.
2. See, for example, Dean, op. cit., n. 1.
3. SI 1994/3159. They apply to contracts concluded after 1 July 1995: Reg. 1. For the two consultation documents which preceded the Regulations, see 'Implementation of the EC Directive on Unfair Terms in Consumer Contracts (93/13/EEC): A Consultative Document' (DTI, October 1993) and 'Implementation of the EC Directive on Unfair Terms in Consumer Contracts (93/13/EEC): A Further Consultative Document' (DTI, September 1994).
4. See for example, Brownsword and Howells, 'The Implementation of the EC Directive on Unfair Terms in Consumer Contracts: Some Unresolved Questions' (1995) JBL 243.
5. Of course, if that rate is under the control of the lender, its alteration by the lender is, in effect, a unilateral alteration by the creditor of the contractual rate of interest.

there is the term giving the bank an absolute discretion to alter *any* term in the loan contract unilaterally. Until the advent of the Regulations, credit and charge card agreements in particular traditionally contained such a term[6] and this proved particularly useful when, a few years ago, annual fees were unilaterally imposed on unsuspecting cardholders.

Until the Regulations were enacted, it was trite law, in keeping with our traditional *laissez-faire* approaches to our contract law, that such terms, if clearly incorporated[7] and clearly expressed,[8] were prima facie effective. There was trenchant confirmation of this, albeit in the special context of a variable interest rate loan where the borrower could settle the debt early, by Staughton LJ in *Lombard Tricity Finance v Paton*.[9] Moreover, in that case the Consumer Credit (Agreements) Regulations 1983[10] were held not to affect the ability, at common law, of a creditor to provide for unilateral variation of the interest rate at will.[11] However, the case is not such a strong endorsement of the lawfulness of a unilateral variation clause as it might be, in that it concerned a power to vary interest rates where, as the court acknowledged, market forces would restrain its capricious exercise.[12] In addition, the creditor was also no doubt constrained by the need to retain its consumer credit licence which, as will be noted below, can be withdrawn for improper business practices which fall short of unlawfulness.[13]

6. For example, the Access card issued by Midland Bank used to provide: 'We may vary these conditions by written notice to you, by a general notice in our branches or in the national press.' The old Barclaycard agreement provided: 'The Bank may vary this Agreement at any time or times whether or not a similar variation is made to the agreement(s) with any other Cardholder(s). Subject to the requirements of statute, notification of any such variation shall be given to the Principal Cardholder by the Bank either in writing or by publication thereof by such means as the Bank may select and a variation so notified shall be binding on the Cardholder.'
7. *Thornton v Shoe Lane Parking* [1971] 2 QB 163. The more unusual and onerous the term, the greater the steps needed for its notification: *Interfoto Picture Library Ltd v Stiletto Visual Programmes Ltd* [1989] QB 433.
8. The *contra proferentem* rules operates to minimise the impact of an ambiguously drafted term (and see now, Reg. 6 of the Regulations). Moreover, in *Lombard Tricity Finance v Paton* (see note 9 *infra*), Staughton LJ expressed the view that it was unusual for a contract to enable a party to change its terms unilaterally and 'in general one would require clear words to achieve that result' (at p. 923b).
9. [1989] 1 All ER 918. The point was conceded by counsel (p. 923a) but given its importance, the court explained why it thought the concession was rightly made. An analogy was drawn with the situation where the buyer in a sale of goods contract reserves the right to fix the price of the goods: *May & Butcher Ltd v R* [1934] 2 KB 17. (However, this type of term is now suspect, in being on the 'grey list', under the Regulations: Sch. 3, para. 1(1), see *infra*.)
10. SI 1983 1553 (made under the Consumer Credit Act 1974), in particular, Sch. 1, para. 19, considered further below.
11. See further n. 26 *infra*.
12. At p. 923c–d, in that the debtor could terminate the contract.
13. Consumer Credit Act 1974, s. 25(2)(d), noted *infra*.

Unilateral variation clauses also appeared unobjectionable, in principle, to the framers of the Consumer Credit Act 1974. That statute was enacted on the basis that unilateral variation was possible[14] and while it does outlaw certain objectionable terms in the credit agreements it regulates,[15] it merely imposes notification constraints on the exercise of a power of unilateral variation. These constraints take the form of requiring notice to be given in a manner prescribed by regulation.[16] The regulations generally require the serving[17] of a notice on the debtor seven days before the variation is to take effect,[18] although in certain circumstances notice of variation in interest rate may (only) be given by announcement in the press and display at the creditor's premises.[19] In addition, in relation to variable rate agreements, any advertisements[20] must state (if this is the case) that the interest rate[21] (in the case of credit agreements) and the charges (in the case of hire agreements) are variable.[22]

14. Ibid., s. 82(1): 'Where, under a power contained in a regulated agreement the creditor or owner varies the agreement.' Similarly, the Agreements Regulations (see n. 10 *supra*, Reg. 2(1) and Sch. 1 assume that the creditor is permitted to vary the interest rate (see Sch. 1, paras 9(c), 18) and the amounts of repayments (see Sch. 1, para. 13) by requiring the information as to their calculation to be given. See also ibid., Sch. 1, para. 8 (variation of credit limit and notification thereof) and Reg. 6(1) and Sch. 6, para. 5 (statement of power of variation of amount of repayments is a 'prescribed term' for the purposes of ss. 61(1)(a) and 127(3)). For analogous provisions in relation to hire agreements, see ibid., Reg. 3(1) and Sch. 3, para. 7 (variable payments) and Reg. 6(1) and Sch. 6, para. 6 (statement of power of variation of amount of repayments a 'prescribed term' for the purposes of ss. 61(1)(a) and 127(3)).
15. See for example, s. 59 (rendering void, agreements purporting to bind a consumer to enter into a regulated agreement), s. 83 (liability of debtor for persons other than agents), s. 93 (interest rate cannot be increased on default).
16. Ibid., s. 82(1): 'the variation shall not take effect before notice of it is given . . . in the prescribed manner'. See the Consumer Credit (Notice of Variation of Agreements) Regulations 1977, SI 1997 /328, as amended.
17. Defined, ibid., s. 176(1), as amended by the Law of Property (Miscellaneous Provisions) Act 1994, to mean deliver or send by post to the last known address or addressed and left at the last known address. See also, Interpretation Act 1978, s. 7, on service by post.
18. SI 1977 /328, Reg. 2.
19. Ibid., Reg. 3. It seems the announcement and display need not also occur seven days before that variation is to take effect as Reg. 3 is stated to operate in substitution for that part of Reg. 2 which imposes the seven days requirement and Reg. 3 makes no mention of *when* the announcement is to take place.
20. See Consumer Credit (Advertisements) Regulations 1989, SI 1989/1125 (hereafter, 'the Advertisements Regulations'). There were similar provisions in relation to quotations, imposed by the Consumer Credit (Quotations) Regulations, 1989/1126, before their revocation.
21. Or, more accurately, 'the rate or amount of any item included in the total charge for credit'.
22. In relation to *credit* agreement advertisements, see Advertisements Regulations, Reg. 2(1) and Sch. 1, part II, para. 7(c) (intermediate credit advertisement); Part III, para.

Further, there are documentation requirements applicable to powers of variation in relation to regulated credit and hire agreements.[23] Thus, for example, variable rate agreements must contain a 'statement indicating the circumstances in which' any variation may occur.[24] In *Lombard Tricity Finance v Paton*[25] this was the provision which was used as the basis of the unsuccessful argument that the creditor was precluded from reserving a power to vary interest rates at will, in that 'circumstances' connoted external circumstances (such as a general increase in market rates) and not the whim or desire of the creditor. Moreover, in *Paton* it was held sufficient compliance with this provision to state that the interest rate was 'subject to variation by the creditor from time to time on notification as required by law' even though there was no express statement that the variation was at the creditor's absolute discretion.[26] Thus, more precision as to the 'circumstances' when variation was permitted was not necessary.

Although there was nothing unlawful at common law in the reservation of a power unilaterally to vary a contract, there are, Unfair Terms in Consumer Contracts Regulations apart, a number of constraints on its inclusion or, at least, on its capricious exercise. The constraint on its exercise are particularly significant because the Regulations only control the inclusion of 'unfair' terms.[27]

First, there are the constraints of market forces. In the consumer context, these can be exaggerated. There is little evidence that the *inclusion* of unilateral variation clauses, even if drawn clearly to the attention of the consumer, operate as a disincentive to enter into the contract. As to constraining the *exercise* of a power to vary unilaterally, it is only in those cases where the consumer may terminate the contract easily and without penalty and obtain the product or service elsewhere at a more competitive rate, that market forces might operate to inhibit a creditor exercising the

---

(continued)

       7(3) (full credit advertisement). In relation to *hire* advertisements, see Advertisements Regulations, Reg. 2(2) and Sch. 2, part III, paras 12 and 14 (full hire advertisements). In addition, in relation to variable *hire* charges, there must be a statement of 'the circumstances in which' variation may occur: Advertisements Regulations, Reg. 2(2) and Sch. 2, part III, para. 12.

23. Imposed by the Consumer Credit (Agreements) Regulations 1983; see n. 10 *supra*.
24. Ibid., Reg. 2(1) and Sch. 1, para. 19 (credit agreements). See also Reg. 3(1) and Sch. 3, para. 7 (variation of payments under hire agreements).
25. '[T]he words . . . here are sufficient to convey, to the average reader of modest intelligence, that Lombard have the right to vary the interest rate at will if they choose to do so, subject only to proper notification': *per* Staughton LJ, at p. 924f.
26. '[T]he words . . . here are sufficient to convey, to the average reader of modest intelligence, that Lombard have the right to vary the interest rate at will if they choose to do so, subject only to proper notification': *per* Staughton LJ, at p. 924f.
27. Reg. 4(2) refers to unfairness 'as at the time of the conclusion of the contract, to all the circumstances attending the conclusion of the contract'.

power.[28] Although the Consumer Credit Act 1974 does confer on the consumer the power to terminate credit agreements early,[29] consumer inertia will normally operate as a countervailing force.

Second, there are a number of further constraints in consequence of the Consumer Credit Act 1974. To begin with, there are the licensing provisions of that Act. In deciding if a creditor should obtain or retain a licence, the Director General may take into account '*any* circumstance appearing to him to be relevant',[30] including engaging in business practices 'appearing to the Director to be deceitful or oppressive, or otherwise unfair or improper (*whether unlawful or not*)'.[31] Thus departures from ethical business behaviour, even if they fall short of unlawful activity, may justify the refusal or revocation of a licence. In *Paton*, the court expressed the hope that if the creditor, under the unilateral variation clause, 'capriciously treated old borrowers unfavourably' in comparison with new borrowers – presumably recouping losses made in charging low rates to new customers by 'capriciously' increasing the rates paid by existing customers – 'the Director General of Fair Trading would consider whether he should still have a licence under the 1974 Act'.[32] The suggestion appears to be that the *exercise* of a power of unilateral variation may constitute such a departure, although there is no indication that the mere *reservation* of such a power would attract similar opprobrium.

There are also the extortionate credit bargain provisions of the Consumer Credit Act 1974[33] which enable a court to rewrite[34] credit agreements if they are part of an 'extortionate' credit bargain. Here again, the wording of the statute appears promising in defining 'extortionate' as including the gross contravention of 'ordinary principles of fair dealing'.[35] However, the epithet 'gross' appears to require something quite heinous to induce the court to intervene and the case law on the existing provisions confirms the reluctance of the courts to intervene too readily.[36]

28 . Acknowledged in *Paton*, see nn. 9 and 12, *supra*.
29. See s. 94 (credit agreements) and s. 101 (hire agreements).
30. Consumer Credit Act 1974, s. 25(2) (my emphasis).
31. Ibid., s. 25(2)(d) (my emphasis). For a (rather out of date) description of the OFT's approach to licensing, see Borrie, 'Licensing Practice under the Consumer Credit Act' (1982) JBL 91.
32. Consumer Credit Act 1974, ss. 137–40. The court in *Paton*, at p. 923e found it 'unnecessary to express any view' on the impact of those provisions on the contract before it, as counsel for the consumer conceded that conduct *after* the agreement was made could not be taken into account (see *infra*).
33. Ibid., s. 139.
34. Ibid., s. 138(1)(a).
35. Ibid., s. 138(1)(a).
36. See the OFT's Report, 'Unjust Credit Transactions' (September 1991), which is under fresh consideration by the Labour government.

103

Indeed, the DTI proposes to change the test to 'unjust credit transaction' in order to make the test 'less restrictive'.[37] Thus the mere *inclusion* of a unilateral variation clause is unlikely to be regarded as *grossly* 'contravening ordinary principles of fair dealing'. Moreover, it is unclear whether how a party exercises its contractual powers as opposed to the contract's original terms, may be taken into account in deciding if the bargain is 'extortionate'.[38] If the agreement must be judged at its inception, then the capricious exercise of a power to vary would not enable the court to re-open the contract.

Finally, there are the constraints under the various regulations made under the Consumer Credit Act 1974, noted above. These do not affect the ability of the creditor to include or exercise a unilateral power of variation but in certain circumstances they do require him to disclose it in a particular way and, in certain circumstances, to give prescribed notice before the variation takes effect.

A third constraining factor is the various good practice codes – for example, the Banking Code[39] – which have been voluntarily adopted by much of the banking sector.[40] Being mere exhortations as to good practice, the codes do not, as such,[41] provide direct remedies for consumers. However, in so far as lenders expressly incorporate provisions in their contracts in compliance with the relevant code, then those provisions become contractual obligations enforceable by the consumer. There is also room for implying terms into contracts on the basis of the relevant code, especially when member institutions advertise their adherence to that code[42] and comply with the exhortation in it that they will make copies of the code available to consumers.[43] However, express terms in

---

37. Ibid.
38. Although it is arguable that the contradistinction between the wording of s. 138(2)(a) ('interest rates prevailing *at the time it was made*' (my emphasis)) and s. 138(2)(c) ('*any* other relevant consideration') suggests conduct during the term of the contract may be relevant.
39. See also the Code of Practice of the FLA (Finance and Leasing Association) and the CCTA (Consumer Credit Trade Association).
40. The Good Banking Code first came into force in March 1992, went into second edition in March 1994 and is now (as 'The Banking Code') in its third edition (in force 1 July 1997). It was a response, no doubt by way of preemptive strike to forestall legislative intervention, to some of the criticisms of banking practice in the Jack Report (1989 Cm 622).
41. However, where the standard of behaviour of a lender is at issue (for example, during an investigation by one of the ombudsmen), the code is likely to be very relevant in determining what this (at least as a minimum) should be.
42. Some banks include the rubric 'a signatory to the Code of Banking Practice' (or something similar) in their contracts.
43. See the Preface to the Banking Code: 'This . . . Code . . . sets standards of good banking practice which are followed as a minimum by banks . . . subscribing to it . . . It

banking contracts which are clearly at variance with the code would, in accordance with general contractual principles, preclude the implication of inconsistent terms complying with the code.[44]

Unsurprisingly, given their provenance, the codes have little by way of constraints on unilateral variation powers reserved by creditors. To take the Banking Code by way of example, there are no limitations on the actual reservation of a power of variation by the banks. On the contrary, there is acknowledgement that 'occasionally terms and conditions may have to be changed'.[45] However, there is an undertaking that the customer will be told how s/he will be notified of these changes and that 'reasonable notice' will be given before any change takes effect.[46] The first part of this requirement implies that the bank must undertake to notify of any charges – but leaves it to the bank to decide how to notify,[47] merely requiring it to inform its customers on the method of notification it has chosen. As to length of notice of variation, it would seem that if all a bank does is to include a clause setting out how variations will be notified and saying nothing about notice, a court could hold, on the basis of the Code, that it is an implied term that reasonable notice will be given.[48] There are more specific provisions concerning changes to 'charges', again merely requiring disclosure and (sometimes) 'reasonable notice'.[49]

(continued)
      should help [customers] understand how banks . . . are expected to deal with them'. See in particular, the 'Key Commitments' (para. 1). Lip service is (apparently) paid to the Regulations in para. 2.6 which states that 'All written terms and conditions will be fair in substance.'

44. If an express term is ambiguous, the courts in interpreting it will no doubt attempt to make it consistent with the Code. This approach is assisted by one of the 'Key Commitments' of the Code which states that subscribers promise to 'ensure that all services and products comply with this Code, even if they have their own term and conditions'. However, it is doubtful if such a general undertaking in the code (in effect) not to rely on express terms which are inconsistent with the Code will be enough to induce the courts to over-ride express terms which are clearly inconsistent with it unless, perhaps, a customer establishes s/he relied on the undertaking.

45. Banking Code, para. 2.9. It is unclear (see n. 49, *infra*) how this very general provision relates to the more specific provisions as to changes in 'charges' and 'interest rates' (considered further *supra*). Again, the code assumes that both of these can change ('If we increase a charge': para. 2.10; 'interest rates . . . may change from time to time': para. 2.11).

46. Ibid., para. 2.9. A fresh copy of the amended contract (or a summary of the changes) must sometimes be issued.

47. Thus this could be by way of display in banking premises or announcement in the press. See the more specific provision in relation to interest rate changes in para. 2.11, noted *infra*, n. 53.

48. See *supra* as to the possibility of implying terms on the basis of the Code.

49. Banking Code, para. 2.1 ('tariff' as to 'basic account services' available), para. 2.3 ('additional charges' in relation to certain loan contracts), para. 2.5 ('other charges').

Similarly, special provision is made in relation to interest. First, the customer must be informed of 'the basis on which interest is calculated'.[50] Arguably, the reservation of a power to vary interest which may be exercised 'at will' would not be in compliance with the Code, as 'at will' may not be regarded as a sufficient 'basis' on which interest may be varied.[51] But, even if 'basis' does connote some objectively justifiable ground, given the lack of direct legal effect of the Code on banking contracts, a consumer would have no contractual remedy on the ground that the Code had been breached, should a bank reserve such an absolute power of variation.[52]

Second, there is an undertaking that changes in interest rates will be notified 'at the earliest opportunity' and that notification will be either by personal or more general notification.[53] It should be noted that there is the conspicuous omission of a 'reasonable notice' requirement before variations of interest rates take effect, suggesting that variations with immediate effect are contemplated – in contrast to variations of 'terms and conditions' and (certain) charges.

In consequence, before the Unfair Terms in Consumer Contracts Regulations, there was little to constrain lenders wishing to reserve and then exercise a power to alter contracts unilaterally. However, the inclusion[54] of unilateral variation clauses is now suspect under the Regulations, although the extent to which they are effective, and how they will dovetail into the Consumer Credit Act 1974, is by no means clear.

(continued)

'Reasonable notice' is only mentioned in relation to an increase in a charge for a 'basic account services': para. 2.10. Thus, it seems, other charges can be varied without more, unless it can be argued that such a variation entails a change in 'terms and conditions', in which case para. 2.9 applies to require reasonable notice (see n. 45, *supra*), in which case para. 2.10 is otiose.

50. Ibid., para. 2.1. The older editions of the Code also required an explanation of 'the basis on which' *variation* of interest rates were to be made (and the basis on which other charges were to be made), but these provisions have been omitted from the third edition.

51. Cf. 'circumstances' in the Consumer Credit (Agreements) Regulations 1983, Sch. 1, para. 19, noted *supra* (see n. 25), although admittedly, this was in the context of Regulations which were held not to have the power to alter the common law. Moreover, para. 2.11 of the Banking Code (see *infra*) contains no hint that there are any constraints as to when interest rates may be varied.

52. The express provision enabling variation 'at will' would not permit the implication of a term, on the basis of the code, only enabling variation of an objectively justifiable ground, see *supra*.

53. Banking Code, para. 2.11. Notification may be by either 'letter/other personal notice' or 'notices/leaflets in branches and press advertisements'. If the latter alternative is adopted, customers are to be told (presumably by personal notification) their interest rate at least once a year.

54. See n. 27, *supra*.

3.   THE UNFAIR TERMS IN CONSUMER CONTRACTS REGULATIONS

As is well known, the Regulations outlaw 'unfair terms' in consumer contracts which have not been individually negotiated.[55] The concept 'unfair', based as it is on the relatively unfamiliar notion of something which 'contrary to the requirement of good faith causes a significant imbalance in the parties' rights and obligations under the contract to the detriment of the consumer',[56] leaves plenty of room for debate.[57] Limited interpretive guidance is given in the Regulations.[58] In particular, in Schedule 3 there is 'an indicative and non-exhaustive list of [seventeen] terms which may be regarded as unfair'.[59] This wording is tantalising in its unhelpfulness. There is no black list[60] of terms which are outlawed without more. There is only a 'grey list' of terms which are prima facie unfair but which may nevertheless be upheld.[61] However, although not providing a litmus test, the list is clearly an invitation to re-consider the inclusion of terms which fall within it.

There are no 'safe harbours' in the Regulations, no indications of when a term may be regarded as not unfair.[62] Nevertheless, some have sought solace in the fact that the grey list and the derogations from it,[63] are drafted, surprisingly, with relative precision. This seems an invitation to re-draft contract terms in the light of that precise wording. For example, as will be explained below, a term permitting unilateral variation 'without a valid reason which is specified in the contract'[64] is on the grey list, sug-

---

55. Regs 3, 5.
56. Reg. 4.
57. See Brownsword and Howells, op. cit., n. 4, pp. 252–8 and generally, Collins, 'Good Faith in European Contract Law' (1994) OJLS 229; Brownsword, 'Two Concepts of Good Faith' (1994) 7 JCL 197.
58. Reg. 4 and Schs 2 and 3.
59. Reg. 4(4).
60. The Federal Republic of Germany adopted, in its Standard Business Terms Act 1976, a statute on unfair terms which contains a blacklist of terms that are void and a grey list of terms that may be declared void: see the EC Commission's Explanatory Report to the Directive (reprinted as annex 3 to the Sixth Report of the House of Lords Select Committee on the European Communities (Session 1991–2; HL Papers 228 at p. 36), cited in Duffy, op. cit., n. 1. Some exemption clauses are, of course, declared void by the UK's Unfair Contract Terms Act 1977.
61. Ibid.
62. As Dean (op. cit., n. 1) points out, this lack of precision precludes the imposition of criminal liability for breach of the regulations.
63 . In Sch. 3, para. 2(a) and (b), considered *infra*.
64. Sch. 3, para. 1(j). Cf. para. 1(k) which lists a term permitting unilateral variation of the 'characteristic of' the product or service 'without a valid reason' – not mentioning specification of reasons in the contract.

gesting that if such valid reasons are so specified, the term is likely to be regarded as not unfair. Similarly, the derogations from the list – that is, circumstances in which terms which are prima facie within the list are nevertheless taken outside it – suggest that terms falling within the precise wording of the derogations are again likely to be regarded as not unfair. Otherwise, why draft the list and the derogations in such detail? It does seems that a green(ish) light is being given to certain terms. However, one must not lose sight of the fact that the list is clearly stated to be 'indicative and non-exhaustive'.[65] Thus rewording a term so that it falls outside the grey list entirely or within a derogation, will not guarantee the term's validity.

In sum, the most that can be said is that if a term falls within the grey list it is likely[66] to be held unfair. If the term falls outside the list because of the list's wording, then it is likely[67] that the term will be upheld as not unfair. Moreover, a term which, in coming within the wording of a derogation, does not fall within the list, is also likely to be upheld.[68]

3.1 Keeping outside the grey list

3.1.1 General

What advice should be given to a bank wishing to retain some power unilaterally to vary its contract? The advice must begin with the mantra that nothing is certain and that even a term falling outside the grey list or within a derogation may still be regarded as 'unfair'.[69] However, bearing in mind the precision with which the Regulations deal with unilateral variation terms, there is some merit in examining those provisions and in trying to draft terms either outside the grey list altogether or within the derogations, in the hope that they stand a good chance of being upheld.

Some agreements will, in any event, be regulated under the Consumer Credit Act 1974[70] and therefore subject to its consumer protection provisions as to notification of any unilateral variation, noted above. The question then arises as to the relationship between the Regulations and the Consumer Credit Act provisions, in particular, whether a term enabling a

---

65. See n. 59, *supra*.
66. But only 'likely' as the list is merely 'indicative': Reg. 4(4).
67. But only 'likely' as the list is 'non-exhaustive': Reg. 4(4).
68. But only 'likely' as the list (including – presumably – the derogations from it) is merely 'indicative and non-exhaustive'.
69. See previous paragraph.
70. For the definition of 'regulated agreement', see the Consumer Credit Act 1974, s. 8.

variation in compliance with the statutory obligation under the Consumer Credit Act as to notification, will be regarded as not unfair.

The Regulations are disapplied in the case of: 'any term incorporated in order to comply with or which reflects (i) statutory or regulatory provisions of the United Kingdom'.[71]

This gives effect to a provision in the directive[72] which disapplies it to 'contractual terms which reflect mandatory statutory or regulatory provisions'. Some have argued that a unilateral variation term which 'reflects' the Consumer Credit Act notification provisions by, for example, enabling variations of interest rates to be made by way of announcement in the press (or on premises) or which enables other variations to be made after seven days' notice, is not subject to challenge under the Regulations. However, closer examination of the directive[73] suggests that the disapplication only applies to terms which contractors are statutorily *bound* to incorporate[74] and that the wider alternative 'or which reflects' is inserted to cover the situation where the precise wording of the clause is not statutorily proscribed but its effect is. In such a case it is obviously desirable to give precedence to[75] the legislative decision that such terms ought to be included. But there is no reason to extend the dispensation further. In particular, the Consumer Credit Act 1974 does not *require* any terms as to variation to be inserted. It merely imposes a modicum of consumer protection by way of requiring notification of any unilateral variation that takes place. It is very much a minimalist measure and there is nothing in that Act to preclude greater protection being given to the consumer whether by the creditor in the contract or by further legislative intervention.

---

71. Sch. 1, para. (e). It is doubtful if the industry's good practice codes, in not having any statutory backing, would be regarded as a 'regulatory provision' of the UK.
72. Art. 1.2 and see the preamble: 'Whereas the statutory or regulatory provisions . . . which directly or indirectly determine the terms of consumer contracts are presumed not to contain unfair terms; whereas, therefore, it does not appear necessary to subject the terms which reflect mandatory statutory or regulatory provisions; whereas in that respect the wording 'mandatory statutory or regulatory provisions' in Art. 1(2) also covers rules which, according to the law, shall apply between the contracting parties provided that no other arrangements have been established.' The preamble is, of course, an aid to the interpretation of a directive: *Marleasing SA v La Commercial Internacional de Alimentacion SA* (Case C-106/89), [1990] ECR I-4135; [1992] 1 CMLR 305.
73. Which is, of course, an aid to the interpretation of implementing legislation; see for example, *Lister v Forth Dry Dock Co. Ltd* [1989] 1 All ER 1134 (HL).
74. See the preamble cited in n. 72: 'the statutory . . . provisions . . . which . . . determine the terms of consumer contracts'.
75. And to presume the relevant terms are not 'unfair': see preamble, cited in n. 72, *supra*.

There is also the question whether the Consumer Credit Act 1974, in more general terms, provides guidance as to what is not 'unfair'.[76] In general, it must be doubted if this is the case, given the Community law provenance of the Regulations. Moreover, as noted above, the Act was passed in the days when unilateral variation clauses were assumed to be valid. Now they are prima facie 'unfair' if a valid reason is not specified.[77] Compliance with UK domestic consumer protection legislation remains necessary, but additional requirements may well now arise under the Regulations. *A fortiori*, compliance with the industry's good practice codes is no guarantee that a term is not 'unfair', although a term falling short of the standards set by the codes may well be regarded as 'unfair'.

3.1.2 Schedule 3, paras 1(j) and (k)

As noted above, on the 'grey' list in Schedule 3 are terms: 'enabling the seller or supplier to alter the terms of the contract unilaterally without a valid reason which is specified in the contract' (Schedule 3, paragraph 1(j)).

As also noted above, this suggests (but no more) that if 'valid reasons' for variation are specified in the contract, the term, in now falling outside the list, is likely (but no more) to be valid. There are also two very precise derogations from this paragraph[78] which will be considered below and which seem an invitation to contractors wishing to have a valid unilateral power of variation to draft clauses falling within them. On the negative side, it seems that if no valid reasons are specified, then the term is prima facie invalid, although the derogations may save it.

Also on the 'grey' list are terms: 'enabling the seller or supplier to alter unilaterally without a valid reason any characteristic of the product or service to be provided' (Schedule 3, paragraph 1(k)).

There are no derogations expressly stated to be applicable to this type of term. The difference in wording between the two contiguous subparagraphs – which must be deliberate – is striking.[79] It suggests that

---

76. For example, it will be seen below that the regulations talk of 'reasonable notice' being given of the variation in certain circumstances and the question arises whether notice in compliance with the Consumer Credit Act provisions would be regarded as 'reasonable'.
77. Sch. 3, para. 1(j), considered below.
78. In Sch. 3, para. 2(b). And note Sch. 3, para. 2(c) excludes certain contracts from, *inter alia*, Sch. 3, para. 1(j).
79. Para. 1(k) does not require *specification* of the valid reason in the contract and applies to a particular type of variation (of 'any characteristic of the product or service').

110

there is prima facie no objection to the reservation of a power unilaterally to alter 'any characteristic of the product or service' if there is a valid reason, even if that reason is not set out in the contract. However, as the derogations to paragraph 1(j) are not extended to paragraph 1(k), this also suggests[80] that prima facie a power unilaterally to vary such 'characteristics' at the bank's absolute discretion is unlikely to be upheld no matter what other safeguards derived by analogy from the derogations are provided.

The relationship between paragraphs (1)(j) and (k) is extremely problematic. The intention may be that either the sub-paragraphs (a) are mutually exclusive in scope or (b) that they partially overlap or (c) that they are co-extensive. Taking each possibility in turn, it may be that special provision is being made in paragraph 1(k) for powers to alter the 'characteristics' of the product or service. If so, it becomes important to know what exactly is meant by 'characteristic' and how this relates to the 'terms' of the contract. Indeed, on one view, the terms on which a product or service is provided determine its 'characteristics'. However, for paragraphs 1(j) and (k) to be mutually exclusive, the view must be taken that 'characteristic' has a meaning which does not extend to all the terms of the contract,[81] that special provision is made for this in paragraph 1(k) and that, accordingly, paragraph 1(j) does not apply.

The second possible interpretation is that again, 'characteristic' has a narrow meaning but that both paragraphs 1(j) and (k) apply to the term in that a power to alter the 'characteristic of the product or service' (within paragraph 1(k)) also inevitably entails a power to alter a 'term' (within paragraph 1(j)). Thus, if it is prima facie outlawed by paragraph 1(k) because variation can occur without a valid reason, it will also fall within and be prima facie outlawed by paragraph 1(j), because inevitably there will be no specification of valid reasons in the contract. However, in also falling within paragraph 1(j), the derogations to that paragraph may prima facie save it.

The third possibility is that paragraphs 1(j) and (k) are co-extensive because alteration of a 'characteristic' inevitably involves the alteration of a term and that one or other (probably paragraph 1(k))[82] is otiose.

But too much agonising over the wording is unprofitable because Schedule 3 is drafted on the shifting sands of the courts' ultimate discretion to decide that, the schedule being merely 'indicative and non-

80. Unless para. 1(j) also applies, see *infra*.
81. In particular, terms covered by the derogations to para. 1(j), *eg*, terms as to interest and charges, see *infra*.
82. Because otherwise the derogations are also otiose.

exhaustive',[83] it is not conclusively determinative of the question of unfairness.

For this reason, there is also no point in agonising over the precise meaning of the phrase 'alter . . . unilaterally' and seeking artificially to take a term outside the strict wording of the schedule. It is obvious – given the courts' discretion and given the opening words of the schedule that it applies to terms 'which have the object and effect' of those listed – that such avoidance devices will not work. For example, it is arguable that when (say) interest rates are automatically linked to a base rate within the control of the creditor, this does not involve the 'unilateral alteration' of the interest rate in that the interest rate is the stated function of the base rate throughout the agreement, whereas 'alteration' connotes some change from a stated norm. But such a term would have the 'object and effect' of enabling the creditor unilaterally to alter the interest rate and so prima facie would fall within the schedule.

3.1.3 'Valid reason'

Given that paragraph 1(j) apparently gives the green light[84] to unilateral alteration powers where valid reasons for the variation are spelt out in the contract, some creditors have redrafted their variation terms so as to list circumstances when the power may be exercised by them.[85] Others have adopted the intermediate position of listing some reasons but then also reserving the power to vary in undefined circumstances,[86] on the basis (no doubt) that the specification of some valid reasons (if they are indeed such) is better than specifying none at all.

This approach requires consideration of what is meant by a 'valid reason'.[87] Broadly speaking, the wording is clearly seeking to outlaw varia-

---

83. Reg. 4(4).
84. But if the agreement is regulated under the Consumer Credit Act 1974 (see n. 70, *supra*), then of course that Act's notification requirements must also be complied with, see above.
85. Thus some agreements state that the interest rate is variable 'to take account of prevailing interest rates, market forces and credit and business risks' or 'variations will normally be to reflect changes in market conditions, good banking practice and legislation'.
86. For example, some agreements permit variation 'as a result of a requirement in law, customer feedback or product development or such reasons as are communicated to you'.
87. The term is also used in Sch. 3, para. 1(k) (see *supra*) and in the derogation in para. 2(b). See also, Sch. 3, para. 1(g), which lists unilateral termination clauses and talks of 'serious grounds' and the derogation to that, in para. 2(a) which talks of termination 'where there is a valid reason'.

tion clauses which enable capricious changes to be made.[88] Moreover, the epithet 'valid' clearly seeks to qualify and narrow the concept 'reason'. But it is hard to pin down what qualifies as 'valid reasons'. An expansive view of 'reason' could be taken – as merely connoting the ground or circumstance when a variation is to occur[89] – in which case the qualification 'valid' would narrow it down to a circumstance which in some way justifies the variation. A narrower view would regard 'reason' as connoting the justification (as opposed to mere circumstance) and therefore 'valid' as narrowing this still further to mean, for example, a justification that could in some way be rationalised. This latter approach would require an unfamiliar value judgement to be made as to when it is appropriate (or fair?) unilaterally to alter the contract. Of course, these two approaches merge into each other and all that can be safely said is that a clause which satisfied the narrowest interpretation is more likely to be regarded as not unfair.

On this point it is interesting to note the discussion in *Paton* on the wording of the Consumer Credit (Agreements) Regulations.[90] As noted above, these require a statement of the 'circumstances' when a variation of interest rate will occur. In the context of a term allowing variation at the absolute discretion of the creditor, the court held that 'circumstances' did not connote grounds which could only be justified by external factors (such as a general increase in market rates). But, of course, in the context of the Unfair Terms in Consumer Contracts Regulations we are in the realm of interpreting legislation with a Community law provenance and a very difference approach may well be appropriate.

Examples of 'reasons' which have been specified in banking contracts as justifying variation are: 'customer feedback', 'product development', 'changes in market conditions', 'good banking practice', 'credit and business risks', 'requirement in law'.

3.1.4 'Specified in the contract'

The question also arises as to the specificity with which the 'valid reasons' have to be set out. Again, all that can be said is that the clearer and more precise the specification, the more likely the clause is to be upheld. However, care must be taken that the term is expressed in 'plain and intelligible language',[91] so a verbose and obscure term – reminiscent of those

88. See n. 96, *infra*.
89. But see n. 87 (referring to Sch. 3, para. 1(g)) which suggests that 'reason' has a narrower meaning than 'ground'.
90. See *supra*, esp. nn. 9 and 25.
91. Reg. 6.

all-embracing exclusion clauses which were the norm before these were brought under control – would be counterproductive. At the other extreme, a vague term permitting such variation as is 'allowable by law' or 'for such reasons as are communicated at the time of notification of the change', clearly does not satisfy the requirement of a 'specified valid reason'.

If the specificity is not regarded as sufficient to take the term out of paragraph 1(j), then reliance may be placed on the derogations.

3.2 The derogations

3.2.1 General

An alternative way of escaping inclusion in paragraph 1(j)[92] is to rely on the derogations. The derogations will be particularly relevant if a bank does not wish to limit its power of variation to one exercisable for 'valid reasons' specified in the contract. Again, it must be reiterated that escaping the grey list via a derogation is no guarantee that the term is valid. Moreover, falling outside the derogation, whether because in the circumstances the situation is outside its general scope or because the proviso to the derogation is not precisely satisfied, is not fatal. It will be seen that the scope of the derogations is narrow. For example, the second one only applies to contracts 'of indeterminate duration' – and thus it is inapplicable to fixed-term contracts. However, it would seem that the derogation, although in terms inapplicable, could provide some guidance to a court considering a fixed-term contract. On the other hand, there is the obvious counter-argument that as the scope of the derogation and/or its proviso is so precisely drawn,[93] this is an indication that nothing less will do.

There are two derogations which are particularly relevant.[94] They have one characteristic in common: they only apply if the consumer is 'free to dissolve the contract'. The rationale appears to be that unilateral variation should only be possible if the consumer has the option of terminating[95]

---

92. As noted *supra*, the derogations do not apply to para. 1(k).
93. This becomes particularly problematic when considering the relationship between Sch. 3, para. 1(j) and (k) in that the derogations do not apply to the latter, see *supra*.
94. See also Sch. 3, para. 2(c) which is in terms applicable to para. 1(j) (and (g) and (l)) and which exempts certain contracts from that paragraph.
95. Elsewhere the term 'terminate' is used (see Sch. 3, para. 1(g) and its derogation in para. 2(a)) but it would seem that 'dissolve' (also used in para. 1(f)) and 'terminate' mean the same. The terms 'cancel' is also used (see para. 1(d), 1(l)) but in the sense (it seems) of 'unravelling' the contract.

the contract, as varied. In the first derogation, the debtor must be able to terminate 'immediately'; the second derogation merely talks of him being able to 'dissolve the contract'. It would seem that this difference stems from the fact that the first derogation covers variations without prior notification – in which case the consumer must be given the chance to terminate immediately – whereas the second derogation covers variation after prior notice.

The fact that the consumer must be 'free to dissolve' the contract raises a number of issues. The most obvious one is whether this right of termination should be unfettered or whether the bank may impose pre-conditions (financial or otherwise). Clearly there is no objection to requiring the debtor to settle his outstanding liability under the contract,[96] but what of penalty-type provisions?[97] And what of requirements as to the form of notice that should be given[98] and other conditions?[99] The most that can be said is that the presence of unjustifiable fetters would tend to suggest that the term is 'unfair'. In any event, the Consumer Credit Act 1974 permits early settlement of regulated credit agreements[100] and any fetters on such a right would be invalid.[101] Moreover, any notice (or other) requirements which preclude the debtor terminating 'immediately'[102] would take the situation outside the proviso[103] which requires the possibility of immediate termination.

In so far as the debtor must have the power to terminate, it seems this must be conferred by the contract. Further, although this is not in terms required by the Regulations, clearly a cross-reference to such a power of termination in the variation clause is desirable.

It will be seen that a major difference between the derogations is that the first is narrower in only applying to variations of interest rates and other charges while the second applies to all types of variations. The question therefore arises[104] whether the derogations are mutually exclusive or whether a power to vary interest rates and other charges can be 'justified' by bringing it within either derogation. In general, the second derogation is

---

96. But, arguably, this should not preclude 'immediate' dissolution; see *infra*.
97. Some penalty clauses are on the grey list: Sch. 3, para. 1(e).
98. For example, written notice.
99. For example, the return of the cards. Some agreements go further and require the return of the cards 'cut in two', some being even more demanding in requiring the cards to be cut 'across the magnetic stripe' or 'vertically'.
100. S. 94, together with a rebate (s. 95 and rebate regulations made thereunder).
101. Consumer Credit Act 1974, s. 173(1).
102. For example, termination is often postponed until the return of the cards and/or settlement of outstanding amounts.
103. Of the first derogation in para. 2(b).
104. See the similar difficulty with Sch. 3, paras 1(j) and (k), considered *supra*.

less generous[105] and therefore it seems that the first derogation is a concession[106] to the narrow situation of banks wishing to vary interest rates and
charges without notice. If that is so, it would seem that a power to vary
interest rates and other charges could alternatively be 'justified' by virtue of
the second, less generous but more general, derogation. Some banks have
made separate provision for the two types of variation[107] while others have
treated them together.

3.2.2   Schedule 3, para. 2(b): the first derogation

The first derogation is narrow in being confined to a 'supplier of financial
services'[108] altering interest rates[109] or 'other charges for financial services'. Its terms are:

(b) Subparagraph 1(j) is without hindrance to terms under which a supplier of
financial services reserves the right to alter the rate of interest payable by the consumer or due to the latter, or the amount of other charges for financial services
without notice where there is a valid reason, provided that the supplier is required
to inform the other contracting party or parties thereof at the earliest opportunity
and that the latter are free to dissolve the contract immediately.

Thus, in essence, the derogation applies to a term whereby a bank may
alter interest rates or other charges, where the proviso is satisfied.

3.2.2.1   Scope

Before examining the proviso, the general scope of the derogation needs
to be considered and the punctuation (which corresponds to that in the

---

105. In that the first derogation 'permits' variation without advance notice whereas the
      second derogation requires 'reasonable [advance] notice'. However, in relation to
      variation of 'other charges', there must be a valid reason for the first derogation to
      apply, whereas there is no such requirement in the second derogation, see *infra*.
106. There is a similar 'concession' to variation of interest rates (only) under the Con-
      sumer Credit (Notice of Variation) Regulations 1977 (see n. 16, *supra*), considered
      supra.
107. Mainly, it would seem, reflective of the Consumer Credit Act requirements (and its
      concession to variations in interest rates).
108. 'Supplier' is defined in Reg. 2(1) as 'a person who supplies goods or services and
      who, in making a contract to which these regulations apply, is acting for purposes
      relating to his business' but there is no definition of 'supplier of financial service'.
      The term clearly covers a banker lending money, or someone issuing credit and
      charge cards, but it is less clear if it covers, for example, finance houses in the busi-
      ness of leasing or hire-purchase finance.
109. Whether payable *by* the debtor or *to* him.

116

directive) noted. The opening of the derogation breaks down into two parts and, because of the comma, the phrase 'without notice where there is a valid reason' only qualifies the second part.

Taking the two parts in turn, the first part of the derogation applies to terms reserving the right to alter interest rates. There is no further qualification here. In particular, there is no requirement of notice[110] or 'valid reason'. That said, obviously if the bank undertakes to give notice and/or undertakes only to alter where there is a 'valid reason', then the term stands a better chance of being held not 'unfair'. Thus, although the derogation in terms applies to a term permitting alteration of interest rates without more, it would be absurd to deny the derogation[111] to a term that had such qualifications which favoured the consumer.

The second part covers the alteration of 'other charges for financial services' and there is the further qualification 'without notice where there is a valid reason'. The 'without notice' phrase is curious in that the derogation does not, in terms, apparently apply to a clause which enables such variation to be made *with* notice. Again, it would be absurd to deny the derogation to a clause which was more favourable to the consumer[112] and therefore the 'without notice' requirement should be viewed as a confirmation that even a term which does not provide for advance notice can be upheld.

However, in this case the derogation only applies 'where there is a valid reason'. This again raises the spectre of the meaning of 'valid reason', considered above.[113] Of course, if valid reasons for variation are actually specified in the agreement, then the term may not fall within the grey list at all.[114] Thus clearly the 'valid reasons' do not need to be specified for the derogation to apply, but there is now the difficulty of knowing whether there must be any reference to a 'valid reason' in the term itself. As the derogation only applies where the bank can vary charges 'where there is a valid reason', it would seem that the term must actually expressly state this to be the case.[115] A term enabling variation of charges without more, would not satisfy the wording as it does not limit the power of variation to when there is a valid reason. Moreover, a vague

---

110. But one may arise if the contract is regulated under the Consumer Credit Act 1974, see n. 70, *supra*.
111. Or, an alternative approach might be to admit that the derogation does not, in terms, apply but to hold the term in any event is not 'unfair', on analogy with the derogation.
112. See previous note. The Consumer Credit Act 1974 may, in any event, impose obligations to notify, see *supra*.
113. Assuming the phrase means the same in both Sch. 3, paras. 1(j) and 2(b).
114. See the terms of Sch. 3, para. 1(j), cited *supra*.
115. *Ie*, the term must say that other charges may be altered 'if there is a valid reason'.

formulation such as 'as permitted by law' is also unlikely to satisfy the derogation in not indicating to the consumer the precise nature of the limitation imposed.

One final point on the scope of the derogation. The derogation applies to the conferment of a right 'to alter' interest rates or charges. A literal interpretation suggests that a power to impose a new charge – for example, a new annual fee for credit cards – would not be covered. This raises the question of whether such a literal interpretation is appropriate and if so, whether it suggests that the confinement of the derogation to alteration is deliberate, and if so, whether this suggests that terms enabling the imposition of new charges are going to be particularly difficult to justify as not 'unfair'.

3.2.2.2   The proviso

The proviso contains two conditions which both have to be satisfied before the derogation, in terms, applies. The first is that the bank 'is required' to 'inform' the customer 'thereof' 'at the earliest opportunity'. Each of these components of the proviso raises questions.

'Is required' suggests that the bank must be under a legal obligation to tell the customer.[116] The most obvious way of satisfying this is for the bank to undertake the obligation in the contract. If the agreement is regulated under the Consumer Credit Act 1974 then, as discussed above, in certain circumstances there will be a statutory obligation to notify the debtor 'in the prescribed manner'. Nevertheless the 'prescribed manner' may not correspond to 'inform[ing]' the debtor 'thereof' 'at the earliest opportunity' and therefore it is suggested that it would be dangerous to rely on the statutory obligation as giving rise to the requirement. Thus, the obligation to inform should be expressly undertaken in the contract.

It is unclear if 'inform' requires personalised notification (and, if so, with what degree of precision)[117] or whether publication in the press or at the bank's premises – as permitted in certain circumstances under the Consumer Credit Act 1974[118] – will suffice. Obviously, the former, narrower interpretation is the safest. If this is regarded as too onerous in practice, then one way of making the publication more likely to satisfy the wording would be to include a provision in the agreement drawing the

---

116. It cannot just mean 'must' (in fact) inform, as it is the contractual term that is being judged, not how it operates in practice.
117. Note the normal meaning of giving 'notice' under English statutes: see n. 17, *supra*.
118. See *supra*. See also the argument above that the requirements of the Act have little bearing on whether the term is or is not 'unfair'.

customer's attention to the fact that notification of variation will be made by publication in the specified manner.[119] It should be stressed that it by no means follows that although notification of interest rates by publication in the press and on premises (as opposed to individual personalised notification) is permitted under the Consumer Credit Act 1974, this means a term providing for such notification will satisfy the proviso.[120] However, many banks have taken the view that complying with that Act as to interest rate variation is sufficient, no doubt hoping that the courts will take the view that if the legislature regards this mode of notification as adequate, the term should not be regarded as 'unfair' under the Regulations.

It is unclear if 'thereof' refers only to the alteration made or whether (when charges are altered and this has to be done on the basis of a 'valid reason') it refers[121] also to the valid reason. Although the matter is by no means free from doubt, it would seem that 'thereof' refers only to the variation.[122] However, it would obviously do no harm (and may help to validate the term) to undertake to notify the 'valid reasons' for which the variations were made.[123]

The final problem is the meaning of 'earliest opportunity'. It is to be contrasted with 'immediately', used elsewhere in the schedule,[124] so some time-lag between variation and notification is apparently permitted although again, the shorter the hiatus, the more likely the clause is to be upheld.[125] If the notification is by way of publication,[126] then clearly this connotes publication as soon as the information can be produced in that form. On the other hand, if personal notification is being used, then the further question arises of whether the bank can wait until it has cause to communicate with the customer (for example, when sending a periodic statement). Again, the most that can be said with certainly is that it would be safer to have a system of sending out notifications separately as soon as they can, in practice, be produced and posted.

---

119. On the other hand, a provision enabling the bank to determine *ad hoc* what constitutes 'informing' the customer is unlikely to be effective.
120. See the discussion *supra*.
121. See *supra*.
122. Although it could be argued that the proviso, in operating in default of there being a valid reason *specified in the contract*, requires the valid reason to be specified subsequently.
123. Even if not notified, as a matter of evidence the bank should keep internal records of the reasons for which it varies charges in order to support any subsequent claim that it varied only for such reasons.
124. In para. 2(a).
125. Of course, giving *prior* notification would be even better (and usually required for agreements regulated under the Consumer Credit Act 1974, see *supra*).
126. Assuming this satisfies the requirement of 'informing' the debtor, see *supra*.

The second condition to the proviso is that the customer is 'free to dissolve the contract immediately'. Some general problems with this phrase have been considered above. However, it should be noted that in this derogation,[127] the customer must be able to terminate without any preconditions as to notice.[128]

3.2.3   Schedule 3, para. 2(b): the second derogation

The second derogation is much wider in scope. It is not confined to a supplier of financial services, but extends to any seller or supplier.[129] It also applies to the unilateral alteration of *any* term[130] and so is not confined to terms concerning the interest rate or other charges.[131] However, it has one major limitation. It only applies to contracts of 'indeterminate duration'. As noted above, this raises the issue of how contracts of fixed duration will be treated and it is suggested that, although not in terms applying, the derogation would be relevant in indicating the circumstances where terms permitting variation of a fixed-term contract would not be 'unfair'. There is no mention of 'valid reasons' having to be satisfied,[132] but again, the articulation or requirement for a reason – especially a 'valid' one – will increase the chances of the clause being upheld.

The terms of this derogation are:

Subparagraph 1(j) is also without hindrance to terms under which a seller or supplier reserves the right to alter unilaterally the conditions of a contract of indeterminate duration, provided that he is required to inform the consumer with reasonable notice and that the consumer is free to dissolve the contract.

Thus, in essence, in the banking context, the derogation applies to a term whereby a bank may unilaterally alter the contract 'conditions', provided reasonable notice is given and the consumer may terminate the contract.

Although the Regulations (and directive) talk elsewhere of 'terms' when they refer to unfair (or potentially unfair) terms and although Schedule 3, paragraph 1(j) talks of terms enabling the alteration of 'the terms of the

---

127. Cf. the second derogation considered *infra*.
128. 'Immediately'. Whether other fetters are possible are considered *supra*.
129. For the definition, see n. 108, *supra*.
130. Para. 2(b) uses the word 'conditions', but it is argued *infra* that this must be a reference to 'terms'.
131. The view is taken above that it probably *also* applies to variations of interest rates and other charges.
132. Cf. the first derogation in relation to variation of 'other charges'.

contract', it would seem that the word 'conditions' in the derogation covers any terms of the contract.[133]

The proviso which must be satisfied for the derogation to apply imposes two requirements. The first is that the bank 'is required' to 'inform' the customer 'with reasonable notice'. The words 'required' and 'inform' have been discussed above in relation to the first derogation and similar considerations apply here. Thus it would seem that the bank must undertake in the contract the obligation to give reasonable notice in order to be 'required' to do so[134] and a strict interpretation of 'inform' suggests that individual notification of the customer – rather than publication in the press or on the bank's premises[135] – is probably needed.

The term 'notice' clearly indicates *advance* notice. Thus whilst in the first derogation the bank need only inform the customer 'thereof' – signifying that notification after the variation of interest rates and charges is sufficient – here it is clear that advance notice is required. As for the notice having to be 'reasonable', given that the rationale appears to be that the customer should have the opportunity to terminate the contract if s/he is unhappy with it, as varied, it would seem that the notice must be of such a length as to give the debtor time to reflect and decide whether to terminate *before* s/he is bound by the altered terms. The question arises whether the seven days' notice prescribed under the Consumer Credit Act 1974 for most unilateral variations of regulated agreements is a legislative indication that normally this is 'reasonable'. Some banks appear to have taken this view but it may be that, particularly in circumstances where obtaining alternative finance will take more time, seven days will not be regarded as sufficient. Again, all that can be said with certainly is that the longer the notice needed, the more likely the term is to be regarded as not 'unfair'. Some banks have agreed to give seven days' notice (no doubt by analogy with the Consumer Credit Act requirement), some fourteen days and some one month. Others have merely said they will act 'subject to any legal requirements about notice' or that they will give 'reasonable notice' in the hope that this formulation cannot be regarded as 'unfair'.[136]

---

133. Sch. 3, para. 1(c) uses 'condition' in the sense of pre-condition of liability but this cannot be the meaning in para. 2(b).
134. As to the relevance of the Consumer Credit Act obligation under s. 82, see *supra* (n. 71 and subsequent text) and *infra*.
135. The Consumer Credit Act 1974 'publication' concession only applies to variations in interest rates, see *supra*.
136. This seems a sensible approach because, even if in practice the courts hold that the notice they are actually giving is not 'reasonable', the clause stands unimpeached although individual variations are ineffective. The bank can then change its practice without changing its documentation.

121

The second requirement of the proviso is that the customer must be free to dissolve the contract. Again, in contrast to the first derogation, there is no requirement that dissolution be possible 'immediately' – giving some leeway towards terms which impose temporal fetters on the right to terminate. However, unreasonable temporal (or other) fetters on termination would obviously run the risk of rendering the clause 'unfair'.

4.   PRESENT PRACTICE

A survey of credit and charge card agreements shows that, in this context, different banks have reacted very differently to the Regulations. Some have barely changed their wide variation clauses, reserving the right to vary at their absolute discretion and merely agreeing to notify as required by the Consumer Credit Act 1974 in the case of agreements regulated by that Act.[137] Others have tried to redraft their agreements so as to increase the chances of their terms being upheld. A few have sought to specify 'valid reasons' for any variation. Others have adopted a compromise, setting out some reasons but reserving a more general discretion. But many banks have chosen to retain a wide power to vary their contracts and have then sought to bring themselves within the derogations by undertaking notification obligations. Again, some have merely agreed to comply with the requirements of the Consumer Credit Act 1974. Others, no doubt mindful that the Regulations have moved consumer protection on to a different plane to that existing when our domestic consumer credit provisions were devised, have gone further.

The multiplicity of approaches demonstrates the lack of consensus amongst advisers as to what is likely to be regarded as 'unfair'. The detailed provisions in the Regulations on the issue of unilateral variation have clearly not helped in enabling the drafter to devise a 'fair' unilateral variation clause. It may be that it would have been better to leave the test of 'unfairness' shrouded in the generalities that normally apply.

---

137.   See n. 70, *supra.*

Chapter Five

DEPOSIT GUARANTEES AND THE INDIVIDUAL BANK CUSTOMER

Peter Cartwright

Chapter Outline

1. Introduction

2. Deposit Guarantees: Definitions and Types of Scheme

3. Deposit Guarantees and Consumer Protection

4. Deposit Guarantees, Bank Safety and Moral Hazard

5. Depositor Protection and Co-Insurance: The European Approach

6. Deposit Guarantees and Informed Consumers

7. The Future of Depositor Protection

8. Conclusions

Consumer Protection in Financial Services (P. Cartwright, ed.: 90-411-9717-6: © Kluwer Law International: pub. Kluwer Law International, 1999: printed in Great Britain)

1. INTRODUCTION

This chapter examines the role of deposit guarantee schemes. In particular, it emphasises the joint aims of bank safety and consumer protection, and examines the difficulties posed by the concept of 'moral hazard'. It is argued that the system of deposit guarantees in the UK fails adequately to take account of the difficulties which depositors face when trying to assess the risks posed by banks. As a result of information deficits, depositors are unable to make rational and informed choices about where to invest their money and are in need of protection. The argument that moral hazard exists, and requires depositors to bear some of the loss should their banks fail has some validity, but it is argued that this is overstated. If depositors, particularly those who are most vulnerable, are to be adequately protected, reform is necessary.

2. DEPOSIT GUARANTEES: DEFINITIONS AND TYPES OF SCHEME

A deposit guarantee scheme is one which provides a payout to a bank's customers where certain circumstances arise: for example, where the bank becomes insolvent.[1] It is sometimes referred to as a deposit insurance or deposit protection scheme, and those phrases appear generally to be used interchangeably.[2] There are two main aims to such schemes. The first is to ensure stability in the banking system. To this extent, deposit guarantee schemes are part of a range of measures which supervise and regulate banking activity.[3] The second aim is to ensure adequate consumer or investor protection.[4] As will be seen later, these two aims are closely linked.

Deposit guarantee schemes take a variety of forms. Some are provided by the government alone, some by banks, and others by a combination of

---

1. For the meaning of insolvency in the UK scheme, see the Banking Act 1987, s. 59(1).
2. The term 'deposit insurance' has been criticised by some, as it is argued that deposit guarantee schemes reduce the risk of bank panics rather than pool risks, in the way that insurance does. In the words of Sjaastad: 'the economic function of insurance is to reduce the liability of the insured, not the risk of an adverse outcome (or liability) . . . a better term would be deposit guarantees'. L. A. Sjaastad 'Deposit Insurance: Do We Really Need It?', Paper at *Preventing Banking Sector Distress and Crises in Latin America*, Washington 1996 (Conference Proceedings, p. 48).
3. They are part of the general supervisory system. See G. Penn, *Banking Supervision* (London: Butterworths, 1989).
4. In this way, the aims of deposit insurance are very similar to those of bank regulation and supervision. See *infra*.

banks and government. Miller has argued that privatisation of deposit insurance would be optimal in a 'first best world'. He continued:

A private deposit insurance system would utilise the price system and the profit motive in order to achieve efficiencies of operation. Banks could be expected to organise private deposit insurance in order to achieve optimal monitoring of risk-taking.[5]

It has been argued that it might be desirable to have a private system of deposit insurance, provided by insurance companies. This would have the advantage of ensuring that banks would, in theory at least, be charged premiums which reflected the risk they were deemed to present, and so they would be under an incentive to act prudently. Sjaastad has similarly seen the arguments against private deposit insurance as over-stated. He argues that:

[t]here is no reason insurance companies should not be able to offer deposit insurance. Privatisation should be particularly attractive to developing countries, where the human and other capital to administer state-run deposit insurance schemes is lacking.[6]

There are, however, difficulties with such schemes. The main problem is that it is extremely difficult to calculate the risk posed by banks in advance, and it has therefore been argued that deposit insurance premiums cannot be objectively related to risk.[7] Further difficulties are noted by MacDonald,[8] who sees three main obstacles to private insurance. First, in many countries, the insurance industry is less developed than the banking industry, and so would lack the capital to provide adequate insurance. Second, insurance companies might be unwilling to provide insurance because of the risk of exposure to a run on the banking system, and the difficulties in assessing the probability of bank failures. Finally, private insurers would want the power to cancel insurance where risks started to become excessive. This would have the dual effect of undermining confidence and depriving depositors of cover when it is most necessary.[9]

Although there are some attractions to private insurance, the practical difficulties make it unlikely for such a scheme to be entirely satisfactory. In

---

5. G. P. Miller, 'Deposit insurance for economies in transition' paper to the conference on Bank Failures and Bank Insolvency Law in Economies in Transition, London, 1997.
6. Sjaastad, op cit., n. 2, p. 49.
7. See C. Goodhart, 'Bank Insolvency and Deposit Insurance: a Proposal', in P. Arestis (ed.), *Money and Banking* (Macmillan, 1993), p. 75. Although it should be pointed that in the USA the FDIC does attempt to take account of risk factors when setting premiums for banks.
8. R. MacDonald, *Deposit Insurance* (Bank of England, 1996), pp. 9–10.
9. Ibid.

the words of one commentator, 'the thought of underwriting banks' deposits fills most insurers with horror'.[10] There is also the significant problem that privatising deposit guarantees may conflict with one of the prime aims of depositor protection: to increase public confidence. If bank customers believe that the deposit guarantees scheme, however it is organised, may be unable to pay out in the event of a banking crisis, they will be more likely to withdraw funds when there is evidence of difficulty. They may also be less likely to invest in the first place.[11] These fears are likely to be particularly pronounced with private insurance schemes.

The discussion above relates to what might be called 'explicit' deposit guarantee schemes. These are schemes which are established by law, and which guarantee payouts where certain conditions arise (for example, where a bank becomes insolvent). In addition, around fifty countries have operated or put in place what have been called 'implicit deposit protection arrangements'.[12] These arise where there is no formal deposit guarantee scheme in place, but the government decides, *ex post facto*, to ensure that depositors of a failed bank are protected, for example, by making payouts to depositors, or by promoting the merger of a failed bank with a successful one. This is seen as implicit depositor protection where it creates a presumption that similar action will be taken in the future.[13] It should be borne in mind that where a government indicates that banks will always be protected, it leads to problems of 'moral hazard' which will be considered later.

3. DEPOSIT GUARANTEES AND CONSUMER PROTECTION

There are strong consumer protection justifications for protecting depositors,[14] and some see consumer protection as the 'direct rationale' for deposit guarantees.[15] A contrast may be drawn here between the approach taken in the United States, where schemes have had the prime aim of preventing runs on banks and the resulting systemic risk, and that in Europe, where the consumer protection aspect of deposit guarantees is often emphasised.[16] In the UK, the governor of the Bank of England has

10. 'International Banking: Coping with the Ups and Downs', *The Economist*, 27 April 1996, p. 37.
11. See Miller, op cit., n. 5, p. 27.
12. MacDonald, op cit., n. 8, pp. 5–6.
13. Ibid.
14. See A. Campbell and P. Cartwright, 'Banks and Consumer Protection: the Deposit Protection Scheme in the UK' (1998) LMCLQ 128.
15. MacDonald, op cit., n. 8.
16. Although the importance of avoiding systemic risk is also important in Europe. The recital to Directive 94/19/EC, OJ 1994 L135/5 (on Deposit Guarantees) refers to

described the country's depositor protection scheme as having 'the essentially *social* purpose of shielding retail customers who may be ill-placed to assess the financial soundness of particular intermediaries', although he recognises that such schemes also play a part in avoiding systemic risk.[17] Depositors are the users of banking services, and as such are aptly described as consumers. There are many examples, of course, of legislation which has the aim of protecting consumers where they are at risk in the marketplace.[18] Depositors are, however, especially in need of protection for two main reasons. First, private individuals have a large proportion of their wealth deposited in banks as opposed to other investments, and this is particularly true of the less financially sophisticated.[19] The failure of a bank is likely to have a far more serious impact on its customers than that of other service providers. There has been a long tradition in many countries of seeking to protect the vulnerable in their financial transactions, and deposit guarantee schemes play a part in this. This may, of course, not always be entirely altruistic. Providing protection has clear political advantages. In the words of *The Economist*: 'governments fear the political backlash that the failure of a big bank would cause . . . Ensuring that Aunt Agatha, Anna and Akiko-san have somewhere safe to invest their savings is widely considered to be the government's responsibility.'[20]

Second, even those who are relatively sophisticated financially may find it difficult to assess the risks posed by making a deposit with a particular institution. As White notes: 'The key problem is one of information. For the vast banking public, that is, households and small businesses, it is very costly to monitor the performance of banks and decide which is the safest among all alternatives.'[21]

It is widely accepted that consumers suffer frequently from information deficits when making decisions,[22] but these are particularly acute where those decisions relate to financial products. It has been argued

(continued)
　　　　deposit protection being 'an indispensable supplement to the system of supervision of credit institutions on account of the solidarity it creates amongst all the institutions in a given market in the event of the failure of any one of them'.

17. E. George, 'Some Thoughts on Financial Regulation' (1996) 36 *Bank of England Quarterly Bulletin*, 213, 213.
18. The most famous example in the finance sphere probably being the Consumer Credit Act 1974.
19. See R. Cranston, *Principles of Banking Law* (OUP, 1997), p. 80.
20. 'International Banking: Coping with the Ups and Downs', op cit., n. 10, p. 6.
21. E. White, *Deposit Insurance*, World Bank Policy Research Working Paper 1541, November 1995, p. 13.
22. There is a significant amount of research about the role of information in consumer protection. see for example W. Whitford, 'The Functions of Disclosure Regulation in Consumer Transactions' (1973) 2 *Wisconsin Law Review* 400, and I. Ramsay, *Rationales for Intervention in the Consumer Marketplace* (OFT, 1984).

that when consumers make decisions about which products to purchase, there are typically three things which they would like to know about them:[23] the price of the product and of other products (substitutes or complements); the quality of the product (relative to substitutes); and the terms of trade. In theory, a consumer with this optimal information would be able to make an optimal decision about the matter in question.[24] In reality, this is unrealistic. Consumers suffer from 'bounded rationality', which means that they have a limited capacity to receive, store and process information.[25] Information relating to financial decisions is often costly for consumers to obtain,[26] and particularly difficult to process, and so optimal decisions are extremely difficult to make. This point has recently been made by researchers for the OFT in the UK, who identified financial services as an area of special difficulty. They stated that it was a market in which consumers could not hope to be fully informed: 'there is simply too much information available, and it is of a complex nature'.[27] Goodhart similarly comments:

The ordinary individual will generally have neither the expertise nor the time to maintain a continuous assessment of the standing, riskiness, and reputation of the several alternative banks . . . In particular the poor were seen as being at a disadvantage.[28]

Although the difficulties of accessing optimal information are especially acute with complex financial products such as pensions, they are also present in simpler transactions. When deciding which bank account to choose, the difficulty is often in assessing the quality and safety that the bank provides. Consumers may be able to understand interest rates and charges, but they will seldom be able to judge the risk of the bank becoming insolvent, although this is a key characteristic of the quality of the product supplier.[29] For these reasons, it is seen as particularly important that depositors are adequately protected.

---

23. See OFT, *Consumer Detriment under Conditions of Imperfect Information* (OFT, 1997), p. 22.
24. See I. Ogus, *Regulation* (Clarendon Press, 1994), pp. 38–41.
25. H. Simon, *Administrative Behaviour*, 3rd edn (Free Press, 1976).
26. Ogus, op. cit., n. 24, 40
27. OFT, op. cit., n. 23, p. 78.
28. C. Goodhart, *The Evolution of Central Banks* (MIT Press, 1988), p. 57.
29. There is evidence that information as to price is less costly to supply and process than information as to quality. This leads to a lowering of standards as consumers are able to differentiate between prices but not quality. See G. Akerlof, 'The Market for Lemons: Qualitative Uncertainty and the Market Mechanism' (1970) 84 *Quarterly Journal of Economics* 488.

4.   DEPOSIT GUARANTEES, BANK SAFETY AND MORAL HAZARD

Banking regulation and supervision have the same two prime aims as deposit guarantees. The first aim is ensure the stability of the banking system and, in particular, to avoid systemic risk. There is a fear that the demise of one, or a number of banks, will lead to a domino-like effect which affects the whole banking system. Banks are particularly prone to runs which can lead to this risk of contagion. This results from the payments system itself, and from the role of banks in maturity transformation (in particular, the fact that banks typically have short-term liabilities, such as deposits repayable on demand, and long-term assets which may be difficult to trade, such as loans).[30] If banks are to be stopped from failing, and systemic risk is to be avoided, it is important that an effective system of regulation is in place. The second aim is that of consumer, or depositor protection,[31] which is discussed above. The two aims are closely related. If customers are to have confidence in their banks then those banks must be subject to effective supervision. If the supervision is to be effective, then customers must have confidence, and be dissuaded from withdrawing their funds in the event of a bank facing difficulties. Bank safety, and consumer protection, are inextricably linked.

Although deposit guarantees help to avoid systemic risk by giving depositors the confidence that they need not withdraw their deposits should banks find themselves in difficulty, there is a way in which deposit guarantees may lead to instability. This is through the risk of 'moral hazard'. Moral hazard refers to the danger that if people are promised payment on particular conditions, they will change their conduct in order to make these conditions more likely to occur. A typical example is that a person whose goods are insured is less likely to take care of those goods than one whose goods are uninsured. The person may even seek the goods' destruction. When applied to deposit guarantees, the implications of this theory are clear. People whose deposits are guaranteed will be less likely to take care in choosing their banks carefully, because they will not be bearing the loss which results from bank failure. There is an incentive for the depositor to choose the bank which offers the best rates, because there is little fear of losing the deposit should the bank collapse.[32] Where 100 per cent protection of deposits exists, there has even been evidence of depositors seeking out those institutions which are most likely to fail. This happened in

---

30.   See George, op. cit., n. 17, p. 213.
31.   See *supra*.
32.   Moral hazard can also apply to bankers, who may be more willing to take risks if deposit guarantees are provided. See Miller, op. cit., p. 10.

Argentina in 1980 when the Argentine Central Bank re-introduced deposit guarantees to cover not only deposits, but also accrued interest.[33] In some cases, governments will exceed the protection given by deposit guarantee schemes for fear that the schemes alone are insufficient to avoid systemic risk. This may give the impression that some banks at least are 'too big to fail', and adds to the risk of moral hazard.[34]

So, are the moral hazard arguments against deposit guarantees compelling? Some have argued so. White, examining the question in the context of deposit guarantees (or deposit insurance as it is more commonly described in the United States), suggests that deposit insurance, is not to be recommended, particularly for developing and transitional economies. He argues that the historical record of the United States in this area teaches three lessons:

First, deposit insurance was not adopted primarily to protect the depositor . . . Second, the historical record of federal and state insurance plans shows that it is all but impossible to escape the moral hazard and other problems inherent in deposit insurance . . . Third, in setting up banking regulations, including deposit insurance, a banking lobby will be created that will campaign in the future to protect the industry as it stands, and the industry will be pushed in a particular direction on a course that will be difficult to alter.[35]

Miller is also admonitory, warning of the risks of depositor protection schemes, particularly in terms of cost, efficiency, and moral hazard.[36] Are the arguments sufficiently strong to refute the need for depositor protection? It is submitted that they are not. First, in relation to White's comments, although depositor protection in the US was not set up to protect the consumer, that has been one of its effects. Second, it is submitted that there is no need for deposit insurance and other banking regulations to lead to unnecessary power to be given to, nor for unnecessary inflexibility to be wielded by, the banking industry. Miller expresses concerns about efficiency and cost. They are matters to be addressed, but must, of course,

33. Sjaastad, op. cit., n. 2, p. 48.
34. Note, for example, the approach of the FDIC in the USA to the insolvency of Continental Illinois in 1984. The Federal Deposit Insurance Corporation (FDIC) made it clear that all depositors, not just those with small deposits, would be protected. Some have, however, criticised the use of the expression 'too big to fail', suggesting that 'too big to liquidate' would be more appropriate (see FDIC, *An Examination of Banking Crises in the 1980s and Early 1990s* (1997: FDIC 249)). The approach to Continental Illinois may be contrasted with that taken by the Bank of England in the UK whose governor, Eddie George, has frequently made it clear that the Bank would be reluctant to intervene to save an ailing institution, and would only do so if there was a clear threat of systemic risk.
35. White, op. cit., n. 21, p. 12.
36. Miller, op. cit., n. 5.

be balanced against the schemes' undoubted benefits. Finally, there is the moral hazard problem, which concerns both White and Miller. But this can be over-stated. Some commentators see the arguments of economists about moral hazard as being removed from the real world. Cranston is particularly critical. He argues that: 'unsophisticated depositors are in no position to be vigilant. Even if the information is available it will generally require expertise to interpret it. Moreover, a reason for the insolvency of banks is dishonesty, and that by its nature tends to be concealed.'[37]

As discussed above, there can be little doubt that it is difficult, if not impossible for the average depositor to make an informed judgement about which bank should receive his or her deposit. Although it is understandable to want to try to encourage depositors to take care, there should be a recognition that there is a limit to the extent to which this can be achieved. Cranston's comments about the role of dishonesty in bank insolvency is also telling. Many of the most significant bank failures in recent years have shown clear evidence of dishonesty.[38] This demonstrates how important it is for regulators to take account of the probity of those in control of banks, something which has been emphasised of late.[39] It also explains why deposit guarantee provisions generally exclude from compensation those who have played a role in a bank's collapse.[40]

It should be emphasised here that Miller does not reject depositor protection out of hand. Indeed, he argues that there may be a place for depositor protection which is explicit and limited, utilises the private sector as far as possible, and funds payouts through an assessment of banks rather than endowed funds.[41] Both Miller and White are writing with developing and transition economies particularly in mind, and suggest that such economies considering introducing depositor protection schemes pay close attention to alternatives.[42]

37. Cranston, op. cit., n. 19, p. 81.
38. Barings and BCCI are amongst the highest profile of these, but they are by no means the only examples.
39. In its Report, *Banking Supervision and BCCI: International and National Regulation* (HMSO March 1992), the Treasury and Civil Service Committee recommended that the Bank of England should be willing to draw a much clearer distinction between questions of solvency and those of probity when supervising banks.
40. See for example Reg. 32 of the Credit Institutions (Protection of Depositors) Regulations 1995.
41. Miller, op. cit., n. 5, p. 1.
42. Miller identifies these as assessable stock, narrow banking and government demand debt. White refers in particular to deposit accounts which are segregated, Treasury bill mutual funds, which, he argues, provide insurance from the government, with the same guarantee as government bonds, but without the wrong incentives for financial institutions that arise from deposit insurance: White, op. cit., n. 21, p. 13. It is not possible to examine these in detail here.

5. DEPOSITOR PROTECTION AND CO-INSURANCE: THE EUROPEAN APPROACH

Although there are strong arguments to suggest that depositors cannot be expected to judge the safety posed by a bank, the concern about moral hazard is still strong. It is largely because of this that the European Union has adopted a policy of what may be described as 'co-insurance'. This approach was found in the UK law which predated, and to a large extent influenced, developments at a European level,[43] and requires the consumer to bear a proportion of the loss which results from bank failure.

The Deposit Guarantees Directive[44] was designed to perform a number of functions. First, it was one of several measures aimed at eliminating restrictions on the right of establishment of and freedom to provide banking services. Second, it was designed to ensure adequate consumer protection alongside stability in the banking system. It is clear from the discussion above that bank safety and consumer protection are very closely linked. If consumers are to be adequately protected then they need their banks to be safe. If banks are to be safe then they depend on the confidence of their depositors. However, the moral hazard problem remains strong. Depositors should be encouraged, it is argued, to choose their banks carefully and responsibly, but they must also be deterred from withdrawing their funds.

The EU's policy of co-insurance seeks to tackle the risks posed by the moral hazard, while still discouraging depositors from creating a run. This is achieved by providing that a proportion (90 per cent) of a depositor's money is protected up to a certain level (currently ECU22,222). The depositor is thus under some incentive to take care in choosing his or her bank, but is, in theory, unlikely to panic in the event of the bank finding itself in difficulty. In reality, however, there is still an incentive to withdraw in the event of an actual or perceived crisis. Bank deposits operate on a first come, first served basis. A depositor knows that he or she can withdraw a deposit in full, if this is done sufficiently early in the crisis. While fear of losing 10 per cent of a deposit is certainly not as great as that of losing 100 per cent, a depositor who fears that a bank is about to collapse is, it is submitted, still likely to withdraw funds in order to protect the remaining 10 per cent. It is questionable whether co-insurance at this level is a sufficient incentive to customers to leave their deposits where they are in the face of a potential collapse.

---

43. See M. Andenas, 'Deposit Guarantee Schemes and Home Country Control', in R. Cranston (ed.), *The Single Market and the Law of Banking*, 2nd edn (LLP, 1995); Campbell and Cartwright, op. cit., n. 14.
44. Directive 94/19/EC.

6. DEPOSIT GUARANTEES AND INFORMED CONSUMERS

There can be little doubt that where 100 per cent of a deposit is protected, and the depositor is aware of that protection, there is little incentive to withdraw that deposit. However, it is unclear whether depositors are actually aware of the protection offered. In the UK, there are restrictions on the extent to which membership of the Deposit Protection Scheme can be advertised,[45] and it appears unlikely that many depositors are aware of the protection they would receive in the event of a bank's insolvency.[46] Deposit guarantee schemes will only help to stem bank runs if there is awareness of the schemes' existence. This lack of awareness is a matter for concern.

If we assume for the sake of argument that depositors have knowledge of the protection which they receive from deposit guarantees, there are still difficulties in deciding the kind of scheme to implement. In particular, there is no simple answer to the difficult question of the level at which deposit guarantees should be set. One hundred per cent protection discourages runs but also discourages care in the choosing of deposits. Low levels of protection encourage runs but also encourage care in decision making. The EU approach of co-insurance attempts to find a compromise position, but arguably achieves no objective satisfactorily. For the consumer lawyer who is concerned about distributive justice and the vulnerable consumer,[47] co-insurance presents some difficulties. It has been argued elsewhere that co-insurance fails to provide adequate consumer protection, particularly to the most vulnerable consumers.[48] All UK depositors, for example, must provide a minimum of 10 per cent of their deposits by way of co-insurance. This rises dramatically where deposits are over £20,000.[49]

---

45. Regulation 48, Credit Institutions (Protection of Depositors) Regulations 1995, SI 1995/1442.
46. A straw poll that I conducted of consumer law academics and consumer law postgraduate students showed little awareness of deposit guarantee schemes. It is submitted that there would be considerably less awareness among the public at large.
47. Issues about which the OFT in the UK has shown itself to be particularly concerned of late. See *Financial Services for Vulnerable Consumers: OFT Launches Inquiry* (OFT Press Release, 16 December 1997).
48. Campbell and Cartwright, op. cit., n. 14.
49. On a deposit of £30,000, for example, the element of co-insurance has risen to 40 per cent. See Campbell and Cartwright, op. cit., n. 14.

7. THE FUTURE OF DEPOSITOR PROTECTION

A solution which may appear attractive from the consumer protection point of view is that proposed by Hall.[50] He has argued that the first £30,000 of a deposit should be fully protected, but that deposits above this amount should be subject to an element of co-insurance. He suggests 95 per cent cover up to a further amount and then no cover above that further amount. Hall accepts that the figures are somewhat arbitrary and that other figures could be substituted. In any case, he was writing in 1987 and, presumably, would adjust these figures in line with inflation. As well as providing a high level of consumer protection, Hall's proposal would play an important role in discouraging runs. It obviates some of the difficulties mentioned above and, in particular, ensures that the most vulnerable consumers, who will often be those with relatively small savings, are given full protection. It must be questionable whether a depositor of modest means should always be subject to a requirement of co-insurance, particularly when it is borne in mind how difficult it is for such a depositor to obtain any meaningful information about the risk posed by a bank.

The main objection to Hall's proposal is that of moral hazard. Perhaps a customer who is subject to 100 per cent protection, even if only up to a particular level, will now be under little incentive to ascertain the degree of risk associated with the deposit in question. But the difficulty in ascertaining this has already been noted, and this may be a risk worth taking.

It is open to the EU Member States to put in place deposit guarantee schemes which exceed the protection required by the directive, as the directive provides only a minimum level of protection.[51] There was concern, however, that Member States might use this as an instrument of competition. In order to avoid this, the directive put restrictions on the extent to which Member States could exceed the minimum protection laid down. First, the emphasis in the directive is on home state control. This means that where a Member State sets up a scheme for its own credit institutions,[52] that scheme will cover depositors at branches which the institution sets up in other Member States.[53] The directive also states that in these circumstances, the home state's cover shall not exceed that offered by the corresponding scheme in the host state.[54] This ensures that the

---

50. M. J. B. Hall, 'The Deposit Protection Scheme: the Case for Reform' (1987) *National Westminster Bank Quarterly Review* 45.
51. Art. 7(3).
52. The directive uses the term 'credit institutions' rather than 'banks'. In the UK, building societies are subject to a similar regime.
53. Art. 4(1)
54. A depositor in state Y cannot receive protection from a branch of state X's bank, superior to that provided by a bank authorised in state Y.

home state's branches do not have an advantage over the host state's banks. The directive also provides that where the host state's laws offer greater protection than the home state's, the home state's bank's branch must be able to join a scheme in the host state to supplement its cover. The branch will thus be able to 'top up', so that it offers protection equal to that provided by banks authorised in the host state.[55]

These provisions mean that provided branches of other Member States' banks were permitted to join the scheme, it would be open to the UK to introduce a scheme similar to that proposed by Hall. The reality, however, is that this is unlikely to occur. The governor of the Bank of England recently demonstrated his views as to the seriousness of the moral hazard problem, and indicated that greater protection for depositors is unlikely. He said: 'if depositors were relieved of all responsibility, deposits would simply flow to the highest bidder regardless of risk, which would undermine market disciplines and greatly increase the dangers of instability'.[56]

8.   CONCLUSIONS

It appears that change to the system of deposit guarantees in the UK along the lines suggested is unlikely. Apart from the perceived risk of moral hazard, there is also concern that by placing protection at too high a level, unnecessary burdens would be placed on banks operating in the UK. This might provide a disincentive for banks to seek authorisation in the UK, and to operate there. Whether this is a price worth paying is, of course, difficult to answer. There can be little doubt that the risk of bank failure is an extremely serious matter for depositors. At the same time, it is submitted that the risk presented by the moral hazard is overstated, particularly in countries which have effective systems of authorisation and supervision which should be able to detect and deal with banks which present an unnecessary risk. The system for deposit guarantees in the UK was introduced to provide 'a degree of protection sufficient to prevent severe hardship among the most vulnerable of depositors.'[57] It is only when a regime is introduced which takes account of the difficulties faced by depositors in assessing the risk posed by banks that this objective will be realised.

---

55. Art. 4(2).
56. D. Turing, 'Deposit Protection', in F. Oditah (ed.), *Insolvency of Banks: Managing the Risks* (FT Law and Tax), p. 17.
57. *Banking Supervision*, Cmnd 9695 (1985) chapter 3.5.

PART THREE

FINANCIAL SERVICES AND INVESTMENTS

Chapter Six

FINANCIAL SERVICES REGULATION: CAN HISTORY TEACH US ANYTHING?*

Sharon Chin

Chapter Outline

1. Introduction

2. A Little History
    2.1   The corporatist system of regulation
    2.2   Reasons for the demise of the corporatist system
    2.3   The 'Big Bang'
    2.4   The Gower Committee

3. The Financial Services Act 1986
    3.1   The regulatory structure
    3.2   The scope of the Financial Services Act 1986
    3.3   Regulation of investment firms
    3.4   Problems with the Financial Services Act 1986

4. The Way Forward
    4.1   The Financial Services Authority: background and scope
    4.2   Policy considerations

5. Conclusion

Consumer Protection in Financial Services (P. Cartwright, ed.: 90-411-9717-6: © Kluwer Law International: pub. Kluwer Law International, 1999: printed in Great Britain)

1. INTRODUCTION

This chapter aims to give a brief history of financial services regulation in the United Kingdom and discusses whether any lessons can be learned from the mistakes of the past, so that future legislation governing this area will be better adapted to cope with the needs of the international market.

The current concerns of financial services regulation, such as the protection of consumers and maintenance of confidence in the integrity of the financial markets can best be understood through following the historical development of financial services regulation in the City, from the corporatist *laissez-faire* model of the nineteenth century, to the system of 'self-regulation within a statutory framework' which was created by the Financial Services Act 1986.

The growing global integration in the financial services sector has changed the nature of its regulation in the 1990s. Future legislation will need to address issues such as internet sales of financial products, the need for better cooperation internationally between regulators, providing the right infrastructure to support investment markets, educating consumers to make the appropriate choices, and encouraging senior management to be more proactive in promoting efficient regulation of their firm's compliance with financial regulation.[1]

Fluid markets which have come about with developments in information technology have meant that traders are able to move capital quickly to different countries at any time, at the touch of a button. A new goal-orientated regulatory philosophy will be needed to regulate such innovative markets as they have developed beyond the rigid confines of the legislation which govern it. It will be important for regulators to work with the industry to gain the information needed for effective oversight as new financial products are brought onto the market.

The convergence of regulatory technique which has resulted from the horizontal and vertical integration in the markets has seen the US and UK work together more closely to facilitate enforcement cooperation.[2] This

---

*   I would like to thank Julia Black, Peter Cartwright, Colin Scott and Professor Gunter Teubner for comments on my draft and advice in the preparation of it. Responsibility for the views and errors contained remains my own.

1. See comments made by Sir Andrew Large to the Australian Securities Commission Electronic Commerce Conference in a speech 'Challenges to Regulation: What Does the Impact of Electronic Commerce Mean for the Regulation of the Financial Markets?' (3 February 1997) SIB website http://www.sib.co.uk/speeches/030297.htm.
2. See remarks made by Chairman Arthur Levitt, United States Securities and Exchange Commission, to the International Organisation of Securities Commissions at a conference in Montreal, Canada (18 September 1996). SEC website: http://www.sec.gov/news/speeches/spch1119.txt.

stands in stark contrast to the battle for comparative advantage in the regulatory markets, in the 1980s, and which characterised the particular regulatory structure set up by the Financial Services Act 1986.[3]

Investor protection in the United Kingdom remains the sum of the different relationships between the state, industry and the private individual. Why these laws were passed in the 1980s and 1990s, and what interests they sought to protect, are pertinent questions which will help us to better understand the system of investor protection that now exists, and to consider if it is a sustainable and satisfactory means of regulating the financial services industry.

2. A LITTLE HISTORY

2.1 The corporatist system of regulation

Corporatism in the City originated in the last quarter of the nineteenth century and continued to regulate codes of practitioner behaviour and entry requirements until the 1980s, when the struggle for comparative advantage in international monetary markets forced reluctant and entrenched interests to accept structural changes to the traditional forms of control.[4] That the regulatory structure set up in the Financial Services Act 1986 retains elements of the prior system of self-regulation is testimony to the reluctance on both the part of the City and the government to stray too far from the well-established meso-corporatist form of practitioner-based regulation.[5]

Why and how this came to be can be attributed to the prevailing political climate of the 1980s that had wearied of the scandal-ridden and monopolistic financial services industry, and had wanted, instead, greater investor

---

3. See M. Moran, *The Politics of the Financial Services Revolution: The USA, UK and Japan* (Macmillan, 1991); M. Reid, *All-Change in the City: The Revolution in Britain's Financial Sector* (Macmillan, 1988).
4. L. C. B. Gower, '"Big Bang" and City Regulation' (1988) 51 MLR 1.
5. Meso-corporatism can be defined as the widespread attribution of public status to interest groups. It gives a more prominent role to formally constituted organisations as evidenced in the financial services sector by the growing influence of law and legal regulatory agencies; and it stands in contrast to the concept of 'corporatism' as a form of partnership or control linking the national representatives of capital and labour with the state. Meso-corporatism is not restricted to the interest groups of labour and capital, but reflects a range of collective interests which run from state agencies to business enterprises. For a more detailed discussion on meso-corporatism see Moran, op. cit., n. 3; A. Cawson, *Organised Interests and the State: Studies in Meso Corporatism* (Sage, 1985); Philippe C. Schmitter and Gerhard Lehmbruch (eds.), *Trends Towards Corporatist Intermediation* (Sage, 1979).

protection to maintain 'market confidence'. Curiously, the government was at the same time reluctant to impose a complete system of statutory regulation on the 'old' corporatist regulatory system which it felt had worked well for the past century.

The genesis of the growth in the UK financial services sector can be traced to developments in the post World War II period, where the increased availability of credit fuelled the corresponding boom in the consumer demand in markets, as evidenced by the growing number of private home owners. London's established position as a leading financial centre and its reputation as a 'clean' place to do business, led to greater participation in the financial services market by private investors, who were not necessarily part of the wealthy elite, but were part of the middle or working classes who had 'some spare cash to put away'.

In the pre-1986 situation, regulation of the financial markets was characterised by informal agreements and understandings, with an emphasis on flexibility in rule-making which operated almost totally without sanctions.[6] This dispersed system of meso-corporatism in which representation and regulation were fused had the Bank of England (hereafter 'the Bank') as its guardian angel. As the 'supervisor' of the City, the Bank coordinated industry representation and codes of practice.[7] Such a regulatory system worked because of the homogeneous social and political nature of the financial oligarchies which ruled the City.

2.2 Reasons for the demise of the corporatist system

Several factors contributed to the decay of the corporatist system: the nationalisation of the Bank of England and its consequences, the competitive battle for comparative advantage in the international financial markets, the need for a regulatory structure which would aid such a struggle, and the increasing demands for change which disaffected interests in a pluralist political system were placing on the scandal-ridden financial services industry of the 1980s.

The nationalisation of the Bank in 1946 made it an independent, 'professionally run' institution, and led to a change in the Bank's relations with the City: the 'Old Lady of Threadneedle Street' would no longer defend the financial oligarchies' interests. The gradual erosion of the

6. See Geoffrey Ingham, *Capitalism Divided: The City and Industry in British Social Development* (Macmillan, 1984); Charles P. Kindleberger, *A Financial History of Western Europe* (Allen & Unwin, 1984).
7. G. Blunden, 'The supervisor of the United Kingdom banking system' (1975) 15 *Bank of England Quarterly Bulletin* 188–94.

Consumer Protection in Financial Services

City's political autonomy became increasingly apparent in the 1980s as the Bank of England began to develop its own policy objectives which were independent of the financial elites' interests.

In 1983, the Bank 'deserted' the Stock Exchange and refused to support the Stock Exchange's anti-competitive practices which were being challenged by the Office of Fair Trading (OFT) and were under threat of legal action. This volte-face was the result of several factors: the abolition of exchange controls, the threat to London's position as a leading financial centre, and the Bank's institutional interest in maintaining its power and influence which were dependent on London's continued pre-eminence in world financial markets. Thus supporting free market and competition ideologies which would put London in a more advantageous position in the world financial markets.[8]

Other pressures were evident: large 'outsider' institutional members from America and Japan resented the profits which were creamed off by the brokers inside the Stock Exchange cartel; in turn, ambitious and efficient members of the Stock Exchange understood that integration with big multi-national firms was the only chance that they would have of competing in the global securities markets which were dominated by capital rich American and Japanese firms. Changes to anti-competitive practices became crucial in order to integrate the new interests created by the expanding global financial markets.

2.3. The 'Big Bang'

The resulting Goodison-Parkinson[9] agreements of 1983 to reform competitive practices on the Stock Exchange can also be attributed to the 'scare' effect which the OFT had in taking a tough stance against the City interests.[10] In January 1976, the Restrictive Trade Practices Services Order extended the jurisdiction of the OFT and widened the scope of fair trading law to the service industries. This brought a range of financial institutions within the ambit of the regulatory authority of the OFT. The OFT demanded that the Stock Exchange register its rule book with the OFT and that it reform any offending rules. Failure to comply with these demands would result in the OFT bringing the Stock Exchange rule book for judgment before the Restrictive Practices Court.

8. Reid, op. cit., n. 3.
9. Cecil Parkinson was the Secretary of State for Trade and Industry in 1984 and Sir Nicholas Goodison was the Chairman of the Stock Exchange.
10. Sir N. Goodison, 'The Stock Exchange at Turning Point' (March 1985) *The Stock Exchange Quarterly.*

144

It was obvious that once the statutory instrument had been published, the government could hardly have had agreed to retreat from enforcing it, or to accept the City's special pleading for exemption from it. Thus when Parkinson offered the concession of exemption from the jurisdiction of the OFT and demanded that the key rules which the OFT had objected to be amended, it was seized upon by the City as a face-saving way to escape from the clutches of the OFT.

In essence the deal consisted of the following reforms: that minimum commission on bargains be abolished by December 1986, that lay representatives be on the council of the Stock Exchange, that the substance of rule changes would be undertaken in consultation and with the agreement of the Bank, and that the implementation of the whole package would be monitored by a group drawn from the Bank and the DTI. In return, the government had to back legislation exempting the Stock Exchange from the Restrictive Trade Practices Services Order.

Naturally the Goodison–Parkinson agreements provoked outrage and accusations of 'pork barrel' politics, particularly at the OFT which regarded it as a blow to its prestige and enforcement capabilities. In practice, the decision to phase out minimum commission on bargains opened up the market by removing the main price barrier to competition and achieved what the OFT had sought to enforce. The abolition of minimum commissions intensified the wider competitive struggle and transformed the rules of business conduct in markets. It soon became clear that the single capacity of firms and the enforced separation of brokers and jobbers could no longer be maintained. It is telling that within a few months of the Goodison–Parkinson agreements the Stock Exchange was willing to abolish these anti-competitive practices.

The 'Big Bang' on the Stock Exchange made it necessary to devise a new set of rules to cope with the friction arising from the shift from a floor-based dealing system to that of single capacity. Other problems could be seen in the City's unfamiliarity with the use of new technology in the Stock Exchange, such as an automated quotation system for stocks and shares, and the 'birthing pains' of new financial markets like the London International Financial Futures Exchange in 1982. Later, the collapse of investment advisers in high risk industries such as that of Johnson Matthey bankers[11] and the Norton Warburg investment management firm, created doubts about the viability of existing trading practices. After successive financial scandals in City markets in the early 1980s, state intervention was

11. The authoritative account of these events can be found in 'The Bank of England and Johnson Matthey Bankers Limited', *Reports and Accounts of the Bank of England*, 1985. See also M. J. B. Hall, 'The Johnson Matthey Bankers Affair: Have Lessons Been Learnt?' (1987) *Journal of International Securities Markets*.

championed by political pressure groups to restore the prestige and high trust environment crucial to London's continued existence as one of the world's leading financial markets.[12]

2.4 The Gower Committee

The 1983 Gower Committee was established to the review of the existing mechanisms of investor protection. It was asked to consider the need for statutory control of dealers in securities, investment consultants and investment managers; and to suggest new legislation.[13] Professor Gower made several recommendations: that the Prevention of Fraud (Investments) Act 1958 should be replaced by a new Act providing for basic policy; that overall surveillance and residual regulation of investment business should be undertaken by the government or a new agency. Thus, entry into the industry would be dependent on a system of licensing, the administration of which would be controlled by a single supervisory body. Regulation on a daily basis would be delegated to a range of self-regulatory organisations (SROs), initially based on existing professional bodies and organisations, which would be specifically recognised by the government or the new agency.

In effect, Professor Gower's proposals preserved corporatism in a more codified and institutionalised form. The Financial Services Act 1986 created a system of practitioner-based regulation within a statutory framework. Self-regulation within the statutory framework was deemed to be cheaper, more efficient, competitive and flexible. It kept costs outside the public purse as the SROs would pay for the administration of the system, and it hived off appallingly complex and detailed tasks from central government to practitioners who would have the technical 'know-how'. In turn it was hoped that this would make the system more responsive to international developments in financial services, and allow the industry to adapt better to the competition.

In summary, the principal objectives of the Financial Services Act 1986 were:

- to facilitate the growth of the financial markets under conditions of fair competition;

12. D. H. A. Ingram, 'Change in the Stock Exchange and the Regulation of the City' (February 1987), *The Bank of England Quarterly Bulletin*.
13. L. C. B. Gower, *A Review of Investor Protection*, part I, Cmnd 9125 (HMSO 1984).

- to provide a set of clearly understood principles and rules to encourage the easy raising of capital in the UK, investments, savings, the sale and purchase of investments;
- to prevent fraud on the markets and malpractice in the industry;
- to involve practitioners in the regulation of the financial markets as their commitment would be invaluable in maintaining the highest standards in the industry;
- to ensure that there was an equivalence of treatment between products and services competing in the same industry, and that the law would not create artificial distinctions or barriers to competition.[14]

The objectives of the Financial Services Act 1986 were undoubtedly influenced by the historical context for the creation of the legislation.[15] Whether these objectives were met will be examined in the following section.

3. THE FINANCIAL SERVICES ACT 1986

3.1 The regulatory structure

The Thatcherite constitutional settlement in the financial services industry created an antithetical regulatory system: a corporatist structure which quickly evolved into a system of bureaucratic control. The competing demands of democratic politics, the role of the courts, and problem of settling jurisdiction between the different SROs resulted in the politicisation and bureaucratisation of the financial services industry. [16]

Despite all the assurances that the Financial Services Act 1986 (hereafter 'the Act') had been set up to protect investor interest, it is telling that the City elites and the government sought to make the regulatory system in United Kingdom financial services more 'self' than 'statutory'. The truth is that 'self-regulation within a statutory framework' was at best a euphemism for regulation in industry interest.[17]

The Act created the Securities Investment Board (SIB) with its delegated statutory powers, and the associated SROs to solve the problem of how to provide a disciplined system of regulation without submitting the

---

14. Ibid.
15. See J. Black, ' Which Arrow? Rule Type and Policy' (1995) *Public Law*, Spring.
16. See C. Graham and T. Prosser (eds.), *Waiving the Rules: The Constitution Under Thatcherism* (OUP, 1988).
17. See A. Ogus, *Regulation: Legal Form and Economic Theory* (Clarendon Press, 1994).

Figure 6.1

The regulatory structure set up by The Financial Services Act 1986

---

s. 115 Financial Services Act 1986
Secretary of State retained the power to resume the delegated power (to SIB) in
whole or in part
↓
delegated powers to the Securities and Investments Board (SIB)
↓
SIB governing board
appointed by the Secretary of State and Governor of the Bank of England
↓
membership of SIB governing board drawn largely from investment industry
↓
SIB had to submit its annual report to Parliament, and the Secretary of State.
SIB recognises, monitors and supervises self-regulatory organisations (SROs),
recognised profesional bodies (RPBs), recognised investment exchanges (RIEs)
and recognised clearing houses

---

markets to public control. The inevitable tensions that arose in the process of trying to meet the different objectives in the Financial Services Act 1986 were never resolved by the regulators.

3.2 The scope of the Financial Services Act 1986

As the senior regulator and 'guardian' of public interest, the 'three-tier' structure of the SIB was deemed to be the most cost-effective way to deliver adequate investor protection. The SIB would set standards, and recognise, monitor and supervise other front line financial services market regulators (see Figure 6.1).

The scope of the basic investment business regime in the new regulatory regime was defined by the prohibition in section 3 of the Act: ' No person shall carry on, or purport to carry on, investment business in the United Kingdom unless he is an authorised person . . . or an exempted person.'

Thus, part I of Schedule 1 to the Act detailed the financial instruments which would be regarded as investments for the purposes of the Act such as company shares, debentures, government securities, options, futures, long-term insurance contracts, share warrants and certificates representing deposits. Part II of Schedule 1 to the Act identified five activities which would constitute 'investment business', namely:

148

- dealing in investment;
- arranging deals in investments;
- managing investments;
- giving investment advice; and
- establishing, operating or winding up collective investment schemes.

3.3 Regulation of investment firms

The regulatory structure set up by the Act was dependent on individuals and firms that were involved in investment business obtaining the requisite authorisation either directly from the SIB, or indirectly from one of the SROs or RPBs supervised by the SIB. However, the SIB's power's of intervention and investigation, such as the restriction of investment business and the freezing of assets, were only exercisable in relation to directly regulated firms but not members of SROs or RPBs.

The Act sought to give a 'light touch' in regulation by allowing for exemptions in part III to Schedule 1 for inter-professional dealings. For example section 43 of the Act gave an exemption for listed money market institutions. The Act also provided for sanctions against errant individuals and firms who carried on unlawful investment business. These had several effects:

- Section 4 of the Act made the contravention of section 3 a criminal offence punishable on conviction on indictment to imprisonment for a maximum of two years; or on summary conviction to imprisonment for a term not exceeding six months or to a fine or to both.
- Section 5(1) of the Act made contracts which were entered into in contravention of section 3 unenforceable against the other party, and also gave the other party the right to recover any money or property transferred, together with compensation for any loss suffered.
- Section 6 of the Act gave the SIB powers to apply to the court for the relevant injunctions and restitution orders to aid the investors who have suffered as a consequence of the unlawful investment business being carried out. [18]

This odd regulatory structure created problems for the SIB: it had not only to monitor and enforce regulations for a wide range of investment

18. The Securities and Investments Board has the power to pursue such restitutionary orders as it has the delegated powers from the Secretary of State (see Figure 6.1).

Table 6.1

Summary of SROs and RPBs regulated by SIB

SROs	RPBs
Regulate persons carrying on investment business	Regulate members in professional body and their investment business activities
1. FIMBRA: Financial Intermediaries, Managers and Brokers Regulatory Association 2. IMRO: Investment Management Regulatory Organisation 3. SFA: Securities and Futures Authority 4. LAUTRO: Life, Assurance and Unit Trust Regulatory Organisation	*eg*, the Law Society, the Law Society of Scotland, the Law Society of Northern Ireland, the Institute of Chartered Accountants in England and Wales, the Institute of Chartered Accountants in Scotland, the Institute of Chartered Accountants in Ireland, the Chartered Association of Certified Accountants, the Institute of Actuaries, and the Insurance Brokers Registration Council

business; it also had to persuade industry operators to cooperate in the new regulatory system, many of whom were not used to being regulated, or had been used to a different regime altogether (see Table 6.1).

3.4 Problems with the Financial Services Act 1986

The undue complexity of the rulebooks and the Act procedures meant that the investors were confused about where they stood before the law, which agency to go to with their complaints, and what interests the law would be willing to protect. Much of the dissatisfaction with the Act regulatory system has been directed at the SIB.

Particular concerns were voiced about the undefined nature of the SIB's role in the regulatory system, its tentative position as supervisor of other regulators like SROs and recognised professional bodies (RPBs), its apparent lack of democratic accountability, and how out of touch the SIB was with industry and consumer interests.[19] While most investors and industry

---

19. See comments made by Sir Andrew Large acknowledging the difficulty which the regulators had in keeping up with developments in the financial services market, and how the Financial Services Act 1986 failed to respond quickly enough to the changing environment: Sir Andrew Large, 'Standards of Market Integrity in the New World: the Big Bang Ten Years on', in a speech delivered at House Magazine Conference (29 October 1996) SIB website http://www.sib.co.uk/speeches/291096.htm.

Table 6.2

Role and responsibilities of SIB

1. The SIB regulates investment business, based on recognition, monitoring and supervision of self-regulating organisations (SROs), investment exchanges and clearing houses.
2. The SIB has extensive legislative functions. e.g. the making of rules and regulations, the issue of statements of principle and codes of practice, the designation of rules to apply directly to SROs.
3. The SIB is given the power to authorise and regulate the carrying out of investment business by firms that choose to be regulated by SIB rather than SROs or RPBs.
4. The SIB is given wide powers of intervention and enforcement. It was able to seek injunctions, restitution orders, issue disqualification directions, and discipline directly regulated firms. It also had limited power to institute criminal proceedings.
5. The SIB has the power to recognise and authorise the various collective investment schemes which carry out the administration of any of Financial Services Act 1986 provisions.

insiders perceived the SIB to be the 'leading' regulator in the system, unlike the United States Securities and Exchange Commission (SEC), the SIB lacked the effective structure and resources to meet this public expectation, and to carry out the enormous administrative task of enforcement and monitoring of standards in recognised bodies as thoroughly and efficiently as everyone wished[20] (see Table 6.2).

Further unhappiness with the regulatory system was manifest in the conflict between the the SIB's interests in maintaining a cooperative working relationship with SROs, and the need to retain an 'objective' distance in order to assess whether the self-assessment reviews (SARs) submitted by SROs met recognition standards. SARs were a particular 'gripe' of investors in relation to the SIB's technique of regulation in the financial markets.[21] The SIB's failure to lay down any guidelines as to the form and content of SARs meant that SROs had a wide-ranging discretion to decide on the approach which it would wish to undertake. This contributed to the perception that the SIB failed to 'catch the crooks', and to protect investors and the public interest.

The SIB's role as a 'rule-maker' and 'standard-setter' was also questioned by Treasury officials as financial scandals such as that of the

20. See Table 6.2 for the role and responsibilities of the SIB.
21. See D. D. Prentice, *EEC Directives on Company Law and Financial Markets* (Clarendon Press, 1991).

Maxwell pensions fraud, reinforced the impression that the SIB failed to properly supervise SROs such as the Investment Management Regulatory Organisation (IMRO).[22] That the SIB's governing board structure closely mirrored that of industry SROs was seen to be undesirable, as it left the SIB vulnerable to 'industry capture'.[23]

The Maxwell case and that of London FOX demonstrated the need for the SIB to supervise all recognised bodies in a more formal and active way, as the present system involving heavy reliance on SROs to do the job of detailed tracking and supervision had been unsatisfactory. The Maxwell case highlighted the limitations of depending on SARs and SROs as a method of 'light touch' supervision, and showed how unsuitable the present trial by jury system was in coping with complex financial fraud cases with voluminous documentation. IMRO itself had failed to be critical enough of Maxwell's behaviour: its monitoring had been too mechanistic and it had failed to pick up 'danger' signals; risk assessment had been absent, and worst of all, when the crisis occurred IMRO had not responded with the urgency required.

Compensation for 'victims' of financial scandals was also not forthcoming, with 'good' industry insiders reluctant to subsidise the 'bad' operators in their midst.[24] Under the Financial Services Act 1986, investors had only two specific rights of action by which they could recover damages, namely: under section 62 which made actionable a breach of a SRO's Conduct of Business Rules; and under section 150/Regulation 14 Public Offer of Securities Regulation 1995, which allowed an investor to recover compensation for false or misleading listing particulars or prospectuses. However, it was unlikely that individual investors who had suffered losses as a result of the activities of rogue traders or firms would be able to bear the cost of expensive and time consuming court proceedings. Whilst the new Financial Services Authority might be able to start prosecutions on behalf of these investors, it would not be able to point to any loss which it had suffered and no damages would be recoverable. The mis-selling of 2 million personal pensions to the public was an example of how the Act failed to protect ordinary investors. Until 1997 not one person or company had been prosecuted under the Act's mis-selling clauses. The DTI even attempted to argue that pensions mis-selling was not covered by the

22. A. C. Page and R. B. Ferguson, *Investor Protection* (Weidenfeld & Nicolson, 1992) p. 227; Alison Smith, ' Treasury Plans to Shake up Financial Services Regulation', *The Financial Times*, 30 January 1996.
23. See Sir Andrew Large, 'Making the Two Tier System Work' (1993) SIB Report, for a succinct account of the problems the Financial Services Act 1986 has created.
24. See D. Brierly, 'City Revolts Against the Regulators', *The Sunday Times*, 21 February 1988.

Financial Services Act 1986, a stance which was quicl
Treasury.

The confusion even among regulators and civil se:
well for investors who became increasingly upset a:
paltry the punishment for errant insurance and pens
As Helen Liddell, Economic Secretary to the Treasury
had ordinary investors when faced with an alphabet s(
ulators?'[25]

Enforcement remained problematic as the SIB had no power to fine
City traders or financial advisers who broke the rules that the SROs had
set. Under section 59 of the Act, the SIB had the power only to ban errant
individuals from being employed as investment advisers. If the SIB wished
to impose a fine on an individual it would have to do so under laws which
required a higher burden of proof in a slow and lengthy court action. The
use of juries in complex financial fraud trials contributed to the difficulty
which the SIB and other regulators had in bringing the criminals 'to book'
as prosecutors were forced to simplify the cases too much until 'the basic
criminality was lost'.[26]

A lack of clarity in the objectives of the Financial Services Act 1986 and
the standards of performance expected of regulators and practitioners
were the pressing problems of the existing regulatory system.[27] The
emphasis on the frequency of 'ritual' inspection visits and quick complaint
handling times seem destined to create a mechanical regulatory culture
that failed to keep up with the development of new products in the financial services industry. Clearly the time for change had come.

4. THE WAY FORWARD

4.1. The Financial Services Authority: background and scope

The new Financial Services Authority remains the 'child' of the regulatory
mishaps in the 1980s and 1990s, such as the personal pensions mis-selling
scandal and the collapse of Barings.[28] Its birth is testimony to the failure of

25. See Caroline Merrell, 'Shake-up for Financial Services', *The Times*, 20 September 1997.
26. See comments made by Rosalind Wright, Director of the Serious Fraud Office, as reported in *The Times*, 15 July 1997.
27. See Baldwin and McCrudden, *Regulation and Public Law* (Weidenfeld & Nicolson, 1987).
28. The Financial Services Authority was launched on 28 October 1997 by the Chancellor of the Exchequer, the Rt Hon. Gordon Brown MP and Howard Davies, Chairman of the new Financial Services Authority. It retains the same status as the Securities and

...i-regulation and reflects political recognition that the old regulatory structure was no longer able to meet the needs of both consumers and industry players. The new single super-regulator stands in stark contrast to the curious legacy of the Thatcher years which left the financial services industry with a system of regulation that was best described as 'self-regulation within a statutory framework'; and which was characterised by a cobweb of confusing interrelationships between the various regulatory agencies.[29]

The 1997 proposals for the reform of financial services regulation deserve to be commended for their bold simplicity.[30] Laws accumulated over the years and contained in statutes such as the Financial Services Act 1986, the Banking Act 1987, the Building Societies Act 1986 and the Policyholders Protection Act 1975, will be repealed and replaced by a single Act where possible.[31] Clearly delineated roles have also been carved out for HM Treasury, the Bank and the Financial Services Authority.[32] The principles of accountability, transparency, and efficiency in regulation as agreed in the Memorandum of Understanding between the HM Treasury, the Bank and the Financial Services Authority should do much to promote financial stability and reduce the risk of systemic failure.[33]

In the new regulatory structure, the Bank will be responsible for the management of monetary policy and the infrastructure and stability of the financial system. The 'super-regulator' Financial Services Authority will authorise and supervise the commercial and retail aspects of financial business that banks, building societies, investment firms, insurance companies and friendly societies are involved in. It will also be a 'one-stop' centre for consumer complaints in financial disputes with the firms it regulates. It has committed itself to making consumer groups involved in the policy-making process and to being alert as to the problems that consumers face in the market as early on as possible. The move away from the simplistic *caveat emptor* principle for non-sophisticated investors, and the

---

(continued)

Investments Board and is a private company limited by guarantee under the Companies Act 1985.

29. Gower, op. cit., n. 14, part I.
30. See the SIB Report to the Chancellor on the Reform of the Financial Regulatory System, 31 July 1997.
31. It is expected that the draft bill, tentatively to be called 'The Treasury Bill', will be published for consultation in summer 1998.
32. The Financial Services Authority will acquire its range of powers in two stages. The Bank of England Bill will transfer from the Bank to the Financial Services Authority the responsibility for supervising banks, wholesale money market institutions, and clearing houses. It is expected to receive the Royal Assent in June 1998.
33. See the Financial Services Authority, *An Outline Prospectus*, 28 October 1997.

recognition that they should not be exposed to risks which they should not be reasonably expected to assume, is a welcome change.[34]

The new regulatory structure will be built in several stages, and not in a single 'Big Bang' as happened under the Financial Services Act 1986. This will involve the publication of the Bank of England Bill in 1998 and consultation with the industry and the public on key issues. During this time, detailed organisational structures will be designed and contractual arrangements made with the various SRO boards to allow for the transfer of staff contracts of employment to the Financial Services Authority (hereafter 'the Authority'), when the Bank of England Bill comes into force.

In the second stage, the Authority will become operational under interim arrangements and directly supervise, authorise and enforce investment business in relation to banks and SRO firms. In the final stage, it is envisaged that the Authority will become responsible for the regulation of all financial firms, which will include the handling of all complaints and any compensation arrangements. The SROs will also be wound up after the financial regulatory reform bill comes into force.[35]

The new Authority will have more extensive powers than the SIB. For instance, it will be able to exercise these powers against an SRO member firm, without the need for the SRO's consent.[36] It will also be given the power to fine and punish all the banks and SROs which it will regulate. This will make the Authority a unique entity in the advanced capitalist world as the single regulator for banking, financial services and insurance. However, the extensive powers that the Financial Services Authority will possess has also raised the uncomfortable spectre that it will be 'prosecutor, judge and jury' rolled into one. This would conflict with Article 6 of the European Convention on Human Rights, which provides that 'In the determination of . . . any criminal charge . . . everyone is entitled to a fair . . . hearing . . . by an independent and impartial tribunal'. The Labour government has recognised the City's fears and has amended the Financial Services Authority Bill to allay such apprehension.[37] It is hoped that the consolidation of the vari-

---

34. See the Financial Services Authority, *Consultation Paper on Consumer Involvement*, 28 October 1997.

35. The Financial Services Authority's timetable for integration was taken from the Financial Services Authority, *An Outline Prospectus*, 8 October 1997.

36. See A. Whittaker, 'The Reform of United Kingdom Financial Services Regulation' (1997) *Butterworths Journal of International Banking and Financial Law*, June.

37. UK Government Press Release date 22 December 1998 set out the amendments to the Financial Services Authority Bill, namely: the Financial Services Authority would be obliged to establish and publish proper procedures governing the trial and appeals processes, and would be obliged to act in accordance with such procedures; that any potential defendant to an action would have the right to view the evidence against him, and that the Financial Services Authority would be obliged to act in accordance with such procedures; that the Financial Services Authority would be

ous regulatory agencies into a single 'super-regulator' will make regulation more efficient and preserve London's comparative advantage in the world financial markets.

4.2. Policy considerations

Given that the traditional distinctions between the banking and securities markets have been eroded in the US and Europe with all the recent mergers in 1998, the old regulatory structure that existed under the Financial Services Act 1986 would no longer be able to cope with the evolution in the business practice. The mergers of big banks such as the Union Bank of Switzerland and SBC Warburg, Travellers Group's $9 billion take-over of Salomon Brothers, and Merrill Lynch's $5.2 billion take-over of Mercury Asset Management, have demonstrated the vertical and horizontal integration that is taking place across the financial services and banking sectors.[38]

Such integration suggests that in the future there will be a few truly global firms that will be increasingly dominant as they seek to provide multinational corporations with a broad range of financial services products such as conventional investment banking advice, aid in market trading, finance lending and institutional fund management.

The changes in the operational structure of the financial markets with the advent of telesales and internet sales of financial products, has meant that the traditional role of the stockbroker is also under attack as consumers become more directly involved in the investment market. The use of websites to sell financial products has made it difficult for regulators to police sales of such products to customers. At present, unregulated firms may sell products to customers on the web.[39]

This could have nasty effects for consumer confidence in the regulatory system if too many scams take place on the net. The SIB has considered the suggestion that so long as consumers in the UK can reach such internet sales sites such as E*trade, this will constitute solicitation and will make such firms liable to the jurisdiction and regulatory laws of the UK. It is a developing area of law and the new Financial Services Authority will have to decide what to do with respect to internet sales of financial products.

(continued)
> barred from publicising an enforcement action until the full process, including any tribunal procedures, had been completed; and the Financial Services Authority would also lose its powers to make rules on when relevant evidence might be admissible before the tribunal.

38. William Lewis 'Leaders of the Pack are Striding out Abroad', *The Financial Times*, 23 January 1998.
39. See 'The Internet's Most Wanted' , *The Economist*, 23 August 1997.

The democratisation of the financial services industry with the slow demise of the traditional stockbroker has posed particular problems for consumers, as choosing between the thousands of stocks, bonds and insurance products available has become a daunting task. This trend of direct involvement on the part of consumers has been evident not only in the UK but also in the US where fund deposits now stand at US$3 trillion and one in three Americans claims to have invested in funds.[40] Thus closing the 'knowledge gap', by demanding better risk disclosure and prospectuses drafted in plain English to enable investors to take calculated risks, will help to boost market confidence and stability.

The push towards greater transparency in the markets through better risk disclosure documents, as suggested by the consultation paper on the reform on financial services regulation, represents a move in the right direction. As McMahon has pointed out, investors should be able to obtain some minimum standard of quality in financial services as guaranteed by an independent 'standard-setter', as these *product defects* cannot be discovered by the ordinary investor with no knowledge or experience of how financial markets work.[41]

Disclosure of information requirements are necessary to ensure that certain investor protection standards are met. The regulators have to ensure that excessive risks are not taken by institutions and brokers alike, thus safeguarding the financial services industry from systemic failure and a widespread loss of confidence by investors.

The globalisation of the financial services market has also contributed to the regulatory dilemma as the various national regulatory authorities have 'competed' to deregulate, and to be the more attractive regime to do business in.[42] The City revolution in the UK and the regulatory changes which accompanied it has been an excellent case in point. However, the danger in 'regulatory competition' has been the risk of 'knock on' systemic failure with the present inter-dependence in the world economy. The Mexican peso crisis, Barings, Daiwa, Sumitomo and the Indonesian rupiah devaluation illustrate the need to be able to deal with such events in an organised manner without endangering market confidence in the soundness of the financial system.[43]

---

40. See Chairman of SEC Arthur Levitt's speech to the Investment Company Institute, Washington DC (22 May 1996) http://www.sec.gov/news/speeches/spch102.txt.
41. McMahon, 'The Business of Financial Supervision' (1984) *Bank of England Quarterly Bulletin*.
42. Margaret Reid, *All Change in the City: The Revolution in Britain's Financial Sector* (Macmillan, 1988).
43. See Sir Andrew Large's paper presented at the 27th Yomiuri Symposium Tokyo, May 1997 http://www.sib.co.uk/speeches/053097a.htm.

The stakes remain high, as the economic crisis in Asia in 1998 has illustrated. Capital moves quickly in international money markets and is capable of precipitating 'runs' on banks and economic panic. What role a regulator like the Financial Services Authority should have in underpinning the confidence in global and domestic markets is of pertinent concern, with the revolution in electronic information technology blurring the boundaries between banking and securities, and between legal entities and national jurisdictions. In the wake of the Asian crisis in 1998, the conventional wisdom that it is a good thing to let capital move freely across borders has been challenged. However, capital controls remain difficult to enforce in practice and the best option for most countries hoping to avoid the destabilising effects from inflows and outflows of capital would be to ensure that their financial systems are sound and strong.[44]

Four lessons stand out if the UK hopes to continue to benefit from the free flow of international capital without falling victim to the costs of such a system:

(i) The UK should ensure that its domestic financial systems remain open and liberalised, before opening it up to foreign capital. This is not a problem as the Financial Services Act 1986 has achieved deregulation in the monopolistic practices of the City.

(ii) Financial liberalisation in turn demands strict bank regulation and supervision. The consultation paper on the reform of the Financial Services Act 1986 has given the Financial Services Authority the power to take over the Bank's role in the regulation and supervision of banks, listed money market institutions and related clearing houses. That the Financial Services Authority will supervise both commercial and retail aspects of financial services will ensure that there is greater cohesion and clarity in the policy-making process. The Financial Services Authority Task Force, made up of members taken from the various SROs, exchanges, banks and clearing houses, will also assist in the coordination of the regulators' dealings with multi-regulated firms, and provide a forum for the exchange of information and expertise between the regulators and the market bodies.[45]

(iii) Exchange rate flexibility is also needed to support the 'liberalised financial market' domestically. This means that the Bank should retain the option of raising interest rates domestically to prevent the economy from overheating. The new regulatory structure

---

44. See 'Keeping the Hot Money out', *The Economist*, 24–30 January 1998.
45. Taken from The Financial Services Authority, op. cit.

devolves the responsibility for monetary policy to the Bank, and it is essential that the Financial Services Authority and Bank should coordinate policy to ensure that any repercussions are anticipated and dealt with in an organised and efficient way.

(iv) Financial markets need reliable information to work well. The Financial Services Authority will be demanding better risk disclosure from all financial players in the market for investors, enabling investors to make intelligent investment decisions.

Supporters of self-regulation have asked important questions that have no easy answers: how will we know whether the well-intended regulation actually moves the imperfect market closer to the second best model and results in a more competitive system? What is the point of introducing comprehensive investor protection measures if they are too costly and time-consuming to implement? The moral hazard in such over-regulation is apparent; it could drive even the honest to be untruthful because the cost of compliance would outweigh the benefits.

5. CONCLUSION

It is vital that the financial system is able to continually reposition itself to deal with the new problems and challenges which arise as the financial services sector develops. The globalisation of firms and the development of international finance has meant that regulators can no longer remain creatures of their national governments, merely concerned with issues of domestic regulation.

Investors deserve to be protected both internationally and domestically. The Financial Services Authority would do well to move beyond the traditional focus that regulators in the UK have on product specific problems such as the mis-selling of pensions, or insurance and unit trusts scams. The increasingly active investor in the UK will demand that the Authority becomes more concerned with markets and market integrity. The establishment of the new Authority demonstrates that regulation is not a commodity which can be bought 'off the shelf'; it remains a tailored made product, to the specific circumstances of jurisdiction and time.

As the pace of consolidation in the investment banking industry has quickened in 1998, the challenge for international regulators has become more acute. Companies are now structured on a global basis – for instance a trader in London could report to a manager in New York to execute a deal in Luxembourg. These global institutions have been particularly difficult to regulate, as they tend to be each other's largest counterparties, have extensive dealings with many of the same customers and are members of the same clearing houses and exchanges. Hence direct and indirect exposures within this group are so complicated and opaque (and change so rapidly), that it is virtually impossible to monitor them effectively.[46]

If the history of financial services regulation has taught us anything, it is that the law can never hope to evolve as rapidly as market practices and that legislation quickly becomes outdated. The new Financial Services Authority will be subject to same relentless pace of change, and whatever operational structure it has, will ultimately fail to meet all the public and business interests.

Further steps beyond the consolidation of the various regulatory agencies in the UK will have to be taken, which necessitate a change in regulatory culture in the public and private spheres. Common international ground rules for management control, coupled with increased disclosure and external audits to ensure compliance with agreed regulatory standards should be established. The development and retention of the confidence of regulators in other countries, rather than the mad rush to obtain comparative advantage in the regulatory market, should be the touchstone to encourage greater cooperation in a global market. In the private sphere, banks should also invest more in risk management systems and set pay scales for compliance officers that are closer to front line bankers. Steps should also be taken to ensure that risk reduction measures such as netting are legally binding in the event of bankruptcy. If the new Financial Services Authority can persuade the City to be committed to adhering to these aims, it will have won half the battle.

---

46. George Graham, 'A World of Difference for the Industry', *The Financial Times*, 23 January 1998.

Chapter Seven

PENSIONS AND THE CONSUMER: LESSONS FROM OVERSEAS*

David O. Harris and Susan P. Jones

Chapter Outline

1.   Introduction

2.   Regulation

3.   Distribution

4.   Product Design

5.   Redress

6.   Disclosure

7.   Public Education

Consumer Protection in Financial Services (P. Cartwright, ed.: 90-411-9717-6: © Kluwer Law International: pub. Kluwer Law International, 1999: printed in Great Britain)

1.   INTRODUCTION

The United Kingdom is not alone when it comes to the difficulties and significant impacts on consumers when a sharp alteration in the existing pensions model occurs. Countries in Asia, Africa, Europe and North and South
America have developed different pension systems with a common theme
that the consumer needs to be proactive in planning for retirement as the
retreat of the state increases in providing solely for welfare in old age. Further, it is argued that the sense of paternalism which is offered by many
countries' social security systems will be eroded even further by the 'baby
boomer' generation's rapid ageing and the significant challenges for
retirement planning for both the private and public sectors. Governments
throughout the world are grappling with social security reform and the
impact of ageing populations. This concern is reinforced by OECD demographic data which indicate that average elderly dependency ratios for all
members (retirees compared with the remaining population) will deterio-
rate from 20.9 per cent in 2000 to 37.7 per cent in 2030.

The political environment of a nation has a critical influence on the
shaping of its pensions framework. The tension to be resolved is always
between economic and political pressures in the short term and future
economic security. Peter Diamond from the Massachusetts Institute of
Technology comments:

The role of government in the provision of retirement income is important for the
well-being of its people. It is also a classic example of a problem in institution
design that must try to solve both a complex economic problem and a difficult
problem of political economy. That is, the optimal provision of retirement income
would be a hard problem for a philosopher king, a problem that would require
repeated changes in benefit formulas and tax rules as economic and demographic
uncertainties were resolved. It is precisely this need for additional legislation for
optimal design that makes the actual behaviour of governments such a critical part
of this institutional design. That is, governments will not reproduce the evolution
of social security that a philosopher king would design.[1]

Nevertheless, various 'philosophies' are apparent in the way that countries
have tackled the problem. An ideological or paternalistic approach can be
seen, for example, in the national provident funds of Singapore and
Malaysia.

---

*   The content, opinions and details expressed are those of the authors and are not
    representative or connected with Watson Wyatt Worldwide and the Office of Fair Trad-
    ing.
1. P. Diamond, *Privatisation of Social Security: Lessons from Chile* (1993), National
    Bureau of Economic Research Inc., Working Paper 4510, p. 1.

A significant level of employee and employer contributions are mandatory and paid on a monthly basis into varying sub-accounts of a provident fund. This forced saving has resulted in dramatic income improvements and living standards for the average Singaporean and Malaysian pensioner. The funds have also provided the governments with an excellent reserve of cheap capital for major infrastructure projects such as new airports. Some doubt has been expressed, however, over what impact such compulsory contributions will have on future labour costs, job opportunities and the overall competitiveness of each economy. Furthermore, consumer expectation has already outstripped the provident fund accounts. Increasingly both countries are having to deal with greater consumer sophistication and the belief that better returns can be obtained outside the provident funds where returns have been relatively static or declining in recent years. The Central Provident Fund (CPF) of Singapore now encourages members to be more proactive in their retirement planning. In Malaysia the government has gone further and allowed certain members to transfer part of their investments out of the Employee Provident Fund and into authorised managed funds.

Chile is a noted example of how a political structure can shape and implement pension reform. In 1980, Decrees 3500 and 3501 were passed by the military government of General Pinochet. This replaced the pay-as-you-go social security, which had operated in Chile since 1924, with a privatised, mandatory system that requires 10 per cent of each month's wages to be paid into one of thirteen savings accounts held by highly regulated intermediaries, known as AFPs (*administradora de fondes de pensiones*). It is argued, by some academics and researchers, that such reforms could not have been sustained if a democracy had existed in Chile. In 1981, for instance, the government ordered all employers to increase the wage levels by 18 per cent to alleviate any negative personal detriment that might be caused by the introduction of the scheme. Additionally, government--controlled television provided an enormous amount of free access for public education to promote the merits of the reform. The chief architect of the reforms, Jose Pinera, the Minister of Labour, was one of the main spokespeople in this public education campaign.

Similarly, Australians have witnessed a rapid transformation in the last decade, in the way they provide for retirement. The Australians have managed to establish a mandatory contribution system by consensus. Award (wage determination) mandated contribution into the second pillar was implemented in 1987 and further compulsion followed in 1992 under the package of legislation referred to commonly as the Superannuation Guarantee Charge (SGC). Throughout this reform process, active participation was sought from consumer and union movements and vested interest groups representing industry participants, employers and manufacturers of pension products. Annual meetings of the Superannuation Consultative Committee enable such groups to influence policy. Other political strategies have included public education campaigns and the establishment of a parliamentary committee to inquire into the details associated with pension (superannuation) reform. The Senate Select Committee on Superannuation continues to monitor the likely implications of legislation.

The Republic of Ireland has also taken a consensus approach to possible reform of its three-pillar system. The Pensions Board has been consulting all sections of the Irish community to gauge what direction reform should follow. The Irish believe, as do Canada and the Netherlands, that accord among all major stakeholders helps to nurture public confidence in a pension scheme.

In contrast, South Africa has been more concerned about the likely response of industry to any attempts at reform or a move away from the existing system. More pressing priorities have dominated the political agenda post-apartheid, but comprehensive reform will be needed in the future to improve coverage and cope with demographic pressures of a relatively young population. Greater consumer input will be needed to elicit more responsive political decisions on the issues related to the retirement industry.

2. REGULATION

One of the more emotive issues that confront government, industry and consumer groups in the pension field is the level and type of regulation imposed on the industry. Statutory, self- and consensus regulation generally represent the spectrum of approaches. Often the type of regulation found in each country can be linked more to its historical and cultural approach towards legal enforcement than dispassionate and pragmatic innovation. Ultimately, what regulation attempts to achieve is an efficient and competitive market able to provide consumers with sufficient and suitable retirement vehicles. Experience suggests, however, that excessive regulation can be just as detrimental for the consumer as inadequate regulation.

There is no doubt that regulation and its associated cost shape an industry's profile and overall structure. In recent years, pay-as-you-go defined benefit (DB) schemes have been superseded by the more easily managed and flexible defined contribution (DC) plans. Some argue that the defined contribution schemes' popularity stems from their relative cost effectiveness in minimising administrative costs: 'While the possible explanations for the decline in defined benefit plans and shift toward defined contribution plans are numerous, at least part of the reason is the increasing expense of administering defined benefit plans.'[2]

In the past thirty years there has been a more vigorous push for regulation. The United States, Canada, Australia, South Africa, Denmark, Malaysia, Singapore, the Netherlands, the Republic of Ireland and Chile have all witnessed regulatory initiatives which have had both positive and negative effects on the consumer. Regulation, and the way it is administered by government bodies, influences the degree of public confidence in the life insurance and superannuation industries. A high level of public confidence seems not to be dependent on prescriptive regulation such as that found in Singapore and the UK.

Australia's spirit of cooperation between stakeholders, appointed regulatory agencies and the government has meant that future developments and the impact of regulatory changes can be closely scrutinised and commented upon. Bodies such as the Association of Superannuation Funds of Australia (ASFA) have made consistent efforts in education and the assessment of regulatory developments for their members and for employees. As recommended by the recent Wallis Inquiry, the Insurance and Superannuation Commission (ISC), the industry regulator, will be merged with several other financial regulatory bodies. The likely effects on the industry are, at this stage, unclear but criticisms do exist of the complexity and continual modification of regulation. Additional regulatory burdens coupled with severe penalties under trade practices legislation have increased compliance costs significantly in recent years. A worrying development, too, is the possible removal of the Australian Competition and Consumer Commission (ACCC) from regulation of financial services. Despite this, the Australian regulatory model has developed a strong sense of purpose for providing for the retirement needs of all Australians.

Both the Republic of Ireland and Denmark have regulatory agencies which are keen to foster a spirit of consensus and understanding with stakeholders when proposing or implementing new regulations. The system may seem prone to regulatory capture but both the Arbejdsmarkedets Tilloespension (ATP) in Denmark and the Pensions Board in Ireland have had successes in addressing issues that may be expected to impact on the industry in the long term.

Chile's regulations ensure that there are extensive restrictions on investment and distribution by each AFP. Regulation, however, has not prevented many of the problems of distribution. Chile receives praise worldwide for the capital market and economic growth born out of pension

2.   D. M. McGill, K. N. Brown, J. J. Haley and S. J. Schieber, *Fundamentals of Private Pensions*, 7th edn (University of Pennsylvania Press, 1996), p. 40.

reforms, but its regulatory approach undergoes continual refinement and fine tuning. Restrictions have now been lifted on international investments but less than 1 per cent of total pension funds are invested outside Chile. This must have an impact on overall returns from the funds. According to the World Bank:

How well do these regulations serve the affiliates? We find that the net returns to the affiliates in most countries are negative or negligible over the first 4–5 years, and do not beat returns from simple investments such as bank certificates of deposits (CDs), over the long haul. The regulation seems to create profound biases against competition, efficiency, specialisation, or and in favour of excessive direct-marketing expenses. The resulting losses, even if small, can seriously endanger the retirement nest egg, while subjecting the affiliates to inappropriate risk-reward trade-offs in the interim. We attribute these problems to well meaning but counterproductive investment regulation.[3]

In Poland and Hungary, careful attention will have to be paid to whether the new regulatory agencies of the recently reformed pensions industries are proactive or reactive in meeting future challenges. Limited resources, staff shortages and the relative strength of vested interests and lobby groups will need to be considered when implementing planned or existing consumer protection legislation.

The premise of self-regulation is that industry, not government, is best suited to regulating pension funds. In theory, minimal government involvement in regulation may be desirable, but examples exist where such an approach has not worked. South Africa continues to have minimum regulation – an approach which has largely been driven by the industry. Industry groups such as the Life Office Association (LOA) and Institute of Retirement Funds of South Africa (IRFSA) have been very effective in advocating the regulatory direction the Financial Services Board (FSB) should adopt for the industry. This cooperation has been welcomed by the FSB which, like so many of its international regulatory counterparts, is grappling with finite resources. Industry and the FSB are, for different reasons, orientated towards minimising the level of regulation and sanctions. Self-regulation requires a fine balancing act and often the benefits and detriments are difficult to measure.

The life insurance industry in the US, through major industry bodies such as the American Council of Life Insurance (ACLI) and the National Association of Life Underwriters (NALU), has been determined that regulation of pensions products in the third pillar should be minimal and state based. This orientation towards state-based regulation has led to a myriad

---

3. H. Shah, *Towards Better Regulation of Private Pension Funds* (World Bank, 1997), p. 5.

of differing compliance systems. The treatment of a retirement annuity and its associated disclosure requirements in Florida may differ significantly from that found in Montana. Jurisdictional and regulatory distortions often impact on the type of product being sold to the consumer. Some progress is being made by the National Association of Insurance Commissioners (NAIC) but there is reason to be pessimistic of the outcome.

3. DISTRIBUTION

Shifting the responsibility for future retirees' welfare, either by offering tax incentives or by compulsion, may be good economic policy for a government but what effect has it had on the industry? There is evidence that current methods of distribution and, in particular, intermediary remuneration are causing consumer detriment. Distribution methods are crucial to whether a pension system generates acceptance, support and coverage, and is an indicator of regulatory effectiveness. Sales commissions represent an immediate and monetary cost but damage to public confidence through mis-selling has a structural cost on the overall system. The direct and indirect costs of providing retirement incomes are a real concern for governments and industry throughout the world. Increasingly, governments are looking to slow down or contain their social security spending in the shadow of the 'baby boomer' generation and its potential impact on budgets. In the US there is increasing argument about whether the federal government is the most efficient provider of retirement vehicles under the current social security program. Concern has long existed over the Social Security Administration's role in providing social security payments because of the costs generated compared with the Federal Insurance Contributions Act (FICA) contributions received.

For example, the Social Security Administration in the United States reports a cost of US$18.70 per person per year on the same basis. However, this includes only a small charge made to the Social Security Administration by the Internal Revenue Service for the collection of payroll taxes, and does not follow good accounting practices for the measurement of capital costs. As a guess that is probably not too far off, the US system probably costs twice what it reports.[4]

A more stark comment about the costs and perceived benefits from social security, compared with alternatives offered by the insurance industry, was given in congressional testimony by Arthur J. Altmeyer, the Chairman of the Social Security Board from 1937–46 and the first Commissioner

---

4. Diamond, op. cit., n. 1, p. 6.

of the programme from 1946–53. This evidence was recently restated to a Senate Budget Committee looking into Social Security by Dr Sylvester J. Schieber of Watson Wyatt Worldwide:

Therefore, the indefinite continuation of the present contribution rate will eventually necessitate raising the employees' contribution rate later to a point where future beneficiaries will be obliged to pay more for their benefits than if they obtained this insurance from a private insurance company. I say it is inequitable to compel them to pay more under this system than they have to pay to a private insurance company, and I think that Congress would be confronted with that embarrassing situation.[5]

Similarly, concern is being expressed by some vocal consumer groups and academics in Singapore and Malaysia that the national provident funds are generating smaller returns compared with alternative fund-managed products. Recognising this, both governments are allowing their citizens to plan more actively for their retirement rather than simply relying on the Employee Provident Fund (Malaysia) or Central Provident Fund (Singapore).

In South Africa, industry and government believe that the conduct of intermediaries and the way they are remunerated has influenced public confidence in the retirement planning and life insurance system. Remuneration in both South Africa and Zimbabwe is determined on a formula basis but essentially commissions are taken in the first five years of a policy. This encourages new sales and can lead to inappropriate selling. A further concern for South Africa is that a high level of illiteracy heightens the risk of mis-selling:

A nation that once was hidden behind the curtain of apartheid is now increasingly exposed to the reality that overseas influences and methodology will impact on the retirement incomes industry. The central challenge for maintaining and nurturing public confidence in South Africa is overcoming the enormous level of illiteracy that exists in the general population and the difficulties this presents for companies who are intending to cater for this 'black' market.[6]

The link between the activities of intermediaries and public confidence was addressed by the Australian government in the 1990s when it mandated contributions into pension (superannuation) accounts. To combat

---

5. I. S. Falk, *Questions and Answers on Financing of Old-Age and Survivors Insurance*, Memorandum to O.C. Pogge, Director, Bureau of Old-Age and Survivors Insurance, 9 February 1945, p. 13.
6. D. O. Harris, *At the Intersection: An International Study of Public Confidence in the Life Insurance and Superannuation (Pensions) Industry* (Winston Churchill Memorial Trust, 1997), p. 29.

mis-selling and churning which had already taken place in indigenous communities in North Queensland, the federal government introduced a rigorous Code of Practice for Advising and Selling of Financial Services Products to be implemented by the Insurance and Superannuation Commission (ISC). The Code covered appropriate conduct, compliance and, crucially, the improvement of competency standards. Under section 53 of the Trade Practices Act 1974, companies can be fined for marketing material or behaviour which misleads or deceives the public. Penalties and charges can be required of both the intermediary and the product manufacturer under this legislation. Further, industry associations have introduced codes of ethics to tackle inappropriate behaviour. Focusing on the conduct and professionalism of intermediaries seems to have worked. Commissions for retirement products have flattened as competition between banks, life insurers and fund management entities has increased and there has been a shift towards fee-based remuneration. Competition has also improved the overall standards of intermediaries and more agents are being recognised as financial planners and directing their business growth into retirement planning.

Canada has also been successful in establishing an efficient and highly competitive distribution for its third pillar retirement products. Registered pension plans (RPP) and the registered retirement savings plan have provided effective supplements to the existing public retirement programmes. Remuneration is moving towards a more flat-rate commission to encourage intermediaries to maintain a close planning relationship with the client. Standards and competency levels are being improved by the Financial Planners Standards Council of Canada (FPSCC), which argues strongly for self-regulation to solve any shortcomings in standards. In the future, commissions may be reduced further if restrictions forbidding banks from offering retirement advice and distribution are removed.

Similarly, the Netherlands and Denmark have largely avoided problems in the distribution mechanisms for the voluntary third pillar while there has been concern about the cost of the large first pillar in relation to the public's acceptance of comparatively high taxation levels.

The US still faces challenges in trying to improve the overall standards of distribution of private provision. Recent litigation and the actions of state-based regulators indicate a need for improved standards in competency and compliance.

It is Chile, however, which highlights a major concern for the methods of distribution. Since the introduction of its largely privatised and mandated system, distribution costs have remained stubbornly high. Captive consumers see a significant percentage of their contributions being eroded by inefficient distribution. Chile has no limits on commission levels such as those that exist in Malaysia and Singapore. Hermant Shah, Senior Financial Economist with the World Bank says:

Initially AFPs were free to charge fixed and variable commissions based on salaries and account balances, as well on commissions for each deposit, withdrawal, etc. Fixed and variable commissions based on balances have been abolished since 1987. Aggregate commissions, including insurance costs, increased from 5.1 per cent of average taxable salary in 1982 to 8.27 per cent in 1983 and 8.69 per cent in 1984, fell gradually to around 3.1 per cent of salary by 1990, and have been stagnant since.[7]

Another worrying feature is the high incidence of switching between AFPs and consequent commissions in a distribution system which supported an estimated 15,432 agents in 1995. Switching seems to offer little benefit to consumers and involves high pressure selling. Often rebates of sales commissions or gifts of pens or microwave ovens are offered to encourage a switch. Even more alarming is the comment made by the World Bank of the quality of distribution found in Chile:

Of the 22,000 agents registered with the Superintendency, as many as 5,000 have been delicensed as sales agents for forging signatures of affiliates on transfer forms or lesser offences such as providing misleading information. Delisted agents can be, and often are, employed in other parts of the AFPs.[8]

The inefficiency of the distribution system was commented on in an article in *The Economist*:

Between them the AFPs employ 18,000 salespeople one for every 300 active workers. Since all civilians with regular jobs are already in the system, the marketers spend their time inducing workers to switch funds. One worker in four did so in 1996. The costs of all this, of course, are included in the fees workers pay.[9]

4. PRODUCT DESIGN

Many of the lessons to be gained from overseas are associated with the product design and innovation stimulated by regulatory direction or competitive pressures.

In Australia, retirement products flooded the market after the introduction of compulsion. The system allows multiple retirement accounts and

---

7. Shah, op. cit., n. 3, p. 5.
8. Ibid., p. 9.
9. 'Chile Finance: Rewriting the Pensions Textbook', *The Economist*, August 1997, p. 78.

171

these currently number approximately 16 million individual accounts in a population of 18 million. Total assets at the September 1997 quarter were A$316.7 billion. One of the more promising by-products of vigorous competition has been product innovation. Fund mangers are offering superannuation products which are more flexible and reflect the changing work roles and employment patterns of Australians. Additionally, the debate on fund choice by individual employees has focused more attention on product design. Companies now recognise that they have to provide products with greater investment options to meet differing degrees of risk and 'bolted-on' insurance riders to satisfy life insurance needs. Index-linked tracker funds by group (employer) schemes are also now available for those who wish to invest in the stock market but minimise risk. Under new legislation, companies can provide accounts which limit the amount of fees or costs passed onto the consumer. These accounts usually have lower returns because the investment is in fixed-interest securities. The intention behind retirement savings accounts (RSAs) was to provide an account that minimised administrative costs for consumers who moved in and out of the workforce on a regular basis.

Product innovation has been enhanced in Australia by the involvement of the trade union movement in the development of industry-sponsored funds. Many unions have strongly supported the need for their members to have suitable pension coverage and have encouraged high employee/member participation. An indirect result of this has been that comparatively low administration charges have been built into the system through active competition between administrators and fund managers for the business of such schemes. Such competition has also partially restricted the growth in associated charges of similar products offered by different types of funds:

There is no doubt that Australia has benefited by the introduction of Industry Schemes. As non-traditional players with a lot of muscle they have forced costs down and generated a more open and competitive system at all levels. The industry funds and the regulators have forced much more responsibility on the trustees to act independently and a great deal more attention has been paid to communicating with members. The industry schemes have revolutionised member communication.[10]

The US has seen a rapid growth in 401(k)[11] retirement plans offered through employers. These products attract generous taxation benefits and

10. Graham E. N. Rogers, *Australian Industry Superannuation: A Model for the UK?* (Offley House Group, 1996).
11. Employer-sponsored retirement vehicle which has developed rapidly in the United States since the 1980s. Such a product is designed to receive payments on a defined contribution basis. The reference to 401(k) is a regulatory reference to the United States Income Tax Code.

good returns and use a variety of investments. In some cases, the individual employee can choose the investment option according to their own risk/return needs. The plans are sophisticated and flexible and have comparatively low cost structures. The individual retirement account (IRA) is another consumer-friendly vehicle which allows people to plan for retirement using a very portable and flexible product with favourable taxation status.

Canada's registered retirement savings product (RRSP) has been a popular retirement product for many years. Good returns, little evidence of mis-selling, portability and a generous taxation status have made it extremely popular with most working Canadians who seek to supplement Old Age Security and their Canada Pension Plan.

In the Netherlands and Denmark occupational pension schemes are innovative and generous in how they address the issues associated with career breaks for women and the vesting periods for all workers.

5.   REDRESS

A remarkable feature of many overseas systems is the lack of any formal consumer redress mechanism. Complaints handling and dispute resolution do exist but are more often a result of the industry's perceived need to encourage public confidence, maintain efficient business practice and limit universal liabilities than as part of the regulation process.

Australia does have a statutory disputes authority, the Superannuation Complaints Tribunal (SCT), which was established by the Superannuation (Resolution of Complaints) Act 1993. It is one of two free redress avenues available to those with a complaint. Yet recent legal challenges cast doubt on the future of this disputes resolution body. The other is the Life Insurance Complaints Service (LICS), a private independent company set up by the industry in 1990 which has government, consumer and industry representatives on its board. The SCT hears complaints about decisions or the conduct of trustees and/or insurers in relation to regulated superannuation funds, approved deposit funds, life policy funds and annuity policies.

Companies pay according to usage of LICS which takes complaints from all policy holders, some beneficiaries, some people with an interest and people rejected for a policy if they have not been rejected for commercial reasons. Redress schemes such as the LICS are bound by terms of reference (TOR) guidelines which state that common law damages cannot be awarded, only the loss on a policy can be recovered and that commercial decisions such as fees, charges, premiums or risk loading cannot be examined unless they relate to an issue such as deceptive conduct. A panel decision is binding on the company but not on the consumer. There is

173

currently some debate in Australia on establishing a one-stop-shop for complaints.

Dispute resolution in Canada has some similarity to the Australian model but there is no formal mechanism like the LICS. Industry associations such as Canadian Life and Health Insurance Association (CL&HIA) and the Life Underwriters' Association, deal with complaints about intermediaries, products and companies. Provincial regulators provide dispute resolution for members of registered pension plans. Bodies such as the Pension Commission of Ontario have a tribunal which deals with consumer matters involving schemes which fall under the commission's guidelines. Additionally a Pension Benefits Guarantee Fund (PBGF) exists which enables the tribunal to allocate funds to a relevant scheme. The Canadian Association of Financial Planners (CAFP) and Life Underwriters Association of Canada (LUAC) have adopted positive and robust disputes handling procedures at the provincial level using complaints and ethics committees. In recent years consumer concerns have related to the financial solvency of some life insurance providers. The Canadian Life and Health Insurance Compensation Corporation (CLHICC) was set up by the industry in 1989 to resolve the losses incurred by consumers as a result of a company becoming insolvent. Canada now has a very high level of public confidence in the pensions industry and a good mix of regulatory, compliance, disclosure, competency and complaints handling systems.

A pensions ombudsman was established in the Netherlands in 1995 with strong industry backing and funding. No legislation was needed and decisions are enforced by goodwill and industry ethics.

The US does not have a formal structure for redress. The main form of dispute handling and consumer redress is generally by litigation which, in some states, may be initiated by the state regulator.

Single points of contact systems exist in the ombudsmen of Denmark and Singapore. In Singapore the Insurance Ombudsman Bureau (IOB) was set up by the Life Insurance Association (LIA) and is made up of representatives from the Insurance Commissioner's Department, the Consumers' Association of Singapore and representatives from the accounting, legal and medical professions. The IOB provides good access for consumers and costs are essentially borne by industry but it will only examine complaints if no legal action or arbitration is pending. Its decisions are binding on the company but not the consumer. In South Africa a Pensions Adjudicator was established in 1996 to resolve complaints relating to company schemes. It can only hear cases after the complainant and trustees have failed to reach agreement concerning a dispute. The adjudicator's judgment is binding on both parties.

There is little doubt that independent, free, accessible and efficient disputes resolution influences public confidence in the industry and its

174

products. Reliance on litigation is costly to both consumer and industry and attendant publicity can only detract from the reputation of the industry and the regulatory system. Industry-based resolution has the attraction of not being a burden on the public purse but, in terms of public confidence, requires the participation of independent assessors. An ombudsman, if capable of speedy resolution and binding judgments, would seem to offer the most effective form of arbitration. Alternatively, a one-stop-shop for initial enquiries and advice may be the solution where disputes need to be resolved by different regulators. As noted in the 1997 OFT report on pensions:

For consumers the most obvious concern is the lack of a single contact point for all pensions problems other than the state pension. We recognise that, with different providers involved in the occupational as distinct from personal pensions, it may be difficult to achieve a single regulator. Indeed were personal pension providers to become subject to a different regulator for their pensions business than for other financial services, there could be confusion of a different nature. We recommend provision of a single initial contact point for all pension problems other than those relating to the state pension.[12]

6. DISCLOSURE

One of the more sweeping consumer protection innovations of the last five years has been disclosure of charges and commissions. The economic argument for this has been to enable consumers to make an informed choice of product suitable to their needs. Sufficient disclosure is said to include key features of the product and a policy illustration which provides the consumer with a guide to how their individual retirement product will develop over time or be matched against their own individual needs. Disclosure requirements should also provide, as a minimum, details of the frequency of information statements to be produced by the manufacturer and information on complaint resolution, both externally and internally.

There has been a wide difference in the way countries have approached this issue. Australia has adopted a rather detailed disclosure regime, implemented through surrogate legal devices (circulars or directions) from the industry regulator. Minimum standards have been prescribed for the documentation given to consumers, primarily in the sales process. This information with a customer information brochure and a fact-find should enable the consumer to make comparisons between products. The criticism of the Australian model is that consumers are often faced with

---

12. Office of Fair Trading: *Report by the Director-General on Pensions* (HMSO, 1997).

'disclosure overload'. Enormous amounts of information are provided but in some cases this seems to intimidate the consumer. Surveys conducted by the industry suggest that large volumes of disclosure information can often make the consumer rely even more heavily on the commission- or fee-remunerated intermediary for interpretation. Nevertheless, the Australian disclosure requirements may seem moderate when compared to those required in the UK.

In the US, disclosure standards on products offered through occupational schemes are generally satisfactory. Tax incentives encourage employers to maintain adequate and efficient systems for the running of these second-pillar schemes and they tend to regard it as their fiduciary and ethical duty to provide sufficient educational material for their employees:

Firms have sole control of a plan as long as it meets Employee Retirement Income Security Act (ERISA) standards. ERISA's fundamental purpose was to ensure that pension promises would be fulfilled. At the very least, the law was written to minimise moral hazard from under funding and faulty and incomplete information.[13]

In contrast, the third pillar of the US retirement system has displayed severe disclosure inadequacies. This has principally been due to variations in the degrees of disclosure mandated by state-based regulators. Disclosure has been avoided by traditional distribution channels and has failed to protect the consumer. Moreover, public confidence has been severely affected by cases of major life insurers being fined many millions of dollars for conduct which breached comparatively low (by world comparisons) standards of disclosure. Inaccurate or distorted policy illustrations and major misrepresentations of product features were some of the problems found.

South Africa seems to have resisted the worldwide pressure towards improved disclosure. Slow but steady progress has been made by industry bodies developing and implementing industry standards for their members, but this has not been enough. Recent scandals on highly geared products such as those offered by Masterbond demonstrated how inadequate disclosure had not revealed the increased risk to the consumer of such retirement/investment products. The Life Office Association (LOA) has reacted by developing and releasing industry guidelines for its members. Disclosure remains minimal, however, and where it exists the motivation is to avoid mandated requirements being imposed by the government regulator.

Canada has adopted a pragmatic and efficient method of implementing disclosure. In a spirit of consensus it has, at provincial level, brought govern-

13. T. Ghilarducci, *Labour's Capital: The Economics and Politics of Private Pensions* (MIT Press, 1992), p. 89.

176

ment, industry and consumer groups together to actively seek ways to meet the needs of consumers purchasing or supplementing retirement provisions under the first and second pillars. Canada has suffered little if any disparities with consumers' expectations and Canadians have enthusiastically embraced retirement saving through occupational and personal pension accounts. High levels of public confidence in the system seem to have been effected by the efficient and lean forms of disclosure required for retirement products.

In summary, the international experience is that non-existent, inadequate or over-enthusiastic disclosure can lead to consumer detriment and lack of competition. Getting it right in terms of disclosure increases public confidence, encourages retirement saving and forces product providers to 'sell' plans on a more equitable basis.

7.   PUBLIC EDUCATION

Public information campaigns have largely been implemented when a government has been faced with the need to introduce compulsion or persuade its people that own provision offers the only comfortable route to retirement. The motivation has often been of persuasion to political and fiscal practicalities rather than consumer protection. Increasingly, though, there is recognition that public education should be fundamental part of a pension system and that it is the natural corollary or partner to disclosure: 'Consumers need access to a source able to deliver unbiased information on all types of pension, in particular to enable them to make at least a preliminary assessment of the adequacy or otherwise of their own pension arrangements.'[14]

Anne McMeehan, Director of Communications at the Association of Unit Trusts (AUTIF), whose AUTIF FACETS index is tracking the progress of government, regulatory and industry efforts to raise awareness and improve overall public understanding in the UK is quoted as saying:

What come apparent is that the public at large has a very poor level of understanding of even the most basic financial matters. The Government's call for an improvement in standards of education generally must now extend into the incorporation of personal finance across the school curriculum. Without this, young people will enter the working life ill-equipped to address the increasing need to make personal provision for their long term financial security.[15]

---

14.   Office of Fair Trading, op. cit., n. 12.
15.   Press release from the Association of Unit Trusts and Investment Funds, 2 February 1998.

It is also recognised that without effective redress, a public information campaign to convince the populace of the need to provide for retirement could simply drive them into the arms of an industry without adequate safeguards or sufficient will to give 'best advice':

There is still a lot of work needed to improve the quality of post sale information to consumers. Charges and commission still rank as the least well explained policy feature. Just over a million people took out a personal pension in 1993. Over 300,000 were no longer paying into it three years later. Two-thirds of complaints to the PIA Ombudsman are about 'unsuitable advice'. It is not enough to give out public information on products, consumers also need to know about regulation and redress.[16]

The governments of Canada, Denmark, Ireland and the Netherlands have coordinated public campaigns to increase general understanding and the need for pension schemes. In Singapore, the Central Provident Fund uses the media, membership magazines and appoints staff able to handle inquiries from members. Regulatory bodies in Chile and Australia, where the choice of scheme is wider, have been active in promoting the need for pension planning and the features of the system. In Australia an A$11million public information campaign using TV, radio and print media was used to persuade individuals to plan for retirement. The Australian Tax Office was commissioned to provide the Superannuation Community Education Campaign with the help of other government agencies. Focus groups were used to assist in determining awareness, attitudes and understanding of superannuation:

A major hurdle to overcome is that superannuation is difficult to understand. Both industry and government need to make it simpler. People are prepared to be educated as long as the information is easy to understand and appropriately targeted. There are doubts about confidence in what the future holds, a function of the fact that: they don't know what will be the long term value of their savings, the rules and regulations are ever changing, there are no signs of bipartisanship. As well as simplicity, greater predictability needs to be injected into the whole subject. The individual is somewhat frustrated because they can exert little control over the final outcome. They are in the hands of government and the industry.[17]

Leaflets delivered to every household in Australia outlined the superannuation system and explained the need to plan for retirement. Groups such as the Association of Superannuation Funds of Australia (ASFA) and

16. Personal Investment Authority, *PIA Consumer Panel Report* (1997), London.
17. Australian Tax Office, *Superannuation Research First Phase Results: Qualitative Study* (Brian Sweeney & Associates, November 1994).

the Life Insurance Superannuation Association (LISA) provided training for trustees and industry participants. The country, where pension coverage is now 81 per cent, has also been active in improving the standards of product information and sales material.

In the US, almost 50 per cent of workers are covered by one of three pensions plans but more than half of workers who did not graduate from high school or are nearing retirement age have no plan at all. Public education is seen to be the responsibility of government and industry and government agencies use industry for distribution of public education material. The majority of states have now adopted consumer education policies and a minority have mandated that high-school students are instructed in household financial decision-making. According to B. Douglas Bernheim, Daniel M. Garrett and Dean M. Maki:

Mandates significantly increase exposure to financial education, and ultimately elevate the rates at which individuals save and accumulate wealth during their adult lives. These results contribute to the growing body of evidence that education may be a powerful tool for stimulating personal saving.[18]

A previous study, published in 1996, looked at the effects of financial education provided by employers during the 1990s:

Participation in and contributions to voluntary savings plans are significantly higher when employers offer retirement seminars. The effect is typically much stronger for non-highly compensated employees than for highly compensated employees. The frequency of seminars emerges as a particularly important correlate of behaviour. We are unable to detect any effects of written materials, such as newsletters and summary plan descriptions, regardless of frequency.[19]

According to a 1995 survey, 88 per cent of large employers were offering some form of financial education, and more than two-thirds had added these programmes after 1990:[20]

Typically employers provide information and guidance on a range of topics related to retirement planning. By promoting adequate preparation for retirement, an employer may also hope to avoid subsequent conflicts (e.g. over demands for more generous pension benefits) with older, poorly prepared workers. Assistance with

18. B. Douglas Bernheim, Daniel M. Garrett and Dean M. Maki, *Working Education and Saving: The Long Term Effects of High School Financial Curriculum Mandates*, Paper 6085, National Bureau of Economic Research (1997).
19. Patrick J. Bayer, B. Douglas Bernheim and John Karl Scholz, *The Effect of Financial Education in the Workplace: Evidence from a Survey of Employers*, Working Paper 5655, National Bureau of Economic Research (1996).
20. 'Employees Getting More: Investment Education, Planning Help on the Increase', in *Pensions and Investment*, 23 January 1995, p. 74.

179

financial planning may also enhance employee loyalty, improve labour relations, and boost morale. Educational offerings are significantly more common among organisations with multiple plans. It is apparent that frequent seminars have a consistently positive and significant effect on participation in self-directed plans. For non-highly compensated employees, frequent seminars are associated with participation rates that are 11.5 percentage points higher than plans with no seminars. The corresponding figure for highly compensated employees is 6.4 percentage points. These are economically large estimates given mean participation rates – 60 to 80 per cent – in the sample.[21]

The survey revealed that no other medium of providing information and education to employees – either through newsletters or summary plan descriptions – had any significant association with participation rates:

Mean (unconditional) contribution rates are around 3.4 per cent of salary, so the estimates imply that contributions are nearly 20 per cent larger in firms offering frequent seminars. This result is consistent with the hypothesis that retirement education – and frequent seminars in particular – positively affect the size of contributions to self-directed plans.[22]

In Chile, AFPs, forced to compete with each other, have adopted information policies which not only offer a benefit to the companies but also provide education for the workforce. Panels at each AFP provide information on commission charges, the pension fund and the AFP. Each AFP must also provide an information brochure covering certain aspects of the system. When a worker joins, a four-monthly statement, information on the individual's capitalisation account yield and a pension balance booklet must be provided.

In Denmark, a strong degree of cooperation between the employers' federation and the confederation of trade unions has resulted in pension coverage of more than 80 per cent and a positive attitude to pension provision. Consumer information is provided by the Ministry of Social Affairs, the ATP and the pension schemes and consumers are given the chance to manage their own pension plans. Government information is focused on what various tiers of the pension system can offer.

The Central Provident Fund in Singapore has taken the view that public education is of prime importance. Publications outline the services offered by the CPF and giving information on the balances of members accounts is considered to be essential to explain the CPF's purpose. Balances can be obtained by telephone or electronically. The cost of this substantial information is borne by the members.

21. Bayer *et al.*, op. cit., n. 19.
22. Ibid.

By contrast, in South Africa, where it is estimated that one in three is illiterate, nothing is provided in terms of public education. Two in five respondents claim to read information given to them by providers which, in most cases, is an illustration or quotation showing how much they would pay and how much they would get back. Even this disclosure is made on an *ad hoc* basis in a system which has no mandatory competency standards, where up-front commissions and direct selling are normal practice and distribution is concentrated in form of tied agents. The termination of 1 billion rand of annual premiums of retirement vehicles is due to lapses and surrenders and 25 per cent of new business is terminated.

International experience suggests that government, industry and consumer groups have mutually supportive roles to play in public education. One-off campaigns designed to convince people that they need to take responsibility for their own retirement income have limited value and without sufficient requirements for disclosure and redress may well lead to consumer detriment. The provision of information and education should not depend on arbitrary allocation of responsibility. A government has future economic stability to gain from persuading people to plan their own retirement incomes, equipping them with the means to choose the most productive scheme, ensuring effective regulation to deliver what is promised and establishing accessible redress mechanisms. Industry, faced with well-informed consumers would have to market its products; and consumer, trade union and employer groups have a role to play in helping people to make comparisons of products which would encourage competition.

Chapter Eight

SOME CONSUMER PROBLEMS RELATING TO THE SALE OF LONG-TERM INSURANCE

Richard J. Bragg

Chapter Outline

1. The Scope of Insurance

2. The Consumer Problem

3. The Independent Financial Adviser and the Tied Agent
    3.1   The Financial Services Act and regulation
    3.2   The independent financial adviser
    3.3   The tied agent

4. The Perceived Failure of IMRO and the Industry Response

5. How Can the Insurers Prevent Problems?

6. Sanctions

7. Conclusion

Consumer Protection in Financial Services (P. Cartwright, ed.: 90-411-9717-6:
© Kluwer Law International: pub. Kluwer Law International, 1999: printed in
Great Britain)

1. THE SCOPE OF INSURANCE

This chapter, while relating to financial services in general, is limited in its scope to the life insurance industry. It should be realised, however, that it is a small part of a much larger problem.

One of the largest markets for financial services in the UK is in endowment insurance policies, sold to back mortgages and to provide pensions. There is also a substantial market in unit trusts, personal equity plans and other securities. What characterises this market is the very wide range of products available – all offering slightly different outcomes dependent on the success of future investment by the company concerned. Clearly the outcomes are important to consumers because a poor result may mean insufficient money to pay off a mortgage or a poor pension. It should be realised from the outset that endowment insurance is only one way to achieve the necessary objectives and not necessarily the best one.

The current mortgage market is such that there are many quite good deals available to the consumer. This has been as a result of the extension of competition, with all the major banks becoming quite large players in the market. Fixed interest deals are widely available. The obvious choice is between a repayment mortgage or an endowment backed mortgage. The great advantage of the endowment mortgage used to be the tax breaks that it allowed, with relief on premium payments. This stopped some years ago. Indeed, there is now a tax on some premium payments. In the high interest (and high inflation) years such policies gave good returns to consumers and the industry was able to introduce the so-called low-cost endowments, where the profit element of the policy is used to make up the capital sum at maturity while ensuring that the full capital sum would be paid off on death. Today there are doubts whether some such policies will meet their capital sums on maturity. This is a risk which was unexpected at the time the policies were taken out and therefore rarely explained to consumers. Today, most policies are giving a return of 2–4 per cent, which is not startling, given that there is a risk element. Indeed, a no-risk repayment mortgage backed by a protection policy (which is essentially a whole life policy, covering some other risks) seems a better bet. However, endowment mortgages still account for a surprisingly high proportion of the market. The only reason for this is the commissions made by building societies, banks and other brokers. These people push the endowment approach hard and there have been times when it has been presented as the only way to get a mortgage, particularly from secondary lenders.

Similarly, with the diminution in value of the state pension and the long-term problems of an ageing population, the provision by an individual of his own pension makes sense. Endowment insurance, perhaps linked to a deferred annuity, is one way to achieve this.

There is little doubt that a company pension scheme is likely to provide the best option. Most such schemes are contributory by both employees and employer and usually guarantee a retirement on around half salary, with a degree of subsequent inflation-proofing. The down side of such schemes is that they require long-term contribution of up to forty years to get the full benefit. In today's labour market, few employees stay with one firm for that length of time. Although some schemes are transferable between employers, many are not. An employee who has four or five part-pensions (left until retirement as paid up) will not do so well. Even so, the important point here is that the contribution level is high. Since the employer is contributing (despite the well-publicised payment holidays), this amounts to a free investment for the employee.

Such schemes do little for the employee who moves firms very regularly, often with periods of unemployment between. Unfortunately, this is an increasingly common scenario in the modern labour market and company pensions are just not relevant to those who are self-employed. It therefore makes some sense for such individuals to have their own personal pension and that is where the endowment policy comes into play. It was this reasoning behind the government's advertising campaign in respect of personal pension schemes a few years ago, since they wished to avoid people having inadequate or non-existent pensions on retirement, which might have to be made up with social security payments. However, most employers are unwilling to contribute to personal pensions and that element of the contribution is therefore lost. It is, therefore, very unlikely that such a policy would ever give as good a return as a straight company scheme.

While the primary aim of the consumer may be to pay off his mortgage at maturity or to get a pension, it should be remembered that the endowment policy is also a life insurance. In suitable circumstances this is appropriate because it provides family protection in the event of death. The wife does not have to worry about the mortgage and/or will have the pension fund. However, this element provides a risk for the insurer, which is reflected in the premium. For a person with no dependants, a straight investment, without the insurance element, is likely to yield a higher return and a policy may not then be suitable.

The taking out of life policies are not generally high on the list of purchases by ordinary consumers, and thus it is a truism that they are 'sold and not bought'. It is in the mortgage and pension areas that the major opportunities are open to the market to sell their wares and it is an opportunity that they have not been slow to take.

The information above is very basic to anyone with a knowledge of the financial services industry; however, it should be remembered that the vast majority of the population is not aware of it. The degree of public ignorance in relation to such matters is high. There is therefore much room for the exploitation of ordinary consumers and it is that with which the core of this paper is concerned.

2. THE CONSUMER PROBLEM

Most, if not all, life insurance companies are highly reputable and do not in any way condone irresponsible behaviour. However, it must be remembered that the companies do need to continually sell life insurance to keep in business. The problems lie in the selling of insurance by the salesman at the sharp end.

The misleading of consumers, in this context, is so widespread, that documenting it all would be a major task. Mis-selling of investment policies is the largest single cause of complaint. The usual problem is that the selling agent has exaggerated the return from the investment. Although there are rules governing the returns that may be quoted, these are often ignored. A particular example of this came to light following the government advertising campaign in respect of personal pension schemes. Large numbers of people opted out of extremely good company pensions schemes and were sold life insurance policies instead. Since they lost the advantage of the employers' contribution it was very unlikely that such a policy would ever give as good a return, but salesmen were representing that it would give far better results. There are also many cases of policies being sold where they are an inappropriate type of investment (*eg*, endowment policies being sold to people with no dependants ostensibly for short-term savings). There is also much 'churning', *ie*, getting people to give up one policy and take out another, which is very rarely a good idea. Consumers do not realise that endowments are long-term investments and policies accrue very little in the early years because of the front end commissions that are taken out.

Beyond mis-selling are some instances of downright fraud. There have been a number of well-documented cases of agents absconding with large single premiums, by forging policy documents.

3. THE INDEPENDENT FINANCIAL ADVISER AND THE TIED AGENT

It is necessary to distinguish between independent financial advisers, who generally act as the agents of the proposer/policy holder and company agents, who have a more or less permanent relationship with one company, and who are generally the agents of that company. Although that distinction had proved unsatisfactory in a number of areas and the Financial Services Act 1986 attempted to replace it with a new system, the old question of 'who's agent?' is still relevant, for the new system was superimposed upon the old, rather than replacing it completely.

The independent financial adviser is independent of any one insurer. It acts on its own behalf in placing business with insurers on behalf of its client member of the public. It is thus the agent of the insured and, subject to the regulatory rules, the insurer is not responsible for the negligent acts of the adviser.

Tied agents may only sell the products of the company to which they are tied. They are not usually employees but act as independent contractors on the authorisation of the insurer. The insurer will be responsible for the negligent acts of its tied agent.

It is commonly believed in the industry, probably correctly, that clients are unclear as to the distinction between the two types of agent. Indeed, many less intelligent people cannot distinguish between intermediaries and insurers at all and think they are the same thing. This causes much confusion.

3.1 The Financial Services Act and regulation

As large sums of money are involved, both in insurance and elsewhere, there has been some attempt at regulation of the industry and this has largely been done through the Financial Services Act 1986. This set up the SIB to oversee the industry. More recently this has been largely subsumed by the Financial Services Agency which has a wider remit.

The initial control was pyramidical. Each person who was engaged in investment business of any sort covered by the Act was required to be authorised. It is an offence under the Act to act without authorisation.

The SIB authorised a series of subsidiary organisations which companies would normally join. Regulation would be on a voluntary basis bound by a contract of membership.

The initial (relevant) self-regulatory organisations were IMRO (Investment Managers Regulatory Organisation), LAUTRO (Life Assurance and

Unit Trusts Regulatory Organisation) and FIMBRA (Financial Intermediaries Managers and Brokers Regulatory Association).

In general terms the IFAs were required to be authorised by FIMBRA and the insurance companies by LAUTRO. They might also be authorised by IMRO for certain types of business. Where the IFA employed people they were required to be directly authorised by FIMBRA. Tied agents were authorised by their own insurer to act on their behalf and the insurer was responsible to LAUTRO for them.

At each level a person can only be authorised if he is a 'fit and proper person' with the necessary training.

3.2   The independent financial adviser

These go by many names. The more reputable are registered 'brokers' under the Insurance Brokers Registration Act 1977. This required that the name 'broker' could only be used by a person who was registered with the Insurance Brokers Registration Council. Registration was only available to a person who had the requisite amount of capital and assets, was of good character and suitably qualified and agreed to abide by the code of conduct.

In practice, this Act was circumvented both by the less reputable businesses and those who simply did not want to pay the Council's fees by calling themselves something other than 'broker'. A common usage is 'adviser'. This piece of consumer protection legislation was a failure, since the public does not appreciate the meaning of the words.

Under the Financial Services Act, all independent financial advisers, whatever they might call themselves, were required to obtain authorisation from FIMBRA and the voluntary element under the 1977 Act disappeared.

The basic duty laid down by the Financial Services Act and echoed by the FIMBRA rules was that IFAs have a duty to give the client 'best advice'. This implies making a survey of the entire range of products to see what is most suited to the client's needs and to consider whether an insurance policy is the appropriate method of protecting the client's interests.

What, then, are the major problems? Although an IFA is not the agent of one company, and is considered to owe his duty to his client, thus reflecting the traditional position of the broker in pre-1986 law, he normally obtains remuneration by means of commission from the company whose product he sells. This means that he is not completely independent. Misselling (as detailed below) is rife. Difficult cases may arise where the IFA is in possession of policy documents issued by the insurer, and has, or

189

appears to have, the insurer's authority to complete these and to issue policies. Thus the consumer can be deceived by the IFA through the actions of the insurer, although it would be difficult to make the insurer liable for it. The only potential action is in negligence[1] or breach of statutory duty under section 64 of the Financial Services Act.

The IFA is supposed to give best advice. This requires a choice between all available policies. In reality the IFA is faced with an impossible task in this respect. Even with modern computerisation, it would be difficult to cover the whole field. He is likely to advise a policy with the company which pays the most commission. There is also much evidence of the sale of policies where these are not the best form of investment.

The reality of the set-up is that it was a rogue's paradise. The IFAs were required by FIMBRA to contribute to a fund to reimburse consumers who lost money through the actions of an IFA. The fund, which started at a low level saw so many payments made that there was a steeply rising level of contribution. As a result many IFAs ceased to have that status and became tied agents for life business. Even under the newer regimes there are far fewer IFAs than there were some years ago.

3.3 The tied agent

The tied agents, especially those concerned with insurance companies, have been guilty of much mis-selling. As a result large numbers of insurers have been required to reimburse consumers either by the regulators or under section 64 of the Financial Services Act. A number have also been fined by LAUTRO and more recently by its replacement, the PIA.

A tied agent must declare to the prospect at the outset of his dealings his status (*ie*, tied agent) and the name of the company which he represents. Tied agents are also required to disclose their status on any business notepaper which they may use. This is frequently not done. Agents are not supposed to use any written material which is not authorised for that purpose by the insurer, but they often do so. The agent must not advise the cancellation, conversion or lapsing of any policy without a proper study of the investor's circumstances, and unless he bona fide believes this to be in the investor's best interests. However, 'churning' is commonplace.

The agent must have regard to the investor's financial circumstances generally, to any rights under occupational pension schemes, if relevant, and to all other relevant circumstances. He must use his best endeavours

---

1. Examples are *Osman v Moss* [1970] 1 Lloyds Rep 313 and *McNealy v Pennine Insurance Co* [1978] Lloyds Rep 18. These are not life cases, but the principle is the same.

to ensure that he recommends only contracts which are suited to the investor, and that there is no other contract available within the marketing group which would secure the investor's objectives more advantageously. It is suggested that the obligations under this paragraph include not recommending investment policies to persons whose needs would be best served by, for example, saving in a building society.

The agent must not fill in proposal forms unless specifically requested to do so by the proposer. This rule is unrealistic and is almost universally disregarded. However, where the agent is in breach of this rule, any error by the agent will be the insurer's responsibility. The so-called transferred agency clauses which were commonplace a few years ago[2] would almost certainly be declared void today under the Unfair Terms in Consumer Contracts Regulations 1994.

4.   THE PERCEIVED FAILURE OF IMRO AND THE INDUSTRY RESPONSE

The major problems of IMRO were exposed by the Maxwell affair, where it appeared that IMRO was totally unable to control what amounted to a large-scale fraud by Mr Maxwell in milking the company pension fund for his own purposes, apparently without restraint by the other trustees. This resulted in a large number of former employees being left without a pension and current employees being left without pension provision.

It is notable that as a result of all these problems (and an unhelpful tax regime), sales of life assurance policies are currently at an all time low. One major insurer (London Life) has withdrawn from the market.

Partly as a response to the obvious failure of regulation, the SIB decided to scrap the tripartite subsidiary organisations and replace them with a single body to deal with all consumer investment. The Personal Investment Authority (PIA) was set up, whose rules are very similar to, but wider than, those of the former organisations.

Prior to the setting up of the PIA, the insurance ombudsman was responsible for overseeing the insurers, with jurisdiction to order repayment to consumers of up to £250,000. This jurisdiction has now been removed and given to a new Financial Services Ombudsman set up under the PIA. This scheme is less satisfactory in that the jurisdiction is narrower and the scheme is limited to £100,000. However, it does now cover IFAs

2. See *Newholme Bros. v Road Transport & General Insurance Co.* [1929] 2 KB 356; *CCE v Pools Finance* [1952] 1 All ER 775; *Stone v Reliance Mutual Insurance Society* [1972] 1 Lloyds Rep 469.

which the previous scheme did not. Within its own limits this scheme now appears to be working quite well.

The PIA's first job was to deal with the huge volume of complaints relating to the personal pension schemes saga. The reaction of the IFAs has been to litigate rather than to pay, which does not bode well as the outcome. None the less, it appears that the PIA does have some measure of control over them. The insurance companies have been required to put right all the injustices. The major problem here is the lack of speed with which they are acting. The PIA has adopted a policy of 'name and shame' in this respect coupled with substantial fines in some cases for not meeting deadlines. There are still a substantial number of outstanding cases today. Whether total justice will ever be done must remain doubtful.

5. HOW CAN THE INSURERS PREVENT PROBLEMS?

Insurers have considerable problems in preventing consumer difficulties. The companies need to sell policies and anything that prevents this happening will cause cashflow difficulties. A constant level of sales is needed, thus the companies need to create an incentive to sell and so the reaction has always been to sell on commission. The difficulty is that this is exactly what causes salesmen to break the rules. When your next meal is dependent on your ability to sell another policy, the willingness to abide by restrictive rules is limited.

The companies are also restricted by the fact that their tied agents are traditionally self-employed and loosely controlled. There are many who think that they can sell, but few who can consistently. After selling to family and friends, they find sales are hard to come by. Thus agents float in and out of the business, often with only a few months' service. There is an annual turnover of up to 80 per cent of representatives, which makes records hard to keep. It also makes training expensive.

The companies only have a limited control over IFAs. Most insurers require that premium cheques are made payable to the insurer by the proposer, but there are still some IFAs who insist on paying with their own cheques. Most IFAs insist that policy documents are sent to the proposer through them, although this has dangers. Companies who insist too strongly on the rules may find their business from that source dries up.

Regulation regimes within companies have improved in recent years, but still leave something to be desired. There is only a limited amount of information available on this. All firms are required to satisfy themselves that new agents are fit and proper persons. Thus detailed application forms, full references, and interviews are the order of the day. Even this can go wrong, as was shown in *Spring v Guardian Assurance plc*.[3] All agents have to be properly trained. There is some evidence that courses are stronger on selling than regulation, but at least agents are told the rules. Thereafter, the task is one of monitoring. Full records need to be kept.

Clearly, all complaints have to be investigated. Enquiries on potentially suspicious topics need to be treated as complaints. Persistency rates need constant attention. The essential 'know your client' details need to be scrutinised to see both that they exist and that what has been sold is appropriate. This is not always done. Spot checks on individual agents, going through all information and interviewing the client will be cautionary. The reality is that companies do many of these things at a minimum level, both because of its cost and because it is an inhibition on selling. The compliance officer is often at loggerheads with sales managers. Where faults do show themselves the reality is that a review of sales figures is likely to be done before dismissal is contemplated.

Some companies have moved away from selling purely on commission. There is now at least a minimal salary element. Since commission only was always inconsistent with good selling practices, it seems a sensible move.

6.   SANCTIONS

Under the rules, the PIA carries out checks on companies, but is not clear how thorough these are. A number of companies have been fined over breaches of the rules. Companies can and are told to put things right for the consumer. Ultimately the sanction is losing approval, which would prevent them operating. However, this is difficult to contemplate in a commercial market, even for a flagrant breach. It is difficult to see what other remedies could be available to the PIA in a voluntary regulation, but the continuing breaches suggest that try as it might its current efforts are somewhat ineffective.

In practice, it seems highly unlikely that the PIA will be particularly effective in the long term. It is a last ditch attempt at voluntary regulation before legislation. The change of government precipitated some change from the start with a new regime of the Financial Services Authority replacing the SIB (with a wider remit) and legislation to come. It is as yet unclear whether voluntary regulation in the form of the PIA will survive this. It seems likely that some statutory regulation will emerge.

---

3.   [1995] 2 AC 996, a case on negligence in the giving of references.

7.   CONCLUSION

It is difficult to foresee the future. Consumers are clearly aware that there is a problem, although most do not really understand what it is. Unless the industry sorts out its problems, some highly profitable business will be lost and it is likely that those with current policies will be adversely affected by a downturn in profit bonuses, thereby making the current situation worse. The cost of putting right the wrongs is bound to affect profits.

Consumers are now more likely to require some very firm promises that their investment is a good one, but it seems likely that legislation backed by criminal sanctions will be required eventually to control the misrepresentations of the inevitably over-enthusiastic salesman.

PART FOUR

INSURANCE

Chapter Nine

INSURANCE LAW REFORM FOR THE BENEFIT OF THE CONSUMER: SOME LESSONS FROM AUSTRALIA*

John Birds

Chapter Outline

1. Introduction

2. The Need for Law Reform

3. The Reform Process in Australia

4. Consumer Protection Provisions in the Australian Legislation
    4.1   Intermediaries
    4.2   Non-disclosure and misrepresentation
    4.3   Utmost good faith
    4.4   Formation issues
    4.5   Prohibition of contract terms
    4.6   General restriction on the insurer's right to avoid a claim
    4.7   Standard cover
    4.8   Protection in non-prescribed contracts
    4.9   Other Australian reforms

5. Reactions to the Australian Legislation

6. Self-regulation in Australia

7. Lessons from Australia

Consumer Protection in Financial Services (P. Cartwright, ed.: 90-411-9717-6: © Kluwer Law International: pub. Kluwer Law International, 1999: printed in Great Britain)

1.   INTRODUCTION

In Britain, the fact that aspects of insurance contract law are capable of operating harshly on the weaker party has been known for years and has attracted the attention of judges and law reform agencies as well as academic commentators. However, despite the attention and the official reports, no real law reform has yet been effected.[1] Instead we have self-regulatory Statements of Practice and the beneficial, but strictly voluntary, practices of the Insurance Ombudsman. It took eight years from when the Law Commission first looked at non-disclosure and breach of warranty[2] to achieve the partial non-statutory 'implementation' of their relatively modest recommendations in the 1986 version of the Statements of Insurance Practice. In contrast, in about the same length of time, the Australian Law Reform Committee conducted a thorough enquiry which led to substantial legislative reform.

The theme of this chapter is that the time has come for us to look seriously at what Australia has done.[3] Our insurance contract law needs proper amendment to be fair to consumers,[4] and the Australian legisla-

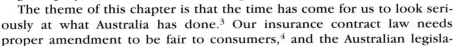

---

*   This is a revised and updated version of a paper presented at the Society of Public Teachers of Law Consumer Law Group conference in September 1996. Much of the work which enabled me to produce this paper was carried out for the National Consumer Council who, based on this work, published their Report *Insurance Law Reform: the Consumer Case for a View of Insurance Law* in May 1997. Obviously my thoughts have benefited from discussions with people there, in particular Frances Harrison, who was jointly responsible for the production of the NCC Report.

1.   The only matter of note is the application of the Unfair Terms in Consumer Contracts Regulations 1994, SI 3159, to insurance contracts, but they are unlikely to be held to apply to many of the problematic aspects of insurance law. For discussion see *Birds Modern Insurance Law*, 4th edn, pp. 3–8, 91–3, 197–9. Also see 'Consumer Protection in Insurance Contracts' by C. Willett and N. Hird in this volume.

2.   Their report *Insurance Law: Non-disclosure and the Breach of Warranty*, Cmnd 8064, was published in 1980, but the earlier Working Paper was published in 1978.

3.   Other countries with a common law background, for example Canada, Australia and the US, have also introduced some statutory reforms of insurance law over the years, although these have not been as comprehensive as the Australian model and, with differences of degree rather than substance, have not covered areas which are not covered by the Australian law.

4.   As to what should be meant by 'consumers' in this context, see below. The fact that the courts have in some recent cases seemingly attempted to reach results which are fairer to the insured than previous case law might indicate does not, it is submitted, remove the need for a general review and statutory reform. For example, even though the House of Lords in *Pan Atlantic Insurance Co. v Pine Top Insurance Co.* [1995] 1 AC 501 introduced the inducement requirement into the test of materiality for the purposes of the duty of disclosure, it seems unlikely to make much difference in practice given the presumption of inducement (quite apart from its somewhat dubious provenance: see Birds and Hird, 'Misrepresentation and Non-disclosure in Insurance Law: Idential Twins or Separate Issues?' (1996) 59 MLR 285. Potentially more significant, perhaps, is the Court of Appeal decision in *Economides v Commercial Union Assurance C. plc* [1997] 3 All ER 639, where it was

tion, passed against the background of an identical common law base to our own, provides a model for this which can teach us a great deal; although there is no doubt that not all aspects of what has happened there should be followed here.[5]

2. THE NEED FOR LAW REFORM

It may be worth attempting briefly to spell out again why the case for law reform remains strong, as there has always been very strong resistance from a very powerful lobby to such reform, even from quarters which are quite happy to 'give up' legal rights under a self-regulatory regime.

A number of reports on insurance have recently been published by organisations representing business, government and the consumer; the National Consumer Council has recently published[6] a general report arguing for law reform with a fair amount of case study evidence of the problems that the law continues to cause consumers. To counter the argument that self-regulation has improved and will continue to improve the lot of consumers, it may be said that it is not clear that consumers have in fact always benefited in practice. By far the most far reaching benefits have probably been due to the Insurance Ombudsman,[7] and clearly of particular value to consumers is his ability to depart from case law to consider what is fair and reasonable in all the circumstances. His decisions, because they are binding on member insurers, have no doubt affected the behaviour and practice of those insurers who have voluntarily signed up to the scheme. However, there remains the gap between those insurers who voluntarily submit to and fully comply with self-regulation and those that do not.

(continued)

    held in effect that proposal form misrepresentations required to be made to the best of the proposer's knowledge and belief (a requirement which derives from the Statements of Insurance Practice) were actionable only if the proposer could be shown to have made them fraudulently, and there are hints that there might not be a duty to disclose matters outside the scope of the questions expressly asked. However, this decision seems a little suspect as a matter of strict law, and it can hardly apply to questions of non-disclosure where there is no proposal form, for example telephone applications and renewals.

5.   To the extent that there is a legal difference this paper concentrates on general, *ie*, non-life, insurance. Protecting the consumer of life insurance raises, of course, many additional issues as most forms of life insurance are investments under the Financial Services Act 1986.
6.   See n. 1 *supra*.
7.   For recent consideration of the Ombudsman, see especially James, chapter 2 in *Private Ombudsmen and Public Law* (Dartmouth, 1997) and Morris and Hamilton, 'The Insurance Ombudsman and the PIA Ombudsman: a Critical Comparison' (1996) 47 NLIQ 119.

Although insurers covering some 90 per cent or so of British insurance consumers belong to the Insurance Ombudsman Bureau (IOB) and/or the Association of British Insurers (ABI), there still exists a substantial minority who are not parties to the self-regulatory devices which exist. Further, this gap between insurers may widen following the opening up of the single European market.[8] This is surely a real cause for concern.

There are perhaps two further reasons why a proper review of the law with a view to reform is necessary, both arising from technological developments. Insurance is increasingly being bought and sold by telephone and machine. Given the central importance of the concepts of utmost good faith and disclosure of information to insurance law, the question arises as to how important these can be in reality when contracts are effected without any personal or written contact; although there will invariably be a contract recorded in writing, this is likely to appear after a binding contract has actually been concluded.

Second, insurers are increasingly using shared electronic data. This may be a legitimate response to a growing problem of fraud, but it could place consumers in a difficult position in that insurers may have access to information which may not be material in the strict legal sense, so that an insured would not legally be obliged to disclose it, but which none the less might prejudice an insurer's view of a particular insured. For example, an insurer may have access to details of a previous accident or claim of which its own underwriting practices do not require disclosure, because they are not sufficiently recent or significant. There may not be an issue of avoiding an existing contract, more one of a contract never coming into being in the first place.

An important question that will need to be addressed in the event of legislation being actively considered by government is the scope of any such legislation, in other words what is meant by 'consumer' in this context. The Australian model does not distinguish between individual consumers and commercial insureds[9] but British practice hitherto, under the Statements of Practice and the jurisdiction of the Ombudsman, has been only to protect the individual insuring in his or her private capacity. It is

---

8. Although the IOB has agreed to extend the membership of the Bureau to cover mainland European insurers transacting personal insurance in the UK, it is not clear how successful this will be. European insurers will be able to ignore the ABI's self-regulatory measures if they wish. Whether or not the Commission will raise again the mater of harmonisation of insurance contract law is as yet unclear. The introduction of freedom of services in insurance was effected in such a way as to remove the necessity for this. Of course the EC's general consumer protection reform in respect of unfair terms applies to consumer insurance contracts, but it is not clear that this will have much effect on insurance contracts in practice: see n. 2, *supra*.
9. Although it exempts some categories of insurance entirely: see *infra*.

arguable that at the very least the small business needs similar protection to the individual consumer.[10]

3.   THE REFORM PROCESS IN AUSTRALIA

It may be helpful to outline briefly the process of insurance law reform in Australia which led to substantial legislation in 1984. It is believed that there was the same general unease and dissatisfaction as here among lawyers, both practising and academic, about aspects of the subject. This was not in any way tempered by the equivalent of our Statements of Insurance Practice. The situation provided sufficient rationale for the Law Reform Committee to look at the subject as a whole as one of their first substantial projects. An issues paper in 1977 was followed by a discussion paper in 1978, two reports in 1982 and two Acts of Parliament in 1984, among which was widespread discussion and consultation involving written and oral hearings and public meetings. It seems clear that the Committee's proposals, and the changes implemented by the Insurance Contracts Act 1984 and the Insurance (Agents and Brokers) Act 1984, had widespread support, and, very importantly, that there was the political will to implement the final recommendations.

In addition, it is thought that Australia has provided a model which appears to have worked well, in the sense that it has been to the benefit of consumers, without any significant financial implications, and has not antagonised the insurance providers. I refer later in this paper to some evidence received which supports this view. Before then, it seems appropriate to describe some of the provisions of the Australian legislation and comment as to their appropriateness as models for law reform here.

4.   CONSUMER PROTECTION PROVISIONS IN THE AUSTRALIAN LEGISLATION

The following paragraphs give a brief overview[11] of those provisions in the (Australian) Insurance Contracts Act 1984[12] and the Insurance (Agents and

10.   See for example the fairly arbitrary treatment of a small businessman in *Spring v Royal Insurance Co. (UK) Ltd* [1997] CLC 70, for which the common law was unable properly to compensate.
11.   A most useful commentary is Mann and Lewis, *Annotated Insurance Contracts Act*, 2nd edn (LBC Information Services, 1997), wherein references can be found to the growing body of case law interpreting the Australian legislation. The following description does not pretend to constitute an authoritative account of the current state of Australian law.
12.   Note that s. 15(1) provides for the Act to be an exclusive statutory code when it applies; so particular state legislation and other Commonwealth legislation does not

Brokers) Act 1984 which can be regarded as having a significant consumer protection focus. It is not felt necessary to examine those aspects which may have brought about a welcome reform of the law, but were either designed to bring the law into line with standard practice[13] or are likely to operate far more for the benefit of commercial insureds than consumer insureds.[14]

4.1 Intermediaries

The law relating to insurance intermediaries was reformed by the Insurance (Agents and Brokers) Act 1984.[15] First there are provisions imposing registration and financial probity requirements on brokers, similar to those contained in the (British) Insurance Brokers (Registration) Act 1977. However, what is notable about the Australian Act is that it defines a broker as someone who carries on the business of arranging contracts of insurance as agent for intending insureds;[16] and thus any independent intermediary is caught by the Act, not simply those who, as in Britain, chose to describe themselves as insurance brokers. Brokers in Australia must operate under a written agreement with the insurer or insurers in question.[17]

In general, the 1984 Act retains the position at common law that brokers are agents of the insured. However, where a broker acts under a binder with authority from an insurer to enter into or deal under insurance contracts, he is statutorily deemed in this respect to be the agent of the insurer.[18]

(continued)
>
> apply except to insurance contracts not covered by the 1984 Act (principally marine, aviation and transport insurances).
>
> 13. For example, the provision amending the law on insurable interest in life insurance (ss. 18 and 19) now further reformed and simplified by the Life Assurance (Consequential Amendments and Repeals) Act 1995. In reality these probably legitimated what has long been common practice in respect of who can insure someone else's life and for what amount. A proper tidying up of British law would no doubt deal with these matters, but the regulation of most forms of life insurance by the Financial Services Act no doubt means that in practice no problems will arise.
> 14. For example, the provisions amending the law on insurable interest in general insurance (ss. 16 and 17). These allow a far broader definition of when someone can insure property than the common law, but it would be extremely rarely that an individual consumer would wish to take advantage of this.
> 15. This Act has been amended by subsequent legislation.
> 16. Insurance (Agents and Brokers) Act 1984, s. 9.
> 17. Ibid., s. 10.
> 18. Ibid., s. 15. This is probably the position in English law, as there are cases holding a broker to be agent of the insurer for such purposes (see specially *Stockton v Mason* [1978] 2 Lloyd's Rep 430, but compare *Winter v Irish Life Assurance plc* [1995] 2 Lloyd's

Australian intermediaries who are not brokers are deemed to be agents of the insurer 'in relation to any matter relating to insurance and between an insured or intending insured and an insurer'.[19] Further, and very importantly, section 11 imposes responsibility on an insurer for the conduct of its agents in relation to any matter relating to insurance where a person in the circumstances of the insured, or intending insured, could reasonably be expected to rely on the agent; and, the insured or intending insured in fact relied in good faith. This responsibility applies notwithstanding that the agent did not act within the scope of his authority, and the insurer is statutorily liable for damages. This provision goes far beyond the common law and dispenses with the need for enquiries as to the agent's actual or apparent authority.[20] It has the clear benefit of imposing on insurers day-to-day responsibility for monitoring the activities of its agents.

4.2 Non-disclosure and misrepresentation

The Australian legislation (the Insurance Contracts Act 1984) dealt with the notorious questions of non-disclosure and misrepresentation in a way which parallels, but in some ways significantly differs from, the English Law Commission recommendations[21] as 'implemented' in the 1986 version of the Statements of Practice and the practices of the Insurance Ombudsman. There is a requirement on insurers to give notice in writing of the general nature and effect of the duty of disclosure, in the absence of which the insurer cannot rely upon anything other than a fraudulent concealment.[22] The duty to disclose is recast as a duty to disclose facts which either the insured knows to be relevant to the insurer's decision or which a reasonable person in the circumstances could be expected to know to be so relevant.[23] Further, an untrue statement made by an insured is not a misrepresentation if the insured honestly believed it to be true and is a misrepresentation in law only if the insured knew, or a reasonable person in his position could be expected to have known, that the statement would have been relevant to the insurer's decision.[24]

(continued)
Rep 274 on imputation of knowledge), but, of course, the benefit of a statutory rule is that the position is made indisputable.
19. Ibid., s. 12.
20. See *Estate of Bottom v Prudential Assurance Co. Ltd* (1992) 7 ANZ Ins Cas 61-129.
21. See n. 3, *supra.*
22. Insurance Contracts Act 1984, s. 22. Statutory references hereafter are to this Act.
23. S. 21.
24. S. 26.

Even if there is a relevant non-disclosure or misrepresentation, the insurer has no remedy if its decision would not in fact have been any different,[25] and the traditional remedy of avoidance of the whole contract is available only for a fraudulent non-disclosure or misrepresentation. For a non-fraudulent non-disclosure or misrepresentation, the insurer's liability is reduced to what would have been its position if there had been no non-disclosure or misrepresentation, basically entitling the insurer only to deduct the extra premium that it would have charged, although it seems that if the insurer would not have taken the risk at all, then its liability can be reduced to nil.

The Australian model thus removes any reference to the judgement of either the prudent or the actual insurer in determining the 'materiality' of facts. It depends entirely on what the insured or a reasonable insured would consider to be relevant. The consequences of a non-disclosure or misrepresentation are not the same as under the proportionality approach adopted by the Ombudsman, and potentially much more beneficial to the consumer.

The basis of the contract clause is abolished, so that statements of existing fact made in, or in connection with, a contract of insurance can only be mere representations[26] and thus, if false, actionable only if material and in accordance with the provisions already described.

4.3 Utmost good faith

Section 14 of the Insurance Contracts Act provides that a party to an insurance contract is precluded from relying on a provision in it if such reliance would amount to a failure to act with the utmost good faith. This supports the general codification of the principle of utmost good faith in section 13:

A contract of insurance is a contract based on the utmost good faith and there is implied in such a contract a provision requiring each party to it to act towards the other party, in respect of any matter arising under or in relation to it, with the utmost good faith.

The full import of this has yet to be seen but it clearly opens the way for the development in Australian insurance contract law of doctrines of good faith and unconscionability being seen in general contract law and long the subject of civil law systems.[27] It has been held that an insurer who

---

25. S. 28.
26. S. 24.
27. Of course it may well be that they are developing in British insurance contract law, but statutory provisions like those in Australia can give a particular impetus.

unreasonably delayed in paying a claim was in breach of contract by virtue of the term implied by section 13,[28] and that the duty of utmost good faith required insurers to bring to the insured's attention the general nature and effect of the insured's obligations under the contract; a failure to do so meant that the insurers could not rely upon the breach.[29]

4.4   Formation issues

A number of provisions made changes to cover particular problems which case law had thrown up regarding the formation of an insurance contract. As far as a contract formed by a cover note or any other interim contract is concerned, its efficacy cannot be made subject to the receipt of a satisfactory proposal[30] and the insured is protected from the expiry or immediate cancellation of a cover note by a provision[31] which ensures that he will have three clear days to arrange alternative insurance.

Section 58 requires insurers to send out notice of renewal of a renewable insurance contract (most non-life contracts). This must give at least fourteen days notice in writing of the expiry of the insurance and indicate whether the insurer is prepared to negotiate or renew the cover. If the insurer fails to do this, and the insured has not obtained alternative cover, cover with the insurer is statutorily extended, potentially for as long as the expired contract (although it may be cancelled before such a period expires). The insured pays a premium calculated according to a formula in the Act.

4.5   Prohibition of contract terms

Under the Insurance Contracts Act, certain terms are declared void and so such terms no longer appear as standard-form provisions in contracts to which the Act applies. The terms in question are as follows:

---

28.   *Moss v Sun Alliance Australia Ltd* (1990) 6 ANZ Ins Cases 60-967. Quaere what the damages were. If they were no more than interest, arguably the common law might provide that anyway.
29.   *Australian Associated Motor Insurers Ltd v Ellis* (1990) 54 SASR 61. See also the unreported decision in *Gutterridge v Commonwealth of Australia*, 25 June 1993, cited by Mann, op. cit., n. 11, para. 13.40.8 (insurer's obligation to communicate its decision in a reasonable time.) A third party who may benefit under a contract of insurance is also subject to the duty: *C. E. Heath Casualty & General Insurance Ltd v Grey* (1993) 32 NSWLR 25.
30.   S. 38(1).
31.   S. 38(2).

- arbitration clauses;[32]

- other insurance provisions, that is provisions which seek to make the insurance ineffective if the risk is covered by other insurance, unless the insurance is genuinely insurance for excess of loss over and above another specified insurance;[33]

- exclusions from or limitations of cover in respect of sickness or disability (in the case of insurance of a person) or in respect of pre-existing defects or imperfections (in the case of a thing) of which the insured was reasonably unaware at the time of entry into the contract;[34]

- cancellation clauses which are not in accordance with the general provisions of the Act concerning cancellation;[35] basically, an insured has to be given at least three days' notice of cancellation in order to find an alternative insurer;

- any provision allowing unilateral variation of policy terms by the insurer to the prejudice of anyone other than the insurer.[36]

4.6 General restriction on the insurer's right to avoid a claim

Perhaps the most important consumer protection measure in the Insurance Contracts Act is section 54 which provides for a general restriction on the insurer's right to deny a claim where there is a breach of some provision of a policy by reason of an act or omission of the insured,[37] typically a breach of warranty or condition. There is a distinction between conduct which cannot in principle cause a loss, and conduct which can cause a loss. As well as being an important consumer protection measure, the section is also causing difficulties of construction.[38]

As far as conduct which cannot cause a loss is concerned, the insurer cannot refuse to pay the claim, but the amount of the claim is reduced by so much as fairly represents the extent to which the insurer's interests were prejudiced. In effect, the insurer is entitled to counterclaim for damages. Typical examples of such situations would be breaches of conditions concerning giving notice and particulars of loss, and breaches of terms requiring a particular qualification, *eg*, the holding of a licence to

32. S. 43(1).
33. S. 45.
34. Ss. 46 and 47.
35. S. 63. These are contained in part VII.
36. S. 53. This does not apply to, among others, life insurance contracts.
37. Or some other person.
38. See the comments of the High Court of Australia in *Ferrcom Pty Ltd v Commercial Union Assurance Co. of Australia Ltd* (1993) 7 ANZ Ins Cases 61-156. Clearly lessons could be learnt if Britain were to contemplate introducing a similar provision.

drive a motor vehicle. In certain cases the insurer may well be unable to show any real prejudice and thus the claim will not or barely be reduced. In other situations, though, it may be able to show that it would have charged an additional premium and/or imposed an additional excess; such sums will determine the 'damages' to which it is entitled and the amount by which the claim is reduced. In certain cases, the prejudice might be such that the insurer would not have insured at all or cancelled the policy, so that the claim is reduced to nil.[39]

Where the insured's act or omission was reasonably capable of causing or contributing to the loss, the insurer may refuse to pay the claim, unless one of the three following qualifications applies:

(i) If the insured proves that no part of the loss was *actually* caused by his act or omission, the insurer cannot refuse to pay the claim. For example, a personal accident policy might exclude liability if the insured suffers injury while intoxicated; if the insured is injured is a car accident when drunk but not driving or in any way responsible, he would be able to recover.

(ii) If (i) applies in relation to a part of the loss, the insured can recover for that part.

(iii) If the act or omission was necessary to protect the safety of a person or to preserve property or where compliance with the policy was not reasonably possible, the insured may recover.

4.7 Standard cover

There are two diametrically opposed ways of trying to ensure that consumers make an informed choice in a competitive insurance market. The current British approach is, of course, to leave it up to market forces, with some general protection for consumers against unfair terms. An alternative, which has been favoured in some mainland European regimes, is to prescribe standard cover and minimum liabilities, so that consumers can choose on the basis of price, extra cover provided and other features. This was the approach favoured by the Australian Law Reform Committee and was enacted in section 35 of the Insurance Contracts Act[40] in respect of the following types of insurance: motor vehicle, home buildings, home contents, sickness and accident, consumer credit and travel. The Act allows an insurer to provide less than the standard only if the insured is notified clearly in writing or, when the insured knew, or a reasonable person in the

---

39. See *Ferrcom Pty Ltd v Commercial Union Assurance Co. of Australia Ltd supra.* See also, *eg, Australian Associated Motor Insurers Ltd v Ellis* [1990] 5 SASR 61.

circumstances could be expected to have known that the insurer was liable only for a lesser amount or that the particular risk was not covered by the contract of insurance.

For example, a motor insurance policy must cover theft of or accidental damage to the vehicle or its accessories,[41] but liability may be excluded in respect of depreciation, wear and tear, rust and corrosion, when the insured is driving the vehicle under the influence of drink or drugs or where the vehicle is being used in various motor sports. This model recognises the consumer protection aspects of standard cover, but equally protects the insurers in accepting the propriety of standard exclusions.

The scheme also provides for minimum monetary liabilities on insurers in respect of compulsory cover. In respect of the above insurances which are contracts of indemnity, this is generally 'the amount sufficient to indemnify the person who made the claim'.[42]

There are aspects about section 35 which may in practice have made it fairly ineffective as a consumer protection measure. First, there is scope for much argument about what the insured knows or a reasonable person would know. Second, it seems that notice in writing of less than the standard cover is satisfied by the handing over of a copy of the proposed contract, *ie*, the insurer's relevant policy. The Act contains no general controls over the comprehensibility of insurance policies; so in a situation where the contract provides for less the statutory minimum, but the insured had a copy in advance, (s)he will be left for protection with whatever common law principles of construction provide, and the general principle of utmost good faith. It remains to be seen whether the latter principle can be used in terms which would affect the basic cover provided under an insurance contract rather than simply dealing with questions of notification. Australia has now dealt with these points in the Code of Practice which is referred to below, and the repeal of the formal legal provisions dealing with standard cover is now being actively considered. As, in Britain, the 1994 Regulations[43] do in effect require 'plain English', so dealing with one of the problems which the Australians have found, we might be better advised, as things stand at the moment, to leave the question of cover provided to market forces.

---

40. Supplemented by the Insurance Contracts Regulations 1985, Regs 5, 9, 13, 17, 21, 25.
41. It must also cover third party liability for property damage, which is of course compulsory in the UK under the Road Traffic Act 1988.
42. Plus, in respect of buildings insurance, sufficient to cover the reasonable cost of emergency accommodation, demolition and removal of debris and identifying and locating the cause of destruction or damage concerned if it is necessary to do so to effect a repair. There is also a permitted excess in respect of earthquake damage.
43. See n. 2, *supra*.

4.8 Protection in non-prescribed contracts

In respect of contracts which are not covered by section 35, section 37 precludes an insurer from relying on a provision of a kind that is not usually included in contracts of insurance that provide similar insurance cover unless, before the loss occurred, the insurer gave to the insured a copy of the policy document or of the provision, or the insurer clearly informed the insured in writing of the effect of the provision. The potential difficulties and costs of litigation in deciding what is 'usually included' no doubt mean that insurers ensure that the insured has a copy of the policy in all cases. This in itself is perhaps no bad thing – there are many instances here where the full contract is not always readily available.

4.9 Other Australian reforms

The Insurance Contracts Act effected some other reforms of a more *ad hoc* nature but clearly intended to benefit the individual consumer insured. There is a general restriction of subrogation rights against members of the insured's family and employees of an insured employer.[44] This provides guaranteed protection which is only available here by virtue of contract terms or insurers' forbearance – neither seems reliable enough. A term excluding or limiting the insurer's liability by reason that the insured is party to a contract which affects the insurer's subrogation rights is ineffective in the absence of a pre-contract warning to the insured of the effect of the term.[45]

Another related issue which the Insurance Contract Act tackled is the relationship between excess clauses and subrogation. Section 67 in essence entitles the insured, where the insurer has successfully pursued a right of subrogation, to recover from the insurer, if appropriate, sufficient to ensure that he is fully indemnified for his loss. This is almost certainly contrary to the common law position[46] and, further, it may be that a similar provision should be sought to deal with cases of under-insurance and average where there are subrogation recoveries.

As far as average clauses in general are concerned, the Australian Act provides a useful model which seems to balance fairly the interests of insured and insurer.[47] It provides first that an average clause may not be relied upon unless the insured had pre-contract notice in writing of its

---

44. S. 65.
45. S. 68.
46. See *Napier v Hunter* [1993] AC 713.
47. S. 44.

nature and effect, and even where this is complied with, the operation of such a clause in a homeowner's policy (covering a principal residence and/or its contents) allows a 20 per cent margin of error in valuation in favour of the insured.

5.   REACTIONS TO THE AUSTRALIAN LEGISLATION

In an attempt to assess the impact of the Insurance Contracts Act and the Insurance (Agents and Brokers) Act 1984, the writer corresponded with a number of people in Australia representing consumer and industry interests as well as with some academic lawyers with an interest in the area. While this clearly was not a scientific survey, the resulting replies gave opinion from a fairly wide spectrum and the result was almost universal satisfaction.

From a consumer point of view, it was said that a much better balance in the law had been achieved and some of the specific points highlighted as constituting major advances were:

- the mandatory notice of the duty of disclosure impacting on the quality of information and attention paid to it;
- the requirement on insurers to issue renewal notices, which has substantially reduced the instance of complaints concerning lapsed insurance coverage;
- the fixing on insurers of responsibility for the actions of their agents even where the latter act outside the scope of their actual or apparent authority has led to much more careful selection and training of agents.

Perhaps more interesting in some ways was the reaction of the insurance industry, in the shape of a very helpful response from Robert Drummond, the National Manager, Technical Services of the Insurance Council of Australia, the equivalent of the ABI. His general view was as follows:

Because of the extensive consultation that took place between the insurance industry and the Australian Law Reform Commission we would have to say that the industry was satisfied it could accommodate the legislation in its final form, and our experience since then has confirmed that to be the case. In some respects the legislation merely reflected or put into words many practices adopted by responsible insurance companies, and otherwise laid down some general rules which were generally considered to be fair and reasonable to all parties. That is not to say however that the industry hasn't had some difficulty with the interpretation placed on some clauses by the courts not some of the less prescriptive or subjective clauses.

Specific points referred to included the following. The industry could live with prescribed cover for standard policies because it persuaded the legislature to allow derogation by providing a copy of the policy in advance. It had, with some difficulty, to learn to live with the watering down of the impact of warranties. The law regarding the duty of disclosure was said to be one of the most difficult areas for both insurers and insureds. In particular, how should the insurer explain the duty to the insured, what level of understanding is the insured expected to exercise in making disclosure, and to what extent should the insurer be permitted to react in the event of non-disclosure? The problem was said to be compounded with regards to innocent co-insureds or people from non-English-speaking backgrounds and by the move into direct telephone selling of insurance. These are understandable difficulties, but the fact that they exist does not, of course, destroy the argument for law reform. They may well, though, assist in assessing the best way in which law reform can be effected.

A further point made on behalf of the industry was the welcome given to the Insurance (Agents and Brokers) Act in its formal separation of the amateur and part-time intermediary from the professional. 'The general public has gradually improved its understanding of the difference between the two groups and can be comforted by the fact that in each case certain security is available in the event of some impropriety or negligence.'

Although reaction in Australia to the 1984 legislation was generally positive, it was recognised that there were improvements needing to be made. One view expressed from the consumer side, albeit this was a minority view, was that the legislation had very little impact on either consumers or industry prior to the establishment of the complaints scheme referred to below. Others thought that the change in the law had had some positive benefits for consumers but were clear that merely changing the underlying law was not enough. One problem was that no appropriate government department had specific authority for overseeing the legislation. As a result the Insurance Contracts Act was amended by the Insurance Laws Amendment (No. 2) Act 1994.[48] This has given the Insurance and Superannuation Commissioner (who has long had responsibility for the financial supervision of insurers) responsibility for administration of the 1984 Act, including giving him the power to take representative legal action on behalf of insureds, and to demand copies of policies and other documentation, including intermediaries' training manuals.

---

48. There have been other minor amendments, some of which have been briefly noted above.

The Australian legislation was also operating in the context of a legal system without appropriate alternative dispute resolution procedures and even though, as mentioned above, the law has been amended to allow representative legal action, individual consumers also need effective means of pursuing individual legal claims. In addition, while the framework for best practice in dealing with insurance consumers can be laid down in legislation, the detail is best spelt out in a more flexible code of practice-type structure. Both of these defects have been addressed in recently adopted practices which may be described as self-regulatory, although government has no doubt been pulling many of the strings. These practices, which have clear parallels with measures in the UK, are described below.

6.   SELF-REGULATION IN AUSTRALIA

The first development in self-regulation was the establishment in 1993 by the Insurance Council of Australia of a General Insurance Enquiries and Complaints Scheme, known as Insurance Enquiries and Complaints Ltd (IEC). This seeks to be both a general enquiries point and an alternative dispute resolution scheme and independence has been assured by the constitution of the overseeing Insurance Industry Complaints Council.

The second measure was the adoption in December 1994 of a General Insurance Code of Practice, designed to complement both IEC and the 1984 legislation. The introduction of this was led by government and compliance with it was made compulsory for all insurers, who are expected to have compliance committees at board level (originally it was to have been a statutory code, but government accepted the arguments for self-regulation, subject to a review after three years). The emphasis of the Code is on the disclosure of information, the wording of policy documents, the content of promotion material, claims handling and internal dispute resolution procedures, and the training and conduct of intermediaries. These points supplement the legal framework. The Code of Practice is an impressive document, which is much more comprehensive in its scope than the sum of the codes and statements of practice in existence in Britain.

7.   LESSONS FROM AUSTRALIA

In conclusion, what lessons can we learn from the Australian experience that could usefully be applied here? Obviously the legal solutions they have adopted can be compared with our own and our own as they apply in practice. I would not advocate wholesale adoption of the Australian solutions to the problems of our insurance law, but all are worth examining so that the many good aspects can be 'pinched'.

A most important lesson is to set up the appropriate support structure for a new legal regime. This includes identifying clear governmental responsibility[49] as well as appropriate codes of practice and complaints procedures. We can learn that law reform must go hand in hand with these other mechanisms. The fact that we already have a version of these would be a great help, although as already indicated, the Australian Code of Practice is a much more impressive document than the total of the various statements and codes that have been issued here. Compliance with appropriate codes and procedures would have to be mandatory, that is a condition of continuing authorisation to transact insurance business. This would involve a substantial change for the IOB, and the Bureau might not like it, but it is difficult to see how the current situation whereby the majority of consumers have the IOB's protection whereas a minority does not can really be justified.[50]

Perhaps most importantly, the Australian experience shows that a thorough reform following a review of all aspects of the legal area in question can work to the reasonable satisfaction of all parties involved. Perhaps it was partly the fact that the whole of the law was reviewed that helped carry the industry along. All we have ever done in this country is look at a few aspects of insurance contract law, chiefly centred around the duty of disclosure. I personally believe that the subject is only properly looked at as a whole. It is rather different from other areas of commercial law (accepting that there are other areas which are also different!).

The insurance industry is a very particular, as well as powerful, industry. The insurance contract is a very odd sort of contract, traditionally badly drafted and laid out, and even now, if plainly worded, often full of legal uncertainty. But it needs to be looked at as a whole, not least because of the fact that different legal techniques can be used to achieve a similar result, for example, what legally might be an exception to the risk in one policy may be the subject of a warranty or a condition (whether or not precedent in some sense) or a clause descriptive of the risk in another. Insurers can, wholly legitimately in my view, decide what risks they will and will not cover and what conditions (using the word in a broad sense) they will impose on people they insure. What is necessary is that everything is set out clearly and legibly, and that insurers do not seek to get out of paying for a claim on purely technical grounds. Tinker-

---

49. Should responsibility vest in the department which has responsibility for financial regulation of insurers under the Insurance Companies Act 1982?
50. There is also the question as to whether or not the IOB (as well as legal and self-regulatory measures) should have jurisdiction over 'small business' complaints, an issue which has been raised by the Ombudsman himself recently.

ing around so that certain odd bits are now at risk of being declared unfair, will not, in my view, achieve real benefits for consumers. We can perhaps use the Australian model to show us the way to go.

Chapter Ten

CONSUMER PROTECTION IN INSURANCE CONTRACTS

Chris Willett and Norma Hird

Chapter Outline

1. Introduction

2. The Common Law
   2.1   Risk and price terms, procedural terms and terms giving a discretion
   2.2   Warranties
   2.3   Rules

3. Legislative Approaches to Fairness

4. Self-regulation
   4.1   The Statements of Practice
         4.1.1   Warranties
         4.1.2   Duty of disclosure
   4.2   Insurance Ombudsman

5. The Way Forward

Consumer Protection in Financial Services (P. Cartwright, ed.: 90-411-9717-6: © Kluwer Law International: pub. Kluwer Law International, 1999: printed in Great Britain)

1.   INTRODUCTION

This chapter considers some aspects of unfairness in the contractual relationship between insurers and consumers. This sort of discussion has been
re-invigorated by three developments which have taken place in recent
years. First, there have been several important decisions dealing with the
duty of disclosure in insurance contract law, and the creation of warranties
in insurance contracts. Second, there has been the Directive on Unfair
Terms in Consumer Contracts[1] implemented by the Unfair Terms in Consumer Contracts Regulations 1994.[2] The Regulations introduce a test of
unfairness. However, this test is not relevant when it comes to some unfairness issues, including the duty of disclosure. In addition, it may not apply
to many terms in insurance contracts. However, the Regulations do introduce a requirement that all terms be drafted in plain and intelligible language. Finally there have been developments in the self-regulatory sphere.
There are Statements of Insurance Practice which set down certain principles as to the presentation of proposal forms and insurance contracts.
These can go some way to mitigating unfairness, by improving on transparency at the stage of contract formation, *ie*, by making it clearer to consumers the sorts of things which should be disclosed and the implications
of non-disclosure, and the implications of giving warranties which are not
adhered to. There is also the Insurance Ombudsman who resolves disputes
after the fact. The Ombudsman has been able to apply fairness principles
which mitigate the harshness of the common law. Importantly in this context, the Ombudsman has been able to limit the rights of the insurer to
avoid all liability when there has been a breach of the duty of disclosure.

2.   THE COMMON LAW

2.1 Risk and price terms, procedural terms and terms giving a discretion

An insurance contract will contain a variety of terms which define the
extent of the cover and deal with procedures for the settlement of claims.
As with many consumer contracts the terms will come in the form of a
package of standard terms which have been drawn up by the other party –
in this case the insurer. It will not be surprising, therefore, if the terms
often tend to favour the interests of the insurer over those of the consumer.

---

1.   93/13/EEC.
2.   SI 94/3159.

For example, the insurer may use terms which significantly limit the sort of risks which are underwritten or the circumstances in which risks are underwritten. Terms can have these effects in a number of ways. Risks can be implicitly or explicitly excluded. Alternatively a risk may be accepted, but conditions may be attached to the claim. There may be some kind of procedural condition, *eg*, that the consumer must claim in a particular way or within a certain period of time. Another possibility is that the insurer gives himself a discretion to decide whether to pursue a particular type of claim. This is most typically invoked where the nature of the claim involves the insurer pursuing a third party for payment. The third party may be an individual or their insurance company. It may be that in the context of the particular claim the insurer's only obligation to the insured is to pay if they can effect recovery from this third party. The term in question may say that it is solely for the insurer to decide as to whether it is worthwhile pursuing the third party.

The modern common law does not recognise any general test of fairness or good faith which could be used to control any of these terms.[3] It could be argued that in the case of price and risk defining terms it is entirely appropriate that there should be no such control. The essence of the insurance contract is that the insurer sets a price based on the package of risks which he is prepared to cover. This price and package of risks can be assessed by consumers by comparison with what other insurers have to offer and consumer choice should regulate what is made available. In such a scenario there might be argued to be no need for a fairness test. However, this scenario only exists if the packages of risks undertaken by various insurers can be easily compared with each other. This requires that the terms be in a decent sized print and in plain language. It also requires that insurance contracts be structured in such a way that the terms defining the risks covered are grouped together. This enables a clear comparison to be made between the packages of cover offered by different insurers. This cannot happen if the risk defining terms are 'dotted around' the contract in among, or perhaps even incorporated into, the terms which deal with procedural matters. The contract must be rationally structured, so that consumers can readily identify the important risk defining terms and compare them to those being offered by other insurers.

There are no express common law requirements on size of print, plain language or rational structuring. There are, of course, rules which may, indirectly, have the effect of achieving some of these things. Rules of construction, which construe ambiguous terms in favour of the consumer, may encourage plain language. However, they will have no impact on the

3. See C. Willett, *The Development of Fairness in Consumer Contracts* (Dartmouth, forthcoming 1999).

size of print used. Terms can be in very small print which is difficult to read, and yet be wholly unambiguous. In addition terms can be structured in a wholly irrational and intransparent way, and yet remain technically unambiguous.

The rule that onerous or unusual terms must be highlighted in order to be incorporated into the contract[4] may also have some effect. If a term is to be highlighted then it must surely be in decent sized print and plain language. However, the focus may only be on one term or a few terms, some of which may be risk terms and others procedural terms. So highlighting of onerous terms does not guarantee rationally structured contracts in which the risk-defining terms are grouped together.

The common law has therefore been deficient in neither applying a general test of fairness to such terms, nor guaranteeing the type of transparency which would aid market discipline.

The issue with procedural terms is different, as it is with terms giving the insurer a discretion. Risk and price terms are the core terms on which decisions to buy insurance are based. If we can make these decisions more rational by enhanced transparency then we can possibly forget about making them fair in any other way (the assumption being that such terms will be disciplined by market forces). However, procedural terms and terms giving the insurer a discretion will rarely, if ever, form the basis of the consumer's decision to purchase insurance. Even if they are transparent they remain secondary to the question of risk, and so it is unlikely that they will be subject to market discipline. They should, therefore, always be subject to a general test of fairness. It seems unacceptable that a consumer should pay for a certain risk to be covered, only to find his claim fail because he has not claimed within some unreasonably short deadline, or because the insurer relies upon a discretion not to pursue a claim. If such a term is onerous or unreasonable then, of course, it should be highlighted.[5] However, this is insufficient; there should be a substantive control over the sort of procedural conditions which can be set, and the extent to which an insurer can give himself a discretion. The common law provides no such control but, as we shall see below, the Unfair Terms Regulations do.

2.2 Warranties

A particularly problematic term for the consumer is a 'warranty'. This is a promise made by the consumer in relation to some matter. It may be, for

---

4. *Interfoto Picture Library v Stiletto* [1989] QB 433 (CA).
5. Ibid.

example, that the consumer warrants that he will keep his car in a road-worthy condition, or keep his house secure. A warranty is created if the parties are taken to have intended to create one. This intention may be inferred from the fact that the term in question expressly states that the consumer 'warrants' something. Another possibility is that certain answers/commitments given in the proposal form are said on the proposal form to represent 'the basis of the contract'. Warranties may be unfair to consumers for several connected reasons. First of all, a warranty can be created on a matter which is not material to the risk being insured. Second, the warranty might be very broad and therefore easily broken. Third, when the consumer is in breach of a warranty the contract is auto-matically discharged[6] and the insurer relieved of liability under the con-tract. This applies even if the consumer has suffered the type of loss insured against and the event causing this loss was unconnected to the breach of warranty. So the consumer may have his car stolen, but be unable to recover because he is in breach of a warranty to keep the car roadworthy, which breach discharges the insurer from liability, but which breach is not in any way causally connected to the theft of the car. A final, but very significant problem with warranties is that consumers may be unaware of these severe consequences.

So what controls might be exerted in relation to warranties? One possi-bility, of course, is simply to reform the law on the matter of breach. The idea would be that a claim should only fail if the event giving rise to it is in some way causally connected to the breach of warranty. Another possi-bility is to develop the rule on highlighting onerous terms so that it requires that a warranty should not only be prominent, but that it should also be specific, and its effects should be explained. If this did not happen then the warranty could be treated as not having been incorporated into the contract. The common law has not yet gone down either of these paths, although as we shall see the Statement of Insurance Practice and the Unfair Terms Regulations have made progress in these areas, although via differing mechanisms.

The common law has, however, been able to make some progress on the question of 'continuing warranties' by *contra proferentem* construc-tion. A 'continuing warranty', as the name suggests, continues to be a fun-damental term going to the root of the contract on each subsequent

---

6. See *The Good Luck* [1992] 2 AC223. Prior to this case, it was thought that the effect of breach was to give the insurer the *option* to terminate. It seems, however, that dis-charge is automatic, so that the insurer need take no positive action. One conceptual problem, however, is that the insurer was always thought to be entitled to waive his right to terminate. Presumably now he is able to choose to bring the discharged con-tract back to life. However, it seems strange to speak of this as 'waiver'.

renewal of the contract. In other words there is no need for it to be expressly renewed; the term will automatically renew itself when the policy is renewed (typically every year for a long period of time). As Birds has said 'it is most unlikely that the insured will remember exactly what he warranted on the original proposal form'.[7] This means that years down the line a claim can be avoided by the insurer because of a promise made which has, in some minor way, ceased to be fulfilled, and which is not relevant to the claim.

There is often ambiguity as to whether a term creates a continuing warranty. If courts are aware of the need to limit unfairness then they can insist on interpretations which favour the consumer. For example in *Kennedy and another v Smith and Ansvar Insurance Co.*,[8] the insured had stated that 'I am a total abstainer from alcoholic drinks', a statement which was true at the time. However, he later went to a cricket match and drank a pint of beer without having eaten. He then drove home with friends in the car. The car was involved in an accident and the two passengers were killed. The insured sought indemnification from the insurer in respect of the delictual damages he had paid. The insurers argued that a continuing warranty had been broken. This argument succeeded in the Outer House of the Court of Session but was rejected by the Inner House. The Lord President said that,

If . . . the insurers seek to limit their liability under a policy by relying upon an alleged undertaking as to the future prepared by them and accepted by an insured, the language they use must be such that the terms of the alleged undertaking and its scope are clearly and unambiguously expressed or plainly implied, and . . . any such alleged undertaking will be construed, in dubio, contra proferentem.[9]

2.3. Rules

Unfairness does not merely arise as a result of terms used by insurers. There are certain rules of insurance contract law which have the potential to operate against the interests of the consumer.

Insurance contracts are viewed by the common law as contracts of the utmost good faith. One corollary of this is that there is a duty on the party seeking insurance to voluntarily disclose material facts to the insurer prior to the formation of the contract.[10] It was said in *Rozanes v Bowen*,[11] to be long established that:

---

7. J. Birds, *Modern Insurance Law* (London: Sweet & Maxwell, 1993), p. 405.
8. 1976 SLT 110.
9. Ibid., at 116–17.
10. *Carter v Boehm* (1766) 3 Burr. 1905
11. (1928) 32 Lloyds Rep 98.

in connection with insurance of all sorts, marine, fire, life, guarantee and every kind of policy that as the underwriter knows nothing and the man who comes to him to insure knows everything, it is the duty of the assured . . . to make a full disclosure to the underwriters without being asked of all the material circumstances.

A breach of the duty of disclosure allows the innocent party to avoid the contract, provided that the non-disclosed fact was material to the underwriting of the risk and that it induced the insurer into the contract.

In *Pan Atlantic Insurance Co. Ltd v Pine Top Insurance Co. Ltd*,[12] the House of Lords was required to make a final ruling on the definition of 'materiality', following considerable uncertainty on this point over recent years. The most recent background to this uncertainty was the Court of Appeal decision in *Container Transport International Inc. v Oceans Mutual Underwriting Associations (Bermuda) Ltd*[13] and the Court of Appeal decision in the *Pan Atlantic* decision itself. In the *Container Transport International Inc. (CTI)* case the Court of Appeal said that it was not necessary for a fact or circumstance to be material that its disclosure would have resulted in the prudent insurer making a 'different decision' as to whether to accept the risk or as to the level at which to set the premium. The Court of Appeal seemed to say that all that was necessary was that the fact or circumstance which was not disclosed would have been of relevance to the mind of the prudent insurer. Such a non-disclosure would be material. However, this seems to be a very low threshold of materiality. As Bennett says it seems to render material any fact or circumstance 'unless a prudent insurer would have immediately disregarded the circumstance as irrelevant'.[14]

However, in *Pan Atlantic* the Court of Appeal took the view that all that the Court of Appeal had done in the *CTI* case was to reject the 'different decision' test, *ie*, that they had not decided in a positive sense what materiality meant. The Court of Appeal in *Pan Atlantic* then went on to take the view that a fact or circumstance was material if a prudent underwriter would have seen it as increasing or changing the risk or as 'probably tending' to do so. This is clearly a higher threshold of materiality than seemed to be considered necessary by the Court of Appeal in the *CTI* case.

The majority in the House of Lords in *Pan Atlantic* rejected this approach in favour of the lower threshold of materiality espoused in the *CTI* case. However, this does not leave the consumer in as vulnerable a

---

12. [1994] 3 All ER 581.
13 [1994] Lloyds Rep. 476.
14. H. Bennett, 'Utmost Good Faith, Materiality and Inducement' (1996) 112 LQR 405 at 406.

position as one might first assume. The House of Lords in *Pan Atlantic* also said that, as in the general law of misrepresentation, the insurer in question must actually have been induced into the contract by the non-disclosure. It had previously been thought that there was no need to establish subjective inducement of the particular insurer.[15] The fact that such a requirement is involved might be thought to go some way to balance out the relatively low level of materiality which now seems to be required.

Lord Mustill indicated that if materiality was established there might be a presumption of inducement.[16] Such a presumption seems a rather strong way of putting the rule, which seems more accurately described in terms of a 'fair inference of fact'. This was the phrase used in *Smith v Chadwick*[17] to describe the connection between materiality and inducement. It was said in the *Smith* case (and approved by Lord Lloyd in *Pan Atlantic*)[18] that material non-disclosure leads to 'fair inference of fact' that the insurer had been induced, and that it was a 'heresy' to talk of an actual presumption of inducement. Certainly an outright presumption would, when allied with the low threshold of materiality required, seem to tip the scales unfairly in favour of the insurer.

The 'inference of fact' approach seems to strike a fairer balance between the interests of the two parties. It is also the approach taken by *Halsbury's Laws of England*[19] and cited with approval by Evans LJ in the Court of Appeal in *St Pauls Fire and Marine Insurance Co. (UK) Ltd v McConnell Powell Constructors Ltd*:

Inducement cannot be inferred in law from proved materiality, although there may be cases where the materiality is so obvious as to justify an inference of fact that the representee was actually induced, but even in such exceptional cases, the inference is only a prima facie one and may be rebutted by counter evidence.[20]

As Bennett says, on this approach there 'is no legal presumption, merely the possibility of a factual inference and the strength of any such inference will vary to reflect the nature and weight of the evidence as to materiality'.[21] So the lower the degree of materiality the weaker the inference of inducement, and the harder for the insurer to establish inducement on the facts.

15. Indeed it may well be that the inducement requirement is bad law: see J. Birds and N. Hird, 'Misrepresentation and Non-disclosure in Insurance Law' 59 (1996) MLR 285.
16. At p. 549.
17. (1884) 9 App. Cas. 187 at 196.
18. At p. 570.
19. 14th edn, vol. 31, para. 1067.
20. [1995] 2 Lloyds Rep. 116 at p. 127.
21. Bennett, op. cit., n. 14 at 410.

Notwithstanding the correct approach to these issues, there are further problems for the consumer. First of all, although he cannot be in breach of the duty of disclosure unless he is aware of the relevant fact (*Economides v Commercial Union Ins. Co. Ltd*),[22] the consumer need not be aware that this is a material fact. How is the consumer to know what facts are likely to be regarded as material? Second, if the consumer fails to disclose a material fact then, as we have said, the insurer may avoid the contract. This is obviously based on the idea that his decision to insure at a certain premium (or to insure at all) has been tainted by his lack of awareness of a material fact. But as we have already said, the consumer may be hard pushed to know what to disclose. In fact the insurer is often in a good position to tell the consumer what kinds of things he wants to know. If he does not do this, it seems unfair that he should be able to avoid liability. This unfairness is all the greater where the fact not disclosed was not, in the event, related to the circumstances giving rise to the claim. This brings us back to the state of the consumer's knowledge at the stage of making the contract. Not only is the consumer *possibly* ignorant as to what might be a material fact, he is *very probably* ignorant as to the severity of the consequences of non-disclosure of such facts.

In the light of these points, one possible reform which might be made would be to say that the insurer will not repudiate for non-disclosure of a fact which the consumer could not have been reasonably expected to disclose; and also to require the insurer to inform the consumer as to what he might regard as material, and as to the consequences of non-disclosure. Another possibility is to introduce a proportionality rule. Under such a rule if there is an innocent failure to disclose a material fact, rather than allowing the insurer to refuse to pay a claim, the law reduces the amount payable in proportion to the amount the premium would have increased if the fact had been known.[23] As we will see the former approach has been adopted by the Statements of Insurance Practice, and the latter by the Ombudsman.

3. LEGISLATIVE APPROACHES TO FAIRNESS

There are two main pieces of legislation applicable to problems of contractual unfairness: the Unfair Contract Terms Act (UCTA) 1977 and the Unfair Terms in Consumer Contracts Regulations 1994. The UCTA does not apply to contracts of insurance, which leaves the regulations. These

---

22. [1997] 3 All ER 636.
23. Rules of this nature are used in France (Code d'assurance, Arts. 113–8 and 113–9), Denmark (Insurance Contracts Act 1930, s. 16(2)), Finland (Insurance Act 1994, ss. 24 and 25), and Ontario (RSO, 1980 C.218, s. 265). See also the discussion in M. Clarke, *Policies and Perceptions of Insurance* (Clarendon Press, 1997), at p. 103.

apply to 'any term in a contract concluded between a seller or supplier [of goods and services] and a consumer where the term has not been individually negotiated' (see Regulations 2 and 3). Insurance is clearly within the definition of a service and so covered by the Regulations. However, what is also clear is that the Regulations apply to 'terms'. They do not apply to rules of law which may operate unfairly or be intrinsically unfair. This means that the Regulations can do nothing to mitigate unfairness problems caused by the duty of disclosure.

What can the Regulations do in relation to the terms of an insurance contract? First, under Regulation 6, all terms must be in 'plain and intelligible language, and any ambiguities will be interpreted in favour of the consumer'. Second, there is a test of unfairness which holds that a term is unfair if 'contrary to the requirement of good faith [it] causes a significant imbalance in the parties' rights and obligations to the detriment of the consumer' (Regulation 4(1)). A term is not binding upon the consumer if it fails this test (Regulation 5). This test does not apply to those terms which constitute the main subject matter of the contract (Regulation 3(2)). In the Preamble to the Unfair Terms Directive (which the Regulations seek to implement) 'main subject matter' terms are described as those which 'clearly define or circumscribe the insured risk and the insurer's liability' (Recital 19).

What, then, are the terms which define the insured risk and the insurer's liability? It would seem to be those terms which set out what is and is not covered in terms of risk. This covers what the insurer, in positive terms, says that he will insure. However, it possibly also covers the warranties given by the consumer, for it is contingent upon the consumer keeping to these promises that the insurer is prepared to offer the cover. There is, of course, something which we must remember about both the warranties and the terms which positively define the risks which are covered. The key justification for excluding them from a test of unfairness is that hopefully they are disciplined by market forces. As we argued above, this can only happen if they are not only in plain language (as all terms must be) but also if they are also in decent sized print, and manifestly grouped together as risk defining terms.[24]

---

24. This approach seems to be supported by the OFT, who have power under Regulation 8 of the Unfair Terms Regulations to investigate complaints about unfair terms and to seek injunctions to prevent their continued use. They publish bulletins which describe their approach to the problem. On the question of main subject matter terms they have said that: 'In our view it would be difficult to claim that any term was a core term unless it was central to how consumers perceived the bargain. A supplier would surely find it hard to sustain the argument that a contract's main subject matter was defined by a term which a consumer had been given no real chance to see and read before signing – in other words if that term had not been properly drawn to

Indeed, if a warranty is to be seen as a risk-defining term, in addition to being physically located in the same section as other risk-defining terms, it is arguable that it should actually speak fully to its own connection with the question of risk. The warranty term should spell out that the under-writing of the various other risks by the insurer is contingent on the consumer keeping to the promise which he is making, *ie*, that if the consumer does not keep his warranty promise the insurer will be discharged from all liability. This sort of approach to the main subject matter issue seems to fit with the idea expressed in the preamble to the effect that main subject matter terms are those which 'clearly' set out risks and liabilities. In taking this kind of approach we are saying that to qualify as a main subject matter term, and so escape the full-scale unfairness test, a high level of transparency must be achieved. In the case of terms creating warranties this should involve explanation of their effect.

If terms do not qualify as main subject matter terms then they are subject to the unfairness test. There would seem to be two possible categories of term which will be so subject. First of all, there are those risk-defining terms which do not clearly enough present themselves as such. Second, there are terms which by virtue of their subject matter could never be main subject matter terms. In this second category, we would suggest, are those terms dealing with the process of a claim, *eg*, terms setting time limits on claims or giving insurers a discretion not to pursue a claim which is in some way dependent on the insurer recovering from a third party. There is no space here for a detailed analysis of the applicability of the unfairness test to such terms.[25] However, we should recall that the test is dependent on whether the term causes significant imbalance to the detriment of the consumer, and is contrary to good faith. All of these concepts go to the substance of the term and its effect on the overall balance of the contract. We must then consider, for example, whether a procedural condition is very difficult for the consumer to comply with; or indeed whether a warranty, if it happens to be covered by the test, is so impossibly vague and broad that it is difficult to comply with. We must then look at the term in the context of the other terms to see what the overall balance looks like.

(continued)
the consumer's attention. We regularly see terms which are claimed to be core terms but which are given no prominence and are indeed rather coyly tucked away in the small print' (Issue No. 2, September 1996, p. 13).
25. See Willett, op. cit., n. 3, and R. Brownsword, G. Howells and T. Wilhelmsson, 'Between Market and Welfare: Some Reflections on Article 3 of the Directive on Unfair Terms in Consumer Contracts', in C. Willett (ed.), *Aspects of Fairness in Contract* (Blackstone, 1996).

There is, however, another aspect to the test. As well as going to the substance of the term, good faith also goes to the bargaining environment surrounding the conclusion of the contract. A term which looks unfair in substance may, in some circumstances, be found to have been incorporated in good faith and therefore be fair. This could happen, for example, if the consumer was in a strong enough bargaining position to look after himself;[26] or, perhaps, if the term had been made very transparent to the consumer at the time the contract was made.

4. SELF-REGULATION

There are two forms of self-regulation which are of relevance here. First of all, there is the proactive regulation effected by the Statements of Insurance Practice. This regulation is proactive in the sense that it is intended to influence the practice of the insurer at the proposal form and contract formation stage – setting down good practice in relation to the sorts of terms offered and the way the relationship is explained to the insured party. The second type of self-regulation operates after the fact. The Ombudsman scheme provides an alternative redress system for consumers; but, as we will see, the ombudsman has also introduced principles which are more favourable to consumers than the common law.

4.1 The Statements of Practice

The first Statement of Insurance Practice was introduced in 1977 by the Association of British Insurers. They had effectively been forced to introduce some form of regulation as the price of being exempted from the controls of UCTA.[27] There was a revised Statement in 1986. The main impact of the Statements of Practice is on warranties and the duty of disclosure.

4.1.1 Warranties

It will be recalled that the common law allows broad warranties to be created on matters which are not material to the risk, and also that if there is a breach of warranty the insurer is discharged of all liability even if the breach is unconnected to the event giving rise to the claim. These are con-

---

26. See Sch. 2 to the Regulations.
27. See discussion by I. Cadogan and K. Lewis, 'Do Insurers Know Best?' (1992) AALR 123.

sequences which the consumer may well be unaware of. The Unfair Terms Regulations may help in some respects. A warranty will have to be in plain language. In order to escape the test of unfairness it may be that it should be situated in a prominent place and explain its effect. If it is subject to the test of unfairness it may be that it will fail if it is too broad. However, the precise demands of the unfairness test are as yet unclear, and are made yet more unclear by the fact that it is not merely the term in question which is relevant, but whether it is balanced out by the other terms, and how fair the bargaining environment was.

The Statements of Practice offer a much clearer and more direct approach to the warranties issue. Paragraph 1(b) (Long Term Statement 1(b)) says that insurers should require specific warranties about matters which are material to the risk. Paragraph 2(b)(ii) goes further by actually effecting a substantive control over the remedy available to the insurer for breach of warranty. An insurer may not repudiate 'where the circumstances of the loss are unconnected with the breach unless fraud is involved'.

4.1.2 Duty of disclosure

We pointed out above that the materiality of a non-disclosure is very important. The greater the degree of materiality the easier it will be for the insurer to establish that the non-disclosure induced him to contract. If he can do this, he escapes liability. However, we made the point that the consumer may well be ignorant as to what he should disclose. The Statement of Practice addresses this problem directly. Paragraph 2(b) of the revised 1986 Statement of General Insurance Practice says that: 'An insurer will not repudiate liability to indemnify a policy holder: (1) on grounds of non-disclosure of a material fact which a policyholder could not reasonably be expected to have disclosed.'

A very similar (although more clumsily drafted) provision applies to long-term insurance (Long Term Statement, paragraph 3(a)).

The effect (if the Statement is followed) is to leave very little of the duty of disclosure. As Birds has said 'if the duty is limited to what a reasonable man would think should be disclosed . . . this would surely . . . [mean] that, except in rare cases, a reasonable man would not . . . [expect] to do more than answer express questions.'[28] At most, then, where the Statement is followed there is a duty to avoid negligent and fraudulent non-disclosure.

28. Birds, op. cit., n. 7, at p. 109.

However, if the insured consumer still happens to fall foul of this standard, the insurer will be able to avoid the contract. The Statement of General Insurance Practice deals with this by the use of rules which require insurers to make it clearer to the insured party what might be regarded as material and what the implications are of a material non-disclosure. Section 1(c) of the General Statement says that,

If not included in the declaration, prominently displayed on the proposal form should be a statement:
(1) drawing the attention of the proposer to the consequences of failure to disclose all material facts, explained as those facts an insurer would regard as likely to influence the acceptance and assessment of the proposal.
(2) a warning that if the proposer is in any doubt about facts considered material, he should disclose them' (see para 1(a) of the Long Term Statement for the equivalent Provision).
These matters which insurers have generally found to be material will be the subject of clear questions in proposal forms (see Long-Term Statement 1(c)).

The idea here is to focus the mind of the consumer on the issues which they should think carefully about – an attempt to make things more transparent for the consumer and reduce the chances of a material non-disclosure.

In addition, paragraph 1(e) says that, 'So far as is practicable insurers will avoid asking questions which would require expert knowledge beyond that which the proposer could reasonably be expected to possess or obtain or which would require a value judgement on the part of the proposer' (see Long Term Statement para. 1(d)).

4.2 Insurance Ombudsman

The Insurance Ombudsman was the first of the private ombudsman schemes to be set up, in 1981. Its stated purpose is 'to resolve disputes between members and consumers in an independent, impartial, cost-effective, efficient, informal and fair way'.[29] The initiative to set up the scheme came from the insurance industry in an attempt to ward off statutory reform.

The Ombudsman has jurisdiction to consider any complaint in connection with or arising out of a policy, or proposed policy of insurance provided that the policy is with a Member of the Bureau.[30] As is common with most private ombudsman schemes, the Insurance Ombudsman is

---

29. *Annual Report 1995*. For an excellent examination of the operation of the Insurance Ombudsman Scheme, see R. James, *Private Ombudsman and Public Law* (Dartmouth, 1997), chapter 2.
30. About 90 per cent of insurers are members, according to the latest *Annual Report*.

not limited to looking at maladministration only, but is able to adjudicate on the merits of a dispute or claim. He cannot, however, concern himself with the underwriting of any policy. As with most schemes, the consumer must first have gone though the insurer's own complaints procedure before he can refer his complaint to the Ombudsman.

In making decisions the Ombudsman must have regard to the terms of the contract between the parties and any relevant legal provisions, and must act in conformity with the general principles of good insurance practice. It is perhaps unclear whether the latter means only the ABI's Statements of Insurance Practice mentioned above, or something more, but, in any event, he is bound to give these precedence over the strict legal rules if this would be in the consumer's favour.[31]

The ultimate role of the Ombudsman is to assess what would be fair and reasonable in all the circumstances. How he interprets this maxim can best be considered by examining his approach to those specific areas of the law which we have pointed out as being the most troublesome.

One area where the Ombudsman has made significant inroads is in non-disclosure. We argued earlier that a fairer approach to innocent non-disclosure would be to disallow the remedy of total avoidance in favour of the doctrine of proportionality. There follows an excerpt from the 1989 Ombudsman report where the Ombudsman discusses a 'proportionality' principle applied to a non-disclosure case:

> The basic solution adopted as equitable was that the claim should be met proportionately taking into account the relative amounts of the actual premium and the appropriate premium. For example in one case had the business use of a house (seasonal bed and breakfast) been disclosed, the premium would have been increased by approximately one quarter (say, from £100 to £125). The proportionality solution meant that the insurer should be liable for 80% of the claim (because £100 is 80 per cent of £125). Similar results have been reached with motoring policies where increased premium rates (*eg*, in the light of the policyholder's claim record) are easily ascertainable. (Insurance Ombudsman Bureau, 1989, para. 2.127)

5. THE WAY FORWARD

We have looked at some of the problems of unfairness in insurance contracts. As far as unfair terms are concerned, the common law has not been able to get beyond rules of construction and a requirement that onerous or unusual terms be highlighted. The common law approach to the duty of disclosure also has the potential to be unfair to the consumer. The Unfair

---

31. Terms of Reference C (1)(c).

Terms Regulations have made advances in protecting the consumer against unfair terms, but are of no help on the problems caused by the duty of disclosure.

In many ways self-regulation has brought the most advanced models for consumer protection. The problems caused by warranties and the duty of disclosure are dealt with in detailed and specific ways. The problem, of course, is that both the Statements of Insurance Practice and the Ombudsman scheme are voluntary. Not all insurers choose to follow the Statements or to be covered by the Ombudsman scheme. It seems unlikely that many consumers choose their insurer on the basis of whether or not they follow the Statements or are covered by the Ombudsman scheme. Consumers are not likely to be sufficiently well informed as to the advantages of dealing with these insurers to enable them to make a choice on this basis.

Many insurers advertise the fact that they are members of the Ombudsman scheme. This obviously conveys a vaguely positive message to the consumer which may encourage him to use that insurer. However, the real problem is those who are not members or who do not follow the Statement of Practice. If consumers do not shop around on the basis that these are important issues then they are unlikely to be deterred from using an insurer who does not advertise membership of the Ombudsman scheme. As far as the Statement of Practice is concerned this is not even an issue which insurers tend to positively advertise, so that choosing on this basis seems even more unlikely.

One possible solution is a 'name and shame' policy under which the ABI or the OFT advertise the advantages of the Statements of Practice and the Ombudsman scheme, and name those insurers who do not adhere. Another possibility is to require insurers who do not adhere to disclose this clearly and prominently themselves. These disclosure approaches fit within an 'informed choice' model of consumer policy.

However in order to ensure a basic threshold of protection for all consumers specialised regulation of warranties and disclosure must ultimately be put on a legal footing. A possible model is the Australian one which is discussed by John Birds in chapter 9.

PART FIVE

CONSUMER CREDIT

Chapter Eleven

SEEKING SOCIAL JUSTICE FOR POOR CONSUMERS IN CREDIT MARKETS*

Geraint Howells

Chapter Outline

Consumer Protection in Financial Services (P. Cartwright, ed.: 90-411-9717-6:
pub. Kluwer Law International, 1999: printed in Great Britain). This chapter first
appeared in I. Ramsay (ed.), *Consumer Law in the Global Economy* © Ashgate
Publishing Limited 1997.

1. INTRODUCTION

A note in the *Yale Law Journal* of 1967 on 'Consumer Legislation and the Poor' opens with the sound truism that 'a family's standard of living is a function of both the size of its income and the way in which that income is spent'.[1] While most people are obsessed with the size of their income (going to extraordinary lengths to increase it by working long hours, gaining qualifications, being nice to their boss, etc.), in contrast the majority are rather poor consumers. Tired and short of leisure time, their purchasing choices tend to be driven by convenience and based on little market research, with the result that they often end up with more expensive and/or lower quality goods or services than could have been obtained in the market. It would be an interesting piece of research to see to what extent wealth could be maximised by working less and shopping more, especially as money gained by sensible purchases is tax free. If people realised how much their living standards could be increased by effective purchasing decisions then consumer law and policy would gain an enhanced status.

2. LOW INCOME CONSUMERS AND MARKETS

Those on low incomes would seem to have even more incentive to maximise the value of their limited spending power. Indeed, there is evidence that many poor consumers are indeed rather careful consumers, and certainly no worse than other groups in society.[2] However, they also have certain structural problems which prevent them from making the best use of the market. They may be physically restricted to certain shopping outlets, because, for instance, they lack a car to travel to out of town supermarkets and shopping complexes. Their limited income also means that they have few opportunities to plan purchases to take advantages of sales and seasonal pricing.

---

*   The reproduction of this paper in the present volume will hopefully assist in the current debate on how to protect vulnerable consumers. The OFT is currently preparing a report on vulnerable consumers and financial services and the Department of Trade and Industry has also asked the Office to consider whether the new government should reconsider its proposals on *Unjust Credit Transactions* (1991).
1.   76 *Yale Law Journal* 745.
2.   See G. Parker, *Getting and Spending* (Avebury, 1990). We shall see below that Karen Rowlingson considers the use made of moneylenders by low income consumers is rational: see *Moneylenders and their Customers* (Policy Studies Institute, 1994).

Rather, their purchasing needs are often dictated by personal crises, which demand that goods and services be purchased immediately without the time to search out the best buy and often require them to use credit for major purchases. These structural barriers probably prevent many of those low income consumers with plenty of time on their hands (because they are unemployed or pensioners) from making the most of this asset (time) when purchasing. However, it should not be thought that all low income people have time on their hands. Many low income earners in fact work long hours and their poverty simply results from low hourly rates, while many low income consumers have family commitments (be they single parents, a couple bringing up children or carers for sick or elderly relatives) which reduce the time they have to devote to being better consumers.

Low income consumers also suffer another disadvantage in the market-place. As they have relatively little to spend they are often treated as being of little interest to mainstream traders. Instead they are targeted by traders who concentrate on 'the bottom end of the market', but charge a premium to make up for the low volume of sales. For most goods and services the careful poor consumer can avoid those who seek to 'exploit' the poorer end of the market and purchase in the mainstream markets. The seller is unable to differentiate between rich and poor consumers and as she will be keen to retain the mass consumer market the poor consumer will be able to benefit from being part of the consumer collective. Only perhaps with regard to after-sales service or complaints may poorer consumers be disadvantaged in general sales, where traders may be less obliging to customers whose repeat business they do not value very highly.

3. THE PARTICULAR PROBLEMS OF THE CREDIT MARKET FOR LOW INCOME CONSUMERS

However, in the credit market poor consumers lose the protection of being part of a wider consumer collective. Whereas in most consumer transactions the interest of the seller diminishes once the sale has been made, in credit transactions the creditor's interest only starts once the bargain has been struck and (s)he starts to receive payments. Thus the supplier of credit has a real interest in the character and circumstances of the party she is contracting with.

It is often said that as poor consumers have a higher risk of default this justifies higher interest rates. This statement needs to be considered carefully. There is no evidence that poor consumers have any less desire to repay loans than other consumers; indeed, as they have fewer opportunities to obtain credit they may be very keen to maintain access to those lines of credits they do have. However, it is true that, as they have less margin for error in their budgets, they may easily have a shortfall one week and events such as illness or unemployment may cause them quickly to fall behind with payments. Thus the risk with poor consumers may well be not so much non-payment as late payment.[3]

Often the collection methods adopted when providing poor consumers with credit will be very expensive. Frequently they involve door to door collections. This is certainly true of the doorstep moneylenders operating on a large scale in the UK, which we consider in detail later on in this section. In part, this reflects the choice of some of these consumers. It also allows the creditor to keep close control on his or her 'investment'. Moreover, it gives this form of creditor an opportunity to persuade the customers to favour him or her over more distant anonymous creditors, such as utilities. It also provides new selling opportunities. Thus the advantages of doorstep collection are mainly for the creditor allowing him or her security and selling opportunities; but it is very expensive way of doing business and the price is paid by the consumer.

Poor consumers tend to borrow small amounts. This results in the administrative costs attached to such loans being very high in proportion to the size of the loan.

Thus the credit market appears to be the ultimate in individualism, stripping consumers of any protection afforded by being part of a crowd and forcing them to seek out the best terms their situation permits. This is often not a very attractive deal given the risk of default (late payment), expensive operating practices and the uneconomic size of loans which such consumers typically require. If, nevertheless, the resulting deal fairly reflected the risk posed by each individual consumer, one might regret the lack of communitarian values, but at least appreciate a certain element of transparency in the workings of the market. However, the market does not even give the poor consumer the benefit of such an individualised assessment. The transaction costs involved would be too expensive. Instead the market's answer is to become stratified with different creditors offering terms for different 'levels' of consumer. Creditors will use various techniques of credit referencing to weed out those consumers who mistakenly apply for credit from too high a level (*ie*, where the interest is too low to cover the risks posed by the category to which the consumer belongs). However, there is no countervailing service warning consumers that they have been too pessimistic about their choice of creditor and that they would have been able to obtain credit from

---

3. For instance, it has been found that default rates in Harlem range from 5–25 per cent, but collection agents obtain default judgments in 97 per cent of cases and execute 75 per cent of these; quoted in Note (1967) 76 *Yale Law Journal* 745 at n. 110.

someone offering better terms. Indeed, there may be a tendency to under-rate one's opportunity of obtaining credit, both in order to avoid embarrass-ment at being turned down and the resulting delay if the application process has to be started over again with another creditor.

Each strata within the credit market will obviously span a range of con-sumers each with a different likelihood of default. Thus, inevitably, some consumers will be forced to subsidise others depending upon where they fall within the range. To the extent that this is made clear by the charge for credit then perhaps it is inevitable and acceptable. However, one benefit often claimed for doorstep moneylenders is that their charges are actually lower than advertised as they do not normally make default charges when payments are missed.[4] Although this seems rather consumer friendly[5] it is in fact an example of lack of transparency, as those who pay on time are paying more than they need to as a certain tolerance to late payment is built into the cost of credit. If one accepts the market approach to transacting, poor consumers ought to obtain the benefits of open market transacting. This requires full transparency of the charge for credit so that consumers can locate the best option for themselves in the market. It also requires no infor-mal rules which may not be known to the body of consumers or which ben-efit those prepared to 'play the system'. Rather than the market mechanism helping consumers to find their best deal, the market system appears deter-mined to give them no more than they are due (and no doubt hopes some-times to give them a little less).

4.   DOORSTEP MONEYLENDERS

In this section we will concentrate on one sector of the credit market in the UK – doorstep moneylending which either takes the form of cash loans or the selling of goods on credit. This case study has been chosen both because it is a market which openly sets out its stall to deal with poor con-sumers and because, conveniently, it has recently been the subject of an empirical study.[6] On the whole the conclusions of this study were rather benevolent to the licensed moneylending industry. It is easy to understand why. The sector has a highly effective trade association – the Consumer Credit Association. Those working at the coal face in this industry are no

---

4. Rowlingson, op. cit., n. 2, p. 126.
5. Indeed, the lenders seemed particularly sympathetic to cases of genuine excuses (per-haps an unlikely example of lenders operating a *de facto* acceptance of social *force majeure*: see T. Wilhelmsson, 'Social Force Majeure: a New Concept in Nordic Con-sumer Law' (1990) 12 *Journal of Consumer Policy* 1.
6. Rowlingson, op. cit., n. 2.

doubt honest folk simply trying to earn an honest living. They may be small businessmen operating with limited capital or agents for large reputable companies, often recruited from not dissimilar backgrounds to the clients.[7] Equally (although there is no data on the profitability of the companies) it seems that the agents are not making exorbitant amounts of money[8] and obtain it by working unsociable hours[9] and placing themselves in vulnerable positions.[10] Many of the agents develop friendly relations with their clients creating a feeling of security in the customer's mind.[11]

The moneylenders not only lend to those who would not have access to other mainstream sources of credit, but also lend smaller amounts and for shorter periods than High Street creditors would be prepared to.[12] The industry would argue that it is meeting a social need (sometimes one almost suspects they want to be seen as a social service), providing credit to sectors of the economy that mainstream financial institutions are not interested in. The industry would point to home collection as the key feature which allows them to lend to these consumers and would point out that this is expensive and justifies their high finance charges.

However, one can accept that the industry is not making excessive profits and yet still feel uncomfortable about it. The interest rates charged by moneylenders is the nub of the problem. Rowlingson found interest rates varying between around 100 per cent annual percentage rate (APR) and 500 per cent APR. The rates varied depending on the length of the loan; for example, with one company a twenty-week loan had an APR of 354 per cent, whilst a fifty-week loan appeared to be a bargain at just 230 per cent! Interestingly, rates vary between companies. Perhaps surprisingly, the smaller companies often offer better rates despite their tending to make

---

7. There are around 1,200 licensed moneylending companies operating in the UK (6 national companies employing at least 1,000 agents, 50–60 medium sized regional companies employing 50–100 agents, 700 smaller companies with an average of 10 agents and 400 sole or small trader with perhaps 1 employee): see, Rowlingson, op. cit., n. 2, at p. 25. Apparently, some companies preferred agents from the same social class as their customers, while others favoured applicants from a slightly more upwardly aspiring and achieving background: see, Rowlingson, op. cit., n. 2, p. 31.
8. Rowlingson found that £300 per week gross was about the best wage of agents.
9. Much of the collecting tends to be evening and weekend work. Part of the skill of collecting was to know the best time to call to secure payment and this would vary from customer to customer: see, Rowlingson, op. cit., n. 2, at pp. 45–6.
10. There was a danger that they would be attacked by people (who knew that they would be carrying sizeable amounts, often in the dark) and dogs! See Rowlingson, op. cit., n. 2, at pp. 48–9.
11. See, ibid., chapter 6.
12. For instance, one of the larger companies offers loans ranging from £50 over 20 weeks to £1,500 over 100 weeks: see, Rowlingson, op. cit., n. 2, at p. 30.

smaller loans for shorter periods.[13] What is astonishing about these extravagant levels of interest rates is that they are charged to people that the moneylenders believe will – perhaps with some defaults – repay the loans! In other words we are concerned with a form of credit available to the poor, but not the poorest consumers. Some firms were, for instance, reluctant to take on the unemployed, the old lone parents (deemed less respectable and trustworthy) as customers and certain housing areas were simply redlined.[14] Not only does this give the lie to any claim that this sector of the credit market is performing a social service, but it also suggests that the high interest rates are perhaps more due to collection costs than default rates.

5.   HIGH INTEREST RATES AND CONSUMER PROTECTION

Does it matter that people are paying such high rates? To the extent that they could strike better bargains in the marketplace, their failure to do so could be ascribed to their apathy rather than any failings in market mechanisms. Where the moneylender was the best choice available to them it could be argued that the customers would prefer this form of, albeit expensive, credit rather than have no alternative. These are powerful arguments against regulating this problem and need to be addressed. For the moment we will leave aside possibilities of improving the lot of poor consumers by reshaping the market by improving competition in their credit market (perhaps by the introduction of new forms of social lending) or altering the basic rules on which the market functions. Instead we will tackle head on the hard question of whether, if this is the best the market can offer, poor consumers should have access to it.

There may not, at first sight, be too much room for sympathy for the consumer who could obtain cheaper credit but does not do so. However, such individuals are likely to be on the borders of acceptability to higher level creditors and there may be many social factors (such as ignorance, complexity and fear) putting them off applying to anonymous, unfamiliar financial institutions and many others (such as security, ease of application, familiarity) encouraging them to maintain their relationship with a moneylender firm, which might have dealt with a family for generations. Indeed, credit is a complex product to appraise. The APR is meant to be a tool to permit comparative shopping, but in one survey carried out by the writer only a little over three-quarters of debtors had heard the term and only one

13.   Ibid., at pp. 28–32.
14.   Ibid., at pp. 52–5.

in seven of those could be regarded as having a reasonable understanding of its meaning.[15] Indeed, some argue (although the present writer demurs) that the APR is not a particularly useful comparator for small loans.[16] Individuals should not be made to pay the price of society's lack of effective consumer education. Thus there are many understandable reasons why consumers do not seek out their cheapest source of credit. Where the variation between creditors is marginal little harm may result from this, but where the difference is between, say, an interest rate of 20 per cent and 500 per cent then this is a serious matter which cannot be simply ignored by blaming the individual.

What of the position of consumers who can only borrow at these high rates of interest? If there is really no alternative should they not be allowed to borrow if they believe to do so is in their best interest? The Crowther Committee on Consumer Credit[17] considered there was a level above which interest rates became socially harmful. This is unfashionable but certainly true. To the extent that there lies behind this statement a claim to know what is best for the individual, such a rule is certainly paternalist and where the sense of one's judgement is self-evidently wiser than that made by a weak and perhaps frustrated consumer one should not perhaps be too shy to admit to being a paternalist.[18] To counter arguments that one's actions might inflict harm on those one is seeking to help, one might wish to distinguish between the acceptability of high cost credit depending upon the use to which it is to be put. Four types of use of credit can be identified:

(i) To permit the purchase of luxuries. Why, the argument goes, should we control the price of goods and services bought on credit when we do not control their cash price? The answer is because the cash price of goods and services is generally controlled by general market pressures, but the price of credit is uniquely high for poor consumers. Expensive credit uses up too much of a poor consumer's limited resources.

(ii) To help manage the budget. However, adding in weekly interest charges is not a long-term solution to budgeting problems and can only escalate the problem.

---

15. See I. Crow, G. Howells and M. Moroney, 'Credit and Debt: Choices for Poorer Consumers', in G. Howells, I. Crow and M. Moroney (eds), *Aspects of Credit and Debt* (Sweet & Maxwell, 1993), at p. 36.
16. Ibid.
17. Cmnd 4596, 1971 at para. 6.6.6.
18. See D. Kennedy, 'Distributive and Paternalist Motives in Contract and Tort Law, with Special Reference to Compulsory Terms and Unequal Bargaining Power' (1982) 41 *Maryland Law Review* 563.

(iii) To act as a form of enforced saving or to prevent savings being used. This is unlikely to be the case with many consumers in this category and it is irrational to protect savings at such an enormous cost.

(iv) The only circumstance where it could be rational to use such expensive credit is where there is a basic need in an emergency and there are no savings. Whilst one might wish to permit a limited high interest rate market to operate for these special cases, it should be recognised that this would lead to a collapse of most of the moneylending industry as they rely on persuading relatively affluent consumers to keep borrowing to buy luxury items.

One problem with an approach based on the use credit is put to is that it may not always be easy to determine what the exact purpose is. This and general criticisms of paternalism (discussed in the next paragraph) might suggest that one ought to adopt alternative techniques for discouraging high interest lending rather than simple prohibition.

Paternalism is a label which is often used to deride social reforms by criticising their proponents for wanting to play God and restricting the liberty of some citizens (in this instance poor people). Looked at another way it is simply common sense to prevent people injuring themselves and the fact that poverty is one of the circumstances causing the danger does not remove the moral imperative to act. However, this charge of arrogance is a dangerous one. Even if it is not true, the mere claim in itself, combined with the fact the paternalist is in the unenviable position of arguing against those she is seeking to help, may weaken the chance of any proposed reforms being accepted. For these reasons I will try to suggest reforms which do not prohibit high interest rates directly, but rather alter the structure of the rules governing the market so that the creditor bears a real risk in such situations (thus giving the consumer some value for the cost of home collections) and ensures the consumer enters into such transaction aware of their expensive nature, with the objective being to restrict the number of high interest loans made to poor consumers. This is not only fair to consumers, but also to society as a whole. Creditors' actions do not take place in isolation. Where there is debt and default the debtor suffers, but society also pays the price of any attendant ill health, marriage break up and homelessness. Where doorstep sellers push expensive goods and services this is at the expense of other more efficient suppliers and creditors. Where doorstep creditors use their weekly presence to ensure priority payment this is often at the expense of other creditors, typically the utilities.

6.   CHALLENGING ASSUMPTIONS ABOUT THE EXISTING VALUES OF THE MARKET

One's attitude to the UK's doorstep moneylending industry must depend upon whether one judges it against the current rules of the market or whether one adopts a more critical stance to a market which is stacked against the poor consumer. The point is that not all legitimate business is socially desirable. Within that statement is an inherent questioning of current notions of legitimacy. How one responds to the activities of moneylenders largely depends upon the sanctity with which one views current market arrangements. It is always hard to propose changes which challenge prevalent values about what is fair business practice, but such a challenge to the rules and attitudes governing the low income credit market is needed. The point can perhaps be made by countering three statements made by Rowlingson in her recent study, in which she states: 'The main conclusion must be that the licensed moneylending industry as a whole does not involve "deceitful or oppressive" practices and so does not come within the bounds of *socially harmful lending.*'[19]

This takes a very narrow view of what amounts to socially harmful lending. The Crowther Committee view of socially harmful lending certainly was that it could cover high interest rates *per se* even if there were no excessive profits.[20] Procuring agreements by deceitful or oppressive techniques offends against one's sense of justice and harms the dignity of contractors, but economic harm is caused by burdensome contracts, however procured. While one might also be uneasy about some of the practices adopted by some doorstep lenders in the privacy of a consumer's home, the real objection is that this is simply a too expensive method of lending money and for that reason is socially harmful to poor consumers. Rowlingson, however, suggests: '[her] research confirms previous work which shows that people on low incomes make rational decisions and act rationally, given the circumstances they find themselves in.'[21]

This assessment is only valid if one is satisfied with leaving poor consumers in blissful ignorance of the impact on their standard of living caused by their use of moneylenders. Given the large percentage of the income of some poor consumers which goes to moneylenders it seems worthwhile trying to educate them (or even regulate) to seek greater happiness by forgoing the services of moneylenders. This would seem

19.   Rowlingson, op. cit., n. 2, at pp. 157–8.
20.   Crowther, op. cit., n. 17, at para. 6.6.6 the report states: 'there is a level of cost above which it becomes socially harmful to make loans available at all, even if the cost is not disproportionate to the risk and expense incurred by the lender.'
21.   Rowlingson, op. cit., n. 2, at p. 161.

worthwhile even if the price is forcing these consumers to break with the security of the routine and known.

However, the linchpin of my argument for reform can be seen in my response to Rowlingson's description of the various arguments about the purpose for which consumers use moneylenders. She claims:

Critics argue that people are desperate for money when they borrow from a moneylender and they use this form of credit to buy basic necessities and pay bills. The industry claims that customers are using a moneylender to obtain consumer durables and improve their quality of life.[22]

My point is that if such expensive credit can ever be justified, it can only ever be so in extreme situations to meet basic necessities. Consumers would have a higher quality of life if they did not purchase consumer durables with such expensive creditors.

7. JUSTIFICATIONS FOR INTERVENTION

If expensive moneylending is undesirable, how can it be eradicated, or at least confined to those limited circumstances where its use may be justified because it is the only practical means of meeting basic needs? Three broad approaches suggest themselves. Two work with existing notions of the market, while a third challenges the basis of the contemporary market structure. I will call these three models the competition, alternative institution and market re-organisation approaches. My view is that all three techniques should be invoked to assist low income consumers, but that a proper solution requires re-organisation of the market by introducing more socially sensitive ground rules for contracting.

7.1 Competition

The competition approach does not simply require the market to be competitive, but also calls on notions of transparency to make the market truly sensitive to consumer demands. This therefore requires information to be provided and consumers to be educated in order to enable them to utilise this information. It also requires rules that prevent the vulnerable from being abused, with the aim being to reproduce the results which otherwise the market mechanisms would have given rise to. All this fits into the traditional model of contract law based on the notion of the voluntary

---

22.   Ibid., p. 70.

exchange of promises in a market which accepts rules which regulate the contract process but not the substance of the contract. Common criticisms of this approach are a lack of trust in competition policy to create competitive market forces and a regret that consumers cannot be sufficiently educated and motivated to participate to their best advantage in the resulting market conditions.

7.2 Market re-organisation

A more fundamental criticism is that the competition model accepts the existing market conditions as pre-ordained. With credit there are special justifications which could be invoked in order to justify government intervention in the ground rules of the market order. Admission to the credit market is typically treated as a privilege granted by way of licence. It would not be unreasonable to grant this licence on conditions which required money to be lent in a manner which was socially acceptable. Such justifications are perhaps strongest in jurisdictions such as the US where applicants have to establish that the granting of the licence is justified on the grounds of 'convenience and advantage' to the community.[23] However, no such special pleading for intervention in the credit market is needed, for the market is not a natural state but one created by a set of basic rules which have been established by society and which therefore can be changed by society.[24] Rules which have been established in the past can be altered. Equally, the failure in the past to establish a rule has been just as much a policy decision dictated by one's view of the market as would be any future decision to enact a rule.

Indeed, as I thought through proposals to reorganise the market rules by, for example, imposing ethical obligations on moneylenders to take the interest of their low income consumers into account or requiring loan transactions to be distinct from supply contracts, it became harder for me to discern a clear boundary between rules which would be justified by the competition model as enhancing the workings of the market and those which sought to interfere in the market order as presently established for

---

23. See R. Jordan and W. Warren, 'The Uniform Commercial Code' (1968) 68 *Columbia Law Review* 387 at 390 who explain the imposition of usury ceilings as being justified by some by analogy to conditions attached to monopoly rights of public utility companies.
24. As Collins has put it 'The law functions . . . to establish the ground rules on which the parties tacitly rely when they enter the market. In this sense, the law of contract constitutes the market order': see H. Collins, *Law of Contract*, 2nd edn (Butterworths, 1993), p. 14.

distributive objectives. This explains why I am discussing the market re-organisation approach immediately after the competition approach, although it might have been more logical to first consider the alternative institution approach which like the competition approach seeks a better solution within existing market conditions.

The current rules regulating fraud, duress and undue influence seem to condemn one type of advantage-taking, but condone the taking of advantages created by inequalities in wealth or the structure of the marketplace. This distinction is not always clear cut or easily defensible.[25] Indeed, as even those committed to the present market structure are prepared to impose prudent lending obligations on lenders, there seems no reason why these obligations should be restricted to ensuring the creditor will be secure in the return of capital and interest and could easily be extended to require considerations of the welfare of the debtor. Thus the ground rules of the market are not pre-ordained. There is nothing to prevent them being changed and these changes will affect the content of the bargains struck with possible redistributive consequences.[26]

Of course there is nothing to say that changes in legal rules will necessarily affect the behaviour of those participating in the moneylending market. Rowlingson suggests that many of the relationships between lender and borrower have long traditions and have often grown into friendships.[27] She cites one example of a manager selling a hamper to a client who ran her own hamper agency![28] Such examples should warn us that legal regulation cannot penetrate all layers of human interaction. It

25. See A. Kronman, 'Contract and distributive justice' (1980) 89 *Yale Law Journal* 472.
26. See D. Kennedy, 'The Stakes of Law, or Hale and Foucault!' in *Sexy Dressing etc* (Harvard University Press, 1993). For a stimulating analysis of these issues in relation to consumer credit see I. Ramsay, 'Consumer Credit Law, Distributive Justice and the Welfare State' (1995) 15 *Oxford Journal of Legal Studies* 177. Ramsay makes the point that the market rules for consumer credit have been established over the years so that they have an impact which is 'cumulative, intersecting with other doctrines and assumptions, so that the effects of the individual decision was not always simple and direct, but was nonetheless significant distributionally' (at 184). This pessimistic analysis of the past, could give rise to optimism for the future. It suggests that the climate for bargaining can be changed over time by a series of progressive reforms. The value to the social reformer lies in the fact that even if radical solutions fail to be accepted (as is usually the case), nevertheless a series of seemingly less radical measures could nevertheless alleviate the plight of the poor. This underlines the need to adopt measures on all fronts (competition, institutional alternatives as well as market organisational).
27. See Rowlingson, op. cit., n. 2, at pp. 140–4. In the language of Sally Falk Moore these might be described as 'fictive friendships': see 'Law and social change: the semi-autonomous Social Field as an Appropriate Subject of Study' (1973) 7 *Law and Society Review* 719.
28. Rowlingson, op. cit., n. 2, at p. 105.

may be that many businesses and customers will ignore as far as possible any legal rules which affect their relationship.

7.3 Alternative institutions

Of course, the market re-organisation approach is contentious. It may be more politically acceptable to wean the poor off expensive moneylenders by introducing new alternative social lending institutions into the marketplace. Some such institutions, like credit unions, have the advantage that their self-help philosophy is in tune with the prevalent fetish for individualism. However, social lending also costs money. Governments either have to provide subsidised loans directly or finance the infrastructure to allow low income consumers to organise themselves into credit unions. This means that social loans are never likely to be more than a marginal player in the credit market servicing low income consumers. Other limitations of social lending will be discussed later, but for now it should be noted that just as moneylenders' established relations with their clients may protect them from legal regulation it may also be sufficient to retain client loyalty even in the face of cheaper social loans. This does not mean that social lending should not be encouraged and that low income consumers should not be educated about its benefits, but rather suggests that faith should not be placed in social lending's ability to remedy market failure to the extent that we neglect to remedy the failings in the market structure.

8.   SOLUTIONS

Everybody would agree that it would be desirable if the cost of borrowing was cheaper for the poor. Differences arise as to whether it is possible to achieve this goal, at least without harmful side effects (such as the expansion of illegal moneylending) or costs which some commentators believe cannot be justified (such as government subsidisation of loans). Regarding the former risk, my view is that it is often overplayed and can be avoided by intelligent interventions in the marketplace; moreover, the response should be to tackle illegal activity rather than accept it and be forced to moderate one's policy. Illegal moneylending is an under-researched topic and enforcement is probably hampered by responsibility being divided between the police (who probably view it as a regulatory matter) and the Trading Standards Authority (who probably feel ill equipped to deal with practices which are more truly criminal than most of the trading practices they regulate). The question of government's subsidising credit institutions which service the poor is essentially a political question about the amount of resources given to the poor and the form in which this is provided. Personally, I would welcome more redistribution of wealth and see advantages in some of this being in the form of loan subsidisation, which helps with long term needs and budgeting problems, rather than direct cash payments which can easily be frittered away. However, I will resist the temptation of straying too far into these wider debates and later on will simply discuss the framework in which alternative credit institutions can best be developed to encourage their use.

What seems clear is that something needs to be done to curb the reliance of many poor consumers on expensive credit and that in striving for this goal one should not be doctrinaire about the techniques used to improve the lot of poor consumers of credit. Policies which are based on competition, market re-organisation and the creation of alternative credit institutions should be experimented with in the hope that a combination of such policies can improve the situation. In the following discussion a critique of the current position in the UK is combined with some comments of relevance to the broader debate about the feasibility and desirability of certain reforms aimed at improving the credit market for low income consumers.

8.1 Competition

Is the market for loans to low income consumers competitive? Certainly it is a discrete market not entered by many of the High Street lenders, but this need not mean that the market is particularly uncompetitive. So long as there is competition between those who operate in the low income credit market the goal of a competitive market need not be threatened. In a study of debtors in Sheffield, several were found to have loans from five or six different doorstep lenders.[29] This seems to be supported by Rowlingson's report where she cites examples of customers having a choice of creditor.[30] However, one gains the impression that the choice of creditor is not based so much on their charges for credit, but rather on the ease of the repayment terms, the attitude of the company to missed payments and the personality of the agent.

Several important consequences flow from these hypotheses. For example, new alternative credit institutions for the poor ought to try so far as possible to meet the preferences of their potential clientele for easy,

29. See Crow *et al.*, op. cit., n. 15, for description of the research and other survey results.
30. Rowlingson, op. cit., n. 2, at pp. 104–8.

flexible repayment terms and a personal service (perhaps even at the expense of some rise in cost). However, as far as the competitiveness of the market is concerned the lack of price sensitivity has serious implications for the traditional measure of competitiveness has been interest rates. Of course, it may be that poor consumers prize facilities such as friendly agents and easy, flexible repayments and are prepared to pay for these services. Thus taking the services offered into account the market may still be price sensitive. However, the suspicion persists that as the consumer's attention is not on the price of the credit there are opportunities for excess charges and, hence, profits to be made.

Much consumer credit regulation has been directed towards increased disclosure of interest rates. Is this policy inappropriate for low income consumers? It may be that poor consumers do not have enough confidence to play the market. Rowlingson points to the fear many customers of doorstep moneylenders have of losing access to what they perceive to be one of their last lines of credit.[31] This may cause them to prize too highly factors such as the apparent kind-heartedness of the collector and repayment terms which they have confidence they can meet and so avoid jeopardising their access to future credit. Such an analysis might be used to support policies such as interest rate ceilings on the basis that they help to simulate competitive market conditions by taking away the 'fear factor'.

However, even if many low income consumers do not presently seek out the cheapest form of loan, there is no reason why they should not be educated to do so. This could be supported by the development of alternative forms of social lending. These institutions might have an explicit educative role, but even their mere existence should help to educate the poor consumer. The low interest rates they offer should form a sharp contrast in the mind of the consumer when compared to the interest rates of the loans being pedalled on her doorstep. In making this comparison the key feature is the annual percentage rate (APR) which seeks to give a true comparator of the real cost of credit, taking into account the interest charged, other costs and the schedule for repayment. Although there are many technical concerns about the way the APR is calculated, the basic principle is sound. However, it is a complex concept. As already noted, in a study of debtors over three-quarters had heard of the term, but only one in seven of those could be regarded as having a reasonable understanding of its meaning.[32] This ignorance should not be accepted, but rather addressed through consumer education directed at those most exposed to high APRs.

Some argue that the APR is not valid for small loans as the proportionately high administration costs exaggerate the APR. However, while it is

31. Ibid., at p. 108.
32. See n. 16.

true that on small loans consumers may in practice be more concerned with the actual amount of interest paid, the APR remains a valuable guide to the cost of that credit, albeit that one may be prepared to accept a high APR on a small amount.[33] The high APRs on small loans exposes the truth that they are expensive! Thus there would seem no justification for the Office of Fair Trading's recommendation that the APR should not need to be disclosed on loans of less than £150.[34] It is to be welcomed that the Consumer Credit Association has recommended that its 800 licensed members continue to disclose the APR on all loans.[35] Although the fact that these companies are willing to be open about the high cost of their credit may also be a testament to the inadequacy of transparency and competition as regulatory tools in this sector.

One aspect of transparency which might be improved relates to connected lending. This involves goods being sold on credit to customers. Rowlingson notes that the cost of credit on connected lending is usually less than on money loans. Doubtless this is because the company is also making a profit on the goods element of the transaction. The consumer may, however, have a better deal by obtaining a money loan (even at a higher interest rate) and then purchasing cheaper goods elsewhere. The difficulty lies in making consumers aware of the choices open to them. I would suggest that connected lending transactions ought to be banned where the interest is high (above a prescribed figure). Doorstep sellers would then still be able to sell goods, but the financing would have to be by a separate loan. There would have to be freedom for consumers to obtain the loan from another source and equally for consumers to be able to purchase the goods for cash.[36] In addition, there would have to be sanctions to control the use of colourable cash prices, so that the regulation was not avoided by low interest rates disguising inflated prices.[37] In practice, the moneylender-client relationship may be such that little changes in reality as a result of the separation of the sale and credit transactions, but at least transparency is improved for those who are concerned to know exactly how much the goods cost and how much the credit costs.

33. The consumer movement and moneylenders share a common interest in explaining the meaning of APR!
34. *Consumer Credit Deregulation* (Office of Fair Trading, 1994).
35. Rowlingson, 'Moneylending and the Disclosure of APRs' (1995) *Consumer Law Journal* 170.
36. This would be an extension of the prohibition on advertisements where the goods are not also sold for cash; see s. 45 of the Consumer Credit Act 1974.
37. S. 138(4)(c) of the Consumer Credit Act 1974.

8.2 Prudent lender

In recent times, consumer credit law in the UK has seen the development of a principle of prudent lending, largely in response to the irresponsible lending practices of the 1980s which left many consumers hopelessly over-indebted when recession took its toll at the end of that decade and the beginning of this. Thus the Code of Practice for banks, building societies and card issuers requires banks and building societies to act responsibly and prudently when marketing.[38] However, the Code stops short of any obligation to be concerned about the ability of the consumer to repay, simply listing the sorts of information that will be taken into account when deciding whether to grant credit. The Director General of Fair Trading has made proposals which would go further. As part of the reforms concerning the replacement of the extortionate credit bargain provisions of the Consumer Credit Act 1974 by the concept of 'the unjust credit transaction' he would make one of the factors for assessing unjustness: 'the lender's care and responsibility in making the loan, including steps taken to find out and check the borrower's credit-worthiness and ability to meet the full terms of the agreement'.[39]

In similar vein one might cite the limited duties imposed on creditors to make sure guarantors understand the commitments that they are entering into.[40] However, while the rules on protecting guarantors are clearly solely motivated by a desire to promote prudent lending practices in order to protect the guarantor, the rules on prudent lending *per se* seek to prevent default. The motivations for seeking to reduce default are more eclectic. While there is doubtless a concern for the consumer, there is also an eagerness to protect the creditor from herself and the consequences of exposure to too many bad debts and equally a feeling that it is against the wider societal interest for there to be too much debt.

The prudent lending principle could, however, be developed from one concerned to protect creditors from over exposure to bad risks into a means for seeking to secure that the interests of debtors are taken into account. It would be unrealistic to expect salesmen voluntarily to dissuade consumers from contracting because they could get a better deal elsewhere or because the purchase did not make much sense given the consumer's position. Nor need one go so far as Ison in suggesting that all retail debts should be unenforceable, with the creditors' only sanctions being possible repossession of goods or the making of a negative report to a credit refer-

---

38. *Good Banking*, 2nd edn, 1994.
39. *Unjust Credit Transactions* (Office of Fair Trading, 1991).
40. *Barclays Bank v O'Brien* [1993] 4 All ER 417.

encing agency.[41] However, I would draw some inspiration from Ison and would give the courts the power of rendering loans unenforceable[42] where the interest charged is high. The courts would have the power to consider the circumstances in which the loan was concluded and the purpose of the loan in the light of the debtor's position and best interests. Such enquiries would only be undertaken when the interest was above a prescribed level so that the creditor would be on guard to the possibility that the loan could be scrutinised by these special criteria. Expensive credit would not be illegal, merely unenforceable at the court's discretion.

The sanction of unenforceablity is a potentially serious one and more severe than the sanction afforded by the extortionate credit bargain provisions, which still requires the court to order repayment of sums fairly due and reasonable. However, such agreements could function until the courts were asked to invoke these new powers by the customer, for instance when the relationship broke down or when the consumer has financial difficulties (other creditors would then be able to exclude such high interest loans from bankruptcy proceedings). The need for a party to invoke the possibility that the credit agreement might be unenforceable could be viewed as a weakness in the proposal. However, all private law rules are only effective if invoked and this approach simply accepts the reality that creditors and debtors may well continue to organise their relationships with little direct influence from the law.[43] However, even those consumers who do not invoke the new laws may benefit if creditors know that if they over step the mark the customer will be able to terminate the relationship and walk away from his or her debts.

At least three goals can be identified for this proposal: (i) improving marketing practices in the low income consumer credit market, (ii) evening up the balance of power between debtor and creditor, and (iii) preferring other debtors, who have not imposed such a burden on the debtor. Thus the proposal would counter blatant marketing abuses. For example, it could be used to challenge those unfair practices singled out for attention by the Director General of Fair Trading, namely, (i) the targeting of consumers who already had county court judgments and inappropriately selling them consolidation loans, and (ii) of particular concern to the moneylending industry, the practice of 'roll over' or 'top up' arrangements.[44]

41. Ison, *Credit Marketing and Consumer Protection* (Croom Helm, 1979), at pp. 284–92.
42. Indeed I would go further than Ison and extend such a power to cover money loans.
43. See Sally Falk Moore, op. cit., n. 27, who comments on the ability of strong social arrangements to resist legal changes.
44. See *Unjust Credit Transactions*, op. cit., n. 39, and also Sir Gordon Borrie, 'Lending to Those in Need: the Responsibilities of Lenders, Borrowers and Regulators', in Howells *et al.*, op. cit., n. 15.

This latter practice involves consumers taking out new loans before the previous loan has expired.[45] In settling the previous loan either no, or little, credit is given for early repayment, because the statutory rules governing rebates are not very generous, particularly for short-term loans. Some moneylending companies actually give more generous rebates than are required by legislation, but this still begs the question of whether such 'top up' arrangements are in the consumers' best interests. A more advantageous route might be to either wait until the existing loan expires or take out a new concurrent loan (the companies seem to have self-imposed restrictions on the number of loans outstanding).

However, my proposal is aimed at effecting more fundamental changes to the ground rules governing creditor–poor debtor relations. In particular, it is aimed at curbing the over promotion of this expensive product, especially when such credit has been used to sell luxury items. For example, I refuse to believe that the highest priority for low income families necessarily include the purchase of first aid boxes, Christmas food hampers and duvet covers[46] and believe it is irresponsible to push such sales with the assistance of extremely high credit. Equally we might question sales procured by suggestions that the condition of the customer's home could be improved[47] or which prey on a customer's loyalty either by suggesting the collector will be in trouble if targets are not met or will gain a bonus if they are[48] or which are induced by a fear that if the customer does not continue to keep an account their access to credit in the future will be affected.[49] Thus, this power would be used to counter some of the sales techniques, which although legal are unethical, especially the provision of expensive credit to the poor for the purchase of 'unnecessary luxuries' at the suggestion of the moneylender.

The proposal could perhaps be viewed as person related and need oriented.[50] It seeks to place into the contract paradigm a concern to respect the needs of the poor consumer and the position she finds herself in. It also requires of creditors an ethical standard in the marketing of their product which goes beyond simply avoiding misrepresentation, or even improvidence, and requires them to acknowledge their responsibilities towards clients whom they dominate economically, socially and psychologically. Inevitably any such principle of unenforceability would leave much to the

---

45. See Rowlingson, op. cit., n. 2, at pp. 109–12 and 161–2 for discussion of renewal practices.
46. Ibid., at p. 57.
47. Ibid., at p. 104.
48. Ibid., at pp. 106–7.
49. Ibid., at pp. 107–8.
50. To use the terminology of T. Wilhemsson in *Critical Studies in Private Law* (Kluwer Law International, 1992).

discretion of the adjudicator. For instance, there might be some circumstances when such contracts would be enforced, *eg*, when the loan had been the only means to meet a genuine need and there had been no undue pressure placed on the consumer. There may be some dangers in leaving this assessment to a judiciary which has proven itself reluctant to use even its present more conservative powers to tackle extortionate credit bargains.[51]

One solution might be a new forum for resolving consumer disputes. Perhaps a credit ombudsman might be established building on the experience of the banking and building societies ombudsmen, or something more imaginative like a consumer tribunal. However, if the judiciary are given this new power there are some grounds for hoping that it will be effective. In part this would be because of the prescribed rate where these powers bite. One reason for a threshold being set was to put creditors on guard that the transaction might be investigated. Another benefit is that it should give the courts the confidence to intervene. This encouragement to intervene ought to be bolstered by the fact that the motives for proposing such a radical solution should be self evident to even the most traditional judge. It can only be hoped that these factors are enough to challenge centuries of contract law ideology based around the sanctity of agreements struck it an allegedly 'free' market.

8.3 Interest rate ceilings

Those, like myself, who are saddened by the exploitatively high interest rates charged to those who can least afford them frequently wish that the introduction of interest rate ceilings could provide a solution. Elsewhere I have favoured consideration of interest rate ceilings, but have tended to hold back from whole-heartedly endorsing such a policy in favour of the use of a presumptive figure attached to an unconscionability standard.[52] This pragmatic approach has been partly due to a feeling that there may be something in the argument that one cannot buck the market (far better to re-fashion it) and the consequences of introducing rate ceilings may be restricted access for the poor to credit (which in itself need not be a bad thing) and forcing them into the hands of illegal moneylenders (which certainly is worrying).

---

51. See L. Bentley and G. Howells, 'Judicial Treatment of Extortionate Credit Bargains' (1989) *Conveyancer* 164 and *Unjust Credit Transactions*, op. cit., n. 39.
52. Howells, 'Enhancing the Choice of Credit for Poor Consumers', in R. Mayer (ed.), *Enhancing Consumer Choice* (ACCI, 1990); G. Howells, 'Controlling Unjust Credit Transactions: Lessons from a Comparative Analysis', in Howells *et al.*, op. cit., n. 15.

However, my main reason for holding back has not been a substantive objection – after all many of the same results would lead from proposals for a presumptively extortionate interest rate and I believe these objections can be overcome by, for example, the development of social lending institutions and effective policing of illegal credit markets. Rather my pragmatic stance is an acceptance of political realities about the resistance there would be to rate ceilings being introduced in the UK, along with nagging concerns about what would happen to those with genuine need for credit if such laws were introduced before alternative social lending institutions had developed sufficiently.

The proposal outlined above for the courts to have the power to render unenforceable high interest credit agreements is in many ways a refinement of the idea of a presumptively extortionate interest rate, but by avoiding the language of interest rate ceilings is hopefully more acceptable. One of the basic tensions surrounding rate regulation, be it by imposing interest rate ceilings or through the use of an unconscionability standard, is whether one is simply seeking to simulate competitive market force conditions or whether one is seeking to ban contracts even where the creditor is acting efficiently within market conditions. My view is that it should be the impact on the debtor which justifies regulation not the economics of the supply side.

Having favoured an unconscionability approach over a fixed ceiling I have attempted to answer the question of when intervention in the market is justified. The answer lies in seeking to do more than a simple act of market transference. Simply trying to look for undue pressure as an excuse for intervention is inadequate. There may be some instances of moneylenders behaving in a manner which can be challenged under traditional contract law principles, *eg*, misrepresentation, economic duress, etc. However, most of the problems arise from more subtle advantage-taking of the superior position the creditor holds in the relationship.

Sometimes this advantage-taking is conscious where, for example, creditors prey on the debtor's loyalty. At other times it is simply arises from the structure of a market which allows the creditor to place all the risk of default on to the debtors. My proposal would refashion the structure of the marketplace by making relevant an assessment of the debtor's true interest in the transaction. This remains paternalist in the sense that it is premised on the belief that there are some transactions which people should not enter into. Their false consciousness may lead them to believe it is in their own best interest, but I disagree so strongly as to what is in their true interest, that I would be prepared to restrict their liberty.

However, the most damning criticism of paternalism is not that it imposes one set of beliefs upon another, but that in so doing it harms the people it seeks to help. I hope to have avoided this by asking the courts to

259

take the purpose of the loan into account. Thus loans to purchase essentials would be less likely to be re-opened (assuming there was no improper behaviour) than credit for luxuries. The poor may have to wait a little longer for their luxuries, but they will be able to afford more of them. Neither does my proposal limit interest rates. A millionaire could agree to buy a first aid box with credit of 500 per cent, but because his ability to meet his basic needs is not threatened the courts need not intervene. It is the situation of the poor person and the impact of the transaction on that situation that justifies the court enquiring about the purpose of the loan and scrutinising the ethics of the marketing of credit.

8.4 Alternative institutions

So far we have considered two possible approaches to improving the lot of poor consumers of credit. With limited optimism, we have considered ways in which the market can be made more competitive and transparent. More ambitiously we have attempted a reformulation of the ground rules for contracting in order to refashion the market so that creditors are not allowed to exploit the economic power they have over debtors without having concern for the situation and interests of the poor debtors. This second approach is controversial as it challenges the assumption that the market is a given state and requires contractors to be aware of their ethical and social responsibilities instead of simply following their own self interest. The third approach which we will consider now is the development of alternative social lending institutions.

Although potentially radical, this approach is likely to be more acceptable than that aimed at re-organising the market by changing the ground rules, for it introduces new players into the credit market for poor consumers without challenging the 'rules of the game' for existing members. Although some might object to subsidies paid to social lenders this approach is relatively uncontroversial, if only because initiatives to date, in the UK, at least, have had limited impact on the low income credit market.

Globally, social banking is having a resurgence with the Grameen Bank in Bangladesh[53] and the Shorebank Corporation in Chicago[54] being well cited examples. Elsewhere within Europe, the Netherlands has a well-

---

53. See Ramsay, op. cit., n. 26, at 187; and G. Howells, 'Contract Law: the Challenge for the Critical Consumer Lawyer', in T. Wilhelmsson (ed.), *Perspectives of Critical Contract Law* (Dartmouth, 1993).

54. Shapiro, 'Shorebank Corporation: a Private Sector Banking Initiative to Renew Distressed Xommunities', in U. Reifner and J. Ford (eds), *Banking for People* (Walter de Gruyter, 1992).

developed system of municipal credit banks and social assistance loans offering loans to the poor and in France social loans continue to be provided through the Caisses de Crédit Municipal which developed out of the *monts de piétés,* which were fifteenth-century charitable pawn-broking institutions.[55] However, I will limit myself to a brief discussion of the two most significant social lending institutions in the UK at the present time: credit unions[56] and the social fund.[57] This will hopefully highlight some of the possibilities for social lending as well as draw attention to some of the limitations to this approach to solving the problems of poor consumers.

It is clear that many of the relationships between moneylender and client are strong and long-standing. We have already noted that this may be an obstacle preventing changes in the legal regime from impacting on actual practice. Equally we have commented that this may be a barrier to the development of social lending institutions if consumers cannot be persuaded to change allegiances. This may be especially so because, as many consumers' choice of creditor does not appear to be very price sensitive, the biggest attractions of social lending institutions – their low interest rates – may not be as attractive to some potential customers as might be expected. Social lenders must therefore try to ensure that so far as possible their services are provided in ways which appeal to low income consumers.[58] The following hypothesise can be suggested: low income consumers require confidentiality, but like dealing with a creditor they know and who will allow them to pay back at a rate they can afford and be flexible if there any difficulties with repayments; many wish to make weekly repayments to a caller or at the creditor's office.

55. See G. Howells and M. Moroney, 'Social Lending in Europe', in Howells *et al.*, op. cit., n. 15.

56. For more detail see R. Berthoud and T. Hinton, *Credit Unions in the United Kingdom,* (Policy Studies Institute, 1989); G. Griffiths and G. Howells, 'Britain's Best Kept Secret: an Analysis of Credit Unions as an Alternative Source of Credit' (1991) *Journal of Consumer Policy* 443; G. Griffiths and G. Howells, 'Slumbering Giant or White Elephant: Do Credit Unions have a Role in the United Kingdom Credit Market?' (1991) 42 *Northern Ireland Legal Quarterly* 199; G. Griffiths and G. Howells, 'Credit Unions in the United Kingdom and Possible Legislative Reforms to the Credit Unions Act 1979', in Howells *et al.*, op. cit., n. 15.

57. Howells, 'Social Fund Budgeting Loans: Social and Civil Justice?' (1990) 9 *Civil Justice Quarterly* 118; J. Mesher, 'The Legal Structure of the Social Fund', in M. Freeman (ed.), *Critical Issues in Welfare Law* (Stevens, 1990); G. Craig, 'Classification and Control: the Role of Social Fund Loans', in Howells *et al.*, op. cit., n. 15.

58. For the purpose of investigating the factors which affected debtors' choice of creditors the present writer undertook an empirical research study: see Howells *et al.*, op. cit., n. 15.

8.4.1   Credit unions

Credit unions are financial cooperatives using members' savings to make loans at no more than 1 per cent per month (an APR of around 12.7 per cent). One per cent a month is an attractive marketing slogan, and even if there are some hidden costs because clients are forced to continue to save (and not withdraw savings) this may not be of great concern to consumers whose only other option is a moneylender. One problem with community-based credit unions targeted at low income consumers is developing the infrastructure to support the union and training members of the community to run it. Local authority funding has helped in some cases, but it is yet to be seen if the unions can be maintained in the long term. The major problem in low income areas is finding consumers with enough money to save so that sufficient funds can be built up for loans to be made. If such a credit union can be established does it meet the needs of low income consumers? As the union is based in the community there will be a local office. However, as most unions are staffed on a voluntary basis the opening hours may be limited and few have the facilities to offer home collections. It would not seem to be a problem for credit unions to offer weekly repayment periods and the level of repayments is kept to what members can afford.[59] As those who run the union would be members of the community, there should be an informality which encourages residents to approach the union to become members, but some may fear a lack of confidentiality if they have to discuss financial affairs with their neighbours. In summary, credit unions can be a positive addition to the options available to poor consumers. But they do have limitations concerning their practical feasibility both to become established and continue to run on a long-term basis and also because they require members to first have a savings record before they can borrow. It may be that credit unions help the relatively rich and well motivated members of low income communities and further isolate those who are less well off.[60]

---

59. Although Berthoud and Hinton, op. cit., n. 56, p. 102 suggest this is due more to the size of the loans taken out by poorer members being relatively small than any significant favouring of poorer members in relation to the rate of repayment.

60. However, the benefits of a credit union are not restricted to the cheap loans they offer. Possibly of even greater significance is the community spirit it can engender; the business skills it teaches the members of the community involved in its management and the confidence they derive from that and the education into savings patterns and about money management which it nurtures.

8.4.2   Social fund

The social fund is a government system aimed, in part, at providing interest free loans to those on income support. A fundamental flaw with the social fund as a social lending institution is that it was not set up to provide additional access to loans, but rather was an attempt to restrict spending on social security by introducing a cash limited loans scheme to meet needs which had previously been met by grants. The scheme is not very popular. Partly this is because claimants do not like having to place themselves at the mercy of social fund officers who have a discretion as to which loans are made. Also although the loans are interest free, the repayments can amount to a sizeable percentage of benefit which is deducted at source, giving the claimants little flexibility to manipulate their finances from week to week. Subsidised loans to the poor may have a role to play, but this should be additional to basic benefit levels. It may even be better for the loans to be at market rates but with repayment schedules being easier. It may also be better for the loans to be administered by a different agency than that which delivers benefits. The poor would then see such loans as less like handouts at the discretion of benefits officers and more like another choice of creditor for them to turn to.

9.   THE CONSUMER LAWYER'S TASK

There may seem little lawyers can do to assist the poor if there is no political desire to adopt policies involving redistribution payments from the rich to the poor. However, one of the aims of consumer law should be to ensure that everyone, but especially the poor, make the best use of the resources which are available to them. Consumer credit is perhaps the most obvious area where poor consumers suffer from a free market philosophy which isolates them from the consumer collective and imposes harsh terms on them. Consumer advocates should promote a more transparent and competitive market so that even poor consumers can be educated to strike the best deal available. Where this is not sufficient social lending institutions should be encouraged to meet the needs of the poor. The unique task of the consumer lawyer is to demonstrate that the legal framework of the market is not pre-ordained and that it is perfectly feasible to have a competitive free market underpinned by principles of social justice which require creditors to be sensitive to the concerns of the disadvantaged in our society.

Chapter Twelve

RACIAL AND GENDER EQUALITY IN MARKETS FOR FINANCIAL SERVICES

Iain Ramsay and Toni Williams

Chapter Outline

Consumer Protection in Financial Services (P. Cartwright, ed.: 90-411-9717-6: © Kluwer Law International: pub. Kluwer Law International, 1999: printed in Great Britain)

[I]n many settings, markets will not stop discrimination . . . Indeed, markets are often the problem rather than the solution. They guarantee that discrimination will persist. Enthusiasm for markets as an anti-discrimination policy is at best wishful thinking.[1]

1.   INTRODUCTION

At the close of the twentieth century, consumer markets for financial services have become a central focus of economic and social policy. Countries of the north are experiencing wholesale restructuring of the welfare state, one element of which process being the re-privatisation of social provisioning. Private insurance, pension plans and bank loans are replacing the publicly funded institutions and social insurance schemes of the mid-twentieth century. In many countries of the south, the austerity packages demanded by the protectors of international capital, such as the International Monetary Fund, have prevented the creation of even rudimentary systems of social welfare.

Financial institutions are also in an era of change, with cross-border mergers of banks resulting in increasingly large units of finance capital and the breakdown of traditional regulatory barriers between differing forms of financial service providers. These developments in financial services should also be related to the dominant role of financial markets. Technology, which links the world's financial markets and which makes possible the instantaneous transfer of large amounts of capital, has facilitated the worldwide search for profitable opportunities for capital. Financial markets are the sites where profits are sucked in to search for the highest returns possible in a globalised trading market. This speeding up of the accumulation process has led to the description of global financial markets as 'the actual collective capitalist, the mother of all accumulations'.[2] It is also a market where there is the continuing possibility of a global crash, notwithstanding the sophisticated techniques of risk management which have been developed over recent decades. Units
subject to the logic of this marke
dominant institutions in the new
twentieth century, these instituti
these markets.

1.   C. Sunstein, *Free Markets and So*
2.   M. Castells, *The Information Ag*
      Millennium (Blackwell, 1997), p.
3.   We take the phrase from Castells,

Within this 'informational capitalism', there is evidence of social inequality and social exclusion where significant numbers of individuals are treated as being of little value as producers or consumers.[4] These patterns are reflected in the increasing segmentation of consumer markets for traditional financial services. There are several dimensions to this inequality of treatment. There is increasing sorting and classification of consumers made possible by sophisticated technology. In this process, high-income consumers reap the benefits of competition as service providers compete in this market of 'relationship banking'. Those consumers at the bottom, by contrast, are treated as discarded goods, and find difficulties in accessing credit and standard financial services from mainstream lenders. This market segmentation is reflected also in differential regulation of markets. More resources are devoted to regulation of services used by middle and upper middle class consumers, such as securities markets and the protection of bank deposits, than to regulation of pawnshops, cheque cashing and income tax rebate services, which services are all part of the growing 'fringe banking' sector[5] in the US. The distributional impact of the stratification of financial services is highlighted by the closure of banks and other financial institutions in lower income areas. Access to financial services, the payments system, and credit is necessary to many aspects of social life so that exclusion from these services represents a significant exclusion from public life and ability to participate fully in society. Communities excluded from access to credit and capital will decline quickly. It is appropriate, therefore, to view the consumer interest here as concerning broader questions of citizenship in contemporary society. Values associated with the public sphere such as democratic participation, accountability and equality are therefore relevant to assessing credit markets and the provision of consumer financial services.

There also has been a large growth in the self-employed, many of whom are women. These small business owners are often highly dependent on financial institutions. In their dealings with banks and other lenders they may confront exclusionary policies and practices that place them in at least as disadvantageous a bargaining position as consumers.

These introductory remarks illustrate some of the ways in which access to credit and capital are significant public issues in the post-welfare state. This chapter explores the implications of market provisioning

4. See Castells, *The Information Age: Economy, Society and Culture* Vol. I: *The Rise of the Network Society* (Blackwell, 1996), chapter 2 and references cited there. In the UK see, eg, Commission for Social Justice (1994) *Social Justice: Strategy for National Renewal*, p. 28, Joseph Rowntree Foundation (1995) *Income and Wealth*, vol. 1, and vol. 11, chapter 5.
5. See John P. Caskey, *Fringe Banking: Check Cashing Outlets, Pawnshops, and the Poor* (Russell Sage Foundation, 1994).

for racial and gender equality in access to financial services. We discuss markets for services related to home ownership, such as mortgage loans and insurance and outline differing responses to discriminatory practices, including human rights legislation, community reinvestment strategies and institutional changes in access to credit and capital. We argue that law has embedded the power to exploit women and racialized persons, and to discriminate against them in the institutional structure of the markets for these services. This is reflected in traditional interpretations of the common law doctrine of freedom of contract and its continuing power should not be discounted. Gender and race inequality have both economic and cultural dimensions, and it is important to recognise that remedies must address both these contributors to exclusion and oppression. If bankers believe media stereotypes about the poor or individuals on welfare then we argue that this may, in the context of financial services, reinforce other factors which lead to credit exclusion for these groups.

An important development of the last fifty years is the increasing awareness of the subtle but powerful ways that social institutions may produce and reproduce racial and gender inequality. The civil rights struggles and women's movements of the mid-twentieth century may have led to the elimination of many explicit forms of exclusions and discrimination, but full social and economic equality has proven to be an elusive goal. Women and racialized persons are still subjected to excessive state and private violence, remaining largely excluded from access to power. Their communities and their lives within those communities continue to be marginalised. Petty barriers to their full participation in civic society endure.

Recognition that the dismantling of overtly discriminatory regimes of private and public power has not brought about racial and gender equality has provoked hotly contested debates about the nature of the problem, and how to proceed. Defenders of the status quo claim that contemporary institutions generally work about as well as might be expected. They insist that non-discrimination principles represent the limit of desirable, or even attainable, reform. If women and racialized persons continue to experience disadvantage despite the protections offered by formal equality, then the fault must lie in their choices, abilities and preferences.

Critics maintain that the limited gains from human rights initiatives demonstrate the weaknesses of strategies that promote formal equality without also addressing the legacy of exclusion and discrimination. They argue that it is not enough to remove contemporary legal barriers to participation if historical patterns of social and economic exclusion are embedded in institutional practices. In such circumstances, the layering of formal equality on top of substantive inequality is likely to conceal but not to displace exclusionary forces. Racial and gender inequality are, in a sense, beyond the reach of the traditional civil rights of liberal regimes within capitalist societies. Their eradication demands a more proactive and systematic disruption of dominant institutions.

2.   FREEDOM FROM CONTRACT: EXCLUSION AND EXPLOITATION

The institutional structure of markets for services is constituted by the various legal regimes that govern the supply of such services. In most parts of North America, the common law of property and contract continue to be constructed as the backbone of the market, even when the market in question is subject to significant public regulation. Common law norms are treated as a set of basic ground rules that operate as a starting point from which departures must be justified, and as an interpretative lens through which to view alternative regulatory schemes. These norms are extraordinarily resilient. Although few North American markets are structured exclusively by the common law, its values and prescriptions continue to dominate contemporary understandings of the market:

[T]he applicability of this theory has been subject over time to several qualifications. First, there are the exclusions: whole areas of law, like family law, labour law, antitrust . . . that were once regarded as branches of a unified contract theory, but gradually came to be seen as requiring a specific set of categories unassimilable to that theory. Then there are the exceptions: bodies of law and social practice . . . that come under an anomalous set of principles within the central area of contract. Finally, there are the repressions: problems like those of long-term contractual dealings that . . . are more often dealt with by ad hoc deviations from the dominant rules and ideas than by clearly distinct norms. When you add up the exclusions, the exceptions and the repressions . . . traditional contract theory . . . seems like an empire whose claimed or perceived authority vastly outreaches its actual power. Yet this theory continues to rule in at least one important sense: it compels all other modes of thought to define themselves negatively, by contrast to it. This intellectual dominance turns out to have important practical consequences . . .[6]

The property/contract system of the common law empowers economic actors to make decisions about the resources they control, such as decisions to permit or to deny access to those resources, and the terms on which they are made available to the market. Common law principles embed a particular pattern of control over resources, authority to make decisions about access, and restraint against interference with authorised

---

6.   Roberto Mangabeira Unger, 'The Critical Legal Studies Movement' (1983) 95 *Harvard Law Review* 563, 617.

decisions. This pattern of material power is represented and reproduced by the ideology of freedom of contract. It generally permits private actors to make arbitrary decisions about access to resources they control without being accountable for their choices, and also to set the terms on which goods or services are made available subject only to what the consumer can be persuaded to accept. State interference, which in this context includes judicial control over access to contract and the substance of contract terms, is generally not permissible, although in limited circumstances judicial protection against harsh contract terms may be available for consumers who are constructed as unable to protect themselves.

Critical scholars in law and in economics have mounted a sustained attack on the ideology of freedom of contract, repeatedly exposing its incoherence. That freedom of contract may have been shown to be radically indeterminate, however, has not diminished its power to justify exclusion. Freedom *from* contract remains the ideological baseline of the common law, which is institutionalised in the permission arbitrarily to refuse to deal with consumers because of their race, sex or other characteristics,[7] and which constructs human rights legislation as interventions designed to secure a competing goal of equality. It is this freedom which is, in classical law, a fundamental aspect of freedom of contract. However, the contrast between freedom and equality might better be replaced by a conflict between two freedoms, freedom from, and consumers' freedom *to,* contract. The ability of an individual to develop life plans may be severely restricted by a pervasive exercise by one group of their freedom from contract. Many aspects of freedom from contract represent permissions granted by the judiciary or legislature, and therefore implicate state action as much as do explicit judicial prohibitions on the use of unfair terms.

3. RESPONSES TO DISCRIMINATION IN ACCESS TO CREDIT AND CAPITAL: HUMAN RIGHTS LAW

Human rights laws in various jurisdictions have to some extent modified the common law in so far as they typically prohibit exclusionary decisions by private actors on the grounds of race, sex and other characteristics associated with discrimination. The traditional model of human rights recognised the idea of equal treatment: that it was wrong for a market provider

---

7. Neil G. Williams, 'Offer, Acceptance, and Improper Considerations: a Common Law Model for the Prohibition of Racial Discrimination in the Contracting Process' (1994) 62 *George Washington Law Review* 183; note 'The Anti-discrimination Principle in the Common Law' (1989) 102 *Harvard Law Review* 1993.

to discriminate between two similarly situated individuals whose only difference was based on an irrelevant characteristic, which the discriminated individual had no power to change. A major development in human rights laws has been the recognition of 'disparate impact' which goes beyond the equal treatment model and recognises the possibility that apparently neutral criteria of exclusion may have a disproportionately disadvantageous impact on groups protected under human rights legislation. The idea of disparate impact, which originated in US employment discrimination cases,[8] has drawn attention to the fact that factors such as the use of stability of home ownership in credit applications may be discriminatory against minority groups who find it necessary to move frequently in order to progress economically.

In Ontario, Canada, a challenge was brought before the Human Rights Commission under disparate impact analysis to the use by landlords of 30 per cent rent to income ratios as a mechanism for screening potential tenants or borrowers.[9] It was argued that these provisions had a disparate impact on protected groups under the human rights code, such as those on welfare, single mothers, refugees, young people and black consumers. The arguments in this case indicate the possibilities and limits of this form of human rights strategy as a response to unequal access to credit.

Landlords and financial interests argued that the rent/income ratios were simply a rational response to the risk of default; that the prohibition on this form of screening could result in more invidious forms of screening, and that tenants might be made worse off because of higher prices and/or greater exclusion of marginal tenants. It was also argued that the relatively objective income criterion was preferable to a more subjective individual evaluation of prospective tenants. This response is the standard neoclassical response to distributional measures in consumer protection. It is not clear, however, based on the evidence in the case whether the actual rental market operated in this fashion. There was some evidence that the income criterion might well be an arbitrary form of exclusion, used to justify discretionary decision making based on stereotyping of lower income consumers as shiftless and unreliable. Landlords, including those involved in the litigation, had rented to tenants who were paying more than 30 per cent of their income towards the rent. The strong opposition to these claims by financial interests might well represent a fear of loss of discretionary (arbitrary) control over

8. See *Griggs v Duke Power Co.* 401 US 424 (1971).
9. See *In the Matter of a Hearing before the Ontario Human Rights Board of Inquiry Board* File Nos. 92-0213/4/6 *Bramalea Ltd and Shelter Corporation ats. Kearney et al.*

whom they wish to deal with (freedom from contract). The case also drew attention to the link between cultural images and exclusion, and the extent to which apparently objective criteria may underline cultural stereotyping of groups.[10] Seen in this light the issues were not simply those of the imperatives of market forces versus attempts to redistribute in the face of market forces. Rather it was a more complex empirical question about the institutional structure and operation of the rental housing market. Since this market diverges significantly from the abstract neo-classical model, economic predictions must be made in the context of the particular empirical circumstances of the market, and it is arguable whether one can make accurate predictions about the impact on the market of the rent/income ratios based on the abstract model of the market. In other words as an empirical matter the economic answer to the allocative and distributional impacts of choice on this issue is unclear.

This case may have had the salutary effect of drawing attention to the extent to which apparently hard economic analysis was premised on misleading cultural images of groups. However, there are limitations to a human rights approach to issues of lending discrimination, particularly where they depend heavily on private actors initiating cases. Developing successful arguments concerning disparate impact depend on the availability of statistical data to support the conclusion of disparate impact. Unless there are publicly available data on lending practices to different groups, it will be difficult to obtain these data. In the US, the existence of the Home Mortgage Disclosure Act, which requires financial institutions to collect data on the race of home borrowers, has permitted greater monitoring and enforcement action against discrimination in mortgage lending. However, without this type of information such actions will be difficult. In addition, the human rights approach protects only those groups identified in the human rights legislation so that it can address only indirectly the issue of economic discrimination. Such an approach may reinforce the exclusionary core of the common law which permits arbitrary exclusion outside those grounds specifically identified in human rights legislation. Any disadvantages which ordinary individuals face in the market (beyond traditional market failure) can be rationalised as simply the consequence of 'the market' as if this referred to some particular, identifiable and pre-political institutional framework. In addition, those groups who are excluded from challenging discrimination may feel that one must belong to a 'special interest group' to obtain protection and the possibility of coalition-building among different groups may be

10. See the discussion of these issues in *Harris v Capital Growth Investors* X1V (1991) 805 P.2d. 873.

reduced. Finally, while the symbolic impact of these cases may be significant, they are unlikely to lead to major or fundamental change in the institutional structure of markets for lending and saving. However, it may well be these structures which have a decisive distributional impact.

4. REDLINING

The struggle over redlining provides an important example of the need for proactive strategies to counteract exclusionary practices in key markets for consumer services. Redlining refers to a process by which goods or services are made unavailable, or are available only on less than favourable terms, to people because of where they live regardless of their relevant objective characteristics.[11] In the US, where the problem has received most attention, redlining is most strongly associated with markets for credit and insurance services related to housing. The consumers who have been denied access to these services are primarily of African–American heritage. While redlining is often seen as a matter of urban policy, the roots of exclusion – and its likely solution – lie in the operation of markets for consumer services.

Redlining is the most recent manifestation of racially exclusionary practices in American housing markets. These practices have a long history, and for many years they were promoted by government institutions. For example, a 1930s' policy manual of the Federal Housing Administration (FHA) clearly indicates that racial minorities were perceived as a threat to federal subsidy programmes rather than beneficiaries of them:

Areas surrounding a location are to be investigated to determine whether incompatible racial and social groups are present, for the purpose of making a prediction regarding the probability of the location being invaded by such groups. If a neighbourhood is to retain stability, it is necessary that properties shall continue to be occupied by the same social and racial classes. A change in social or racial occupancy generally contributes to instability and a decline in values.[12]

This approach towards housing markets was so pervasive in the Federal Housing Administration throughout the middle decades of the twentieth

---

11. Gregory D. Squires, 'Community Reinvestment: an Emerging Social Movement', in Gregory D. Squires (ed.), *From Redlining to Reinvestment: Community Responses to Urban Disinterment* (Temple University Press, 1992). Also see generally, Robert D. Ballard, J. Eugene Grigsby III and Charles Lee, *Residential Apartheid: The American Legacy* (CAAS Publications, 1994).
12. US Federal Housing Administration Underwriting Manual (1938) Washington DC: US Govt Printing Office 937. Quoted in Squires, 'Community Reinvestment: an Emerging Social Movement', op. cit., n. 11.

century that one commentator described the agency as having adopted a racial policy that could well have been culled from the Nuremberg laws. From its inception FHA set itself up as the protector of the all-white neighbourhood.[13]

By the late 1960s, however, a variety of federal initiatives had transformed the government's role in American housing markets. Ostensibly, at least, federal agencies became the main promoters of non-discrimination and fair housing. The Federal Fair Housing Act,[14] introduced in 1968, banned discrimination in housing markets based on a variety of grounds, including race, colour and national origin. This has been reinforced by The Equal Credit Opportunity Act,[15] which outlawed racial and other forms of discrimination in lending markets and the Home Mortgage Disclosure Act 1975 (subsequently strengthened by the Financial Institution Reform, Recovery and Enforcement Act, 1990) which required financial institutions to file detailed annual reports on their lending activity.

Much of this legislation is directed towards changing the ground rules of markets for financial services related to housing. The basic non-discrimination norms seek to prevent creditors from making decisions on the prohibited grounds, while the disclosure requirements attempt to increase the transparency of their decision-making processes. With the reduction of creditor discretion to exclude from these markets, opportunities for minority participation ought to improve.

The persistence of redlining, however, indicates that solutions to the problem of discriminatory exclusion from consumer services markets may require more than these conventional reforms. Each attempt to outlaw reliance on specific characteristics has been met by ever more sophisticated methods of sorting and scoring potential borrowers. These methods, deliberately or not, may further entrench bias against minority consumers. As the indirectly exclusionary impact of one technique is exposed and addressed, another emerges to replace it. In part the problem is the legacy of racial exclusion in these markets, which may result in apparently objective factors being tinged with cultural values that have a racialized impact, as manifested in our above noted example of the use of stability of home ownership in credit applications.

---

13.   Kenneth T. Jackson, *The Crabgrass Frontier: The Suburbanization of the United States* (Oxford University Press, 1985), p. 215, quoting Charles Adams.
14.   42 USC 3601-3619.
15.   USC 1691ff.

5.   COMMUNITY REINVESTMENT AND BEYOND

More effective strategies to increase minority access to markets for consumer services may require that suppliers be compelled to take specific positive steps to bring about change. The Community Reinvestment Act,[16] for example, imposes duties on banks to establish (or not to close) branches in minority areas. It requires banks to meet 'the credit needs of its entire community, including low and moderate income neighbourhoods, consistent with the sound and safe operation' of a bank. The Act has become of increasing significance in relation to US banking. Since mergers may be blocked if a bank has a poor performance record under the Act, it has provided important leverage to community groups to require commitments by banks to lower income communities. The Federal Reserve Board has also developed measures for assessing the performance of banks in meeting the needs of low income communities and these data are publicly available. The Act has increased lending in lower income communities and has added greater democratic accountability to the merger process. One difficulty is that of defining community as banks become nationwide. Since the depression, US banks have been locally based, but the legislative abandonment of restrictions on national banks makes the definition of community more complex and is relevant to attempts to transplant the Act to countries such as the UK. In addition to the Community Reinvestment Act, proactive measures that involve specific changes to advertising, hiring and lending policies are also available under the administrative enforcement provisions of the Fair Housing Act. Recent Consent Decrees to implement these provisions open up the possibility that detailed regulation of particular markets and particular suppliers within those markets may be an avenue for change.[17]

   These reforms have significant potential since they may affect bank culture as well as changing the ground rules of lending policies. Peter Swires argues that those who are in influential positions within the bank will have had little exposure to the issues and problems of low income neighbourhoods.[18] The route to success in banking has been traditionally through involvement in large corporate loans. In addition, there may be significant agency costs in attempting to monitor the conduct of lending

16.   12 USC 2901-2906.
17.   See for example *US v American Family Mutual Insurance Co. NAACP v American Family Insurance Co.* (US Dist. Ct.) Civ. Action No 90-C-0759 (Wis) Consent Decree. *US v Chevy Chase Savings Bank* and *B.F. Saul Mortgage Company* Consent Decree (1993).
18.   See P. Squires, 'The Persistent Problem of Lending Discrimination: a Law and Economics Analysis' (1994–95) 73 *Texas Law Journal* 787.

officers who will often exercise significant discretion in lending decisions. Since this structure is likely to be relatively common within the banking industry, banks may rationally calculate that other banks with similar structures will be unwilling to invest in underprivileged areas. A combination of these factors may result in underinvestment in low income and disadvantaged areas. It is possible therefore that legislation such as the Community Reinvestment Act may over time change these perceptions, and have both an economic and cultural impact in reducing stereotyping of low income consumers as uncreditworthy. Once a bank is established in an area, the simple motivation to maximise profits may provide a significant incentive to adapt lending policies to the characteristics of the local community

There are, however, potential limitations with this approach. The early development of the Community Reinvestment Act in the US is often conceptualized as a model of affirmative action. It was open therefore to the interpretation that, but for government coercion, banks would not invest in these communities, because the logic of market profitability would result in investment in more profitable investments. This argument is partly based on the assumption that 'market forces' drive the activity of banks towards a single investment and not the alternative explanation that there are a menu of potential choices, all of which might bring similarly profitable levels of return. The Act could help change this perception by showing that low income lending is profitable, but the affirmative action ideology could reinforce those cultural stereotypes about the lack of creditworthiness of low income consumers. Just as liberal models of the welfare state which provide residual aid to the targeted poor may stigmatise and solidify class divisions, so the affirmative action model of the Community Reinvestment Act may have similar consequences for low income borrowers.

A further approach which is reflected in more recent developments under the Community Reinvestment Act and other programmes are the greater variety of approaches which banks may take to comply with their obligations under the Act. These include investment in private sector financial intermediaries whose goal is community development, or investment in community banks and community venture capital funds. One of the advantages of this approach is that banks can harness the greater knowledge which these institutions have of their communities. This approach provides greater autonomy to community institutions which may demonstrate that, given the right circumstances, it is profitable to invest in traditionally depressed areas. One particular approach is micro-lending and micro-enterprise funds which has been used in several countries and draws on a variety of models such as the Grameen Bank in Bangladesh. These institutions generally provide small loans to individuals to permit them to start their own businesses. In Canada, the Women's Rural Enterprise Loan Fund provides capital to individuals who are not considered eligible for loans by lending institutions due to credit history, insufficient collateral or the small amount requested. A conventional response of lenders for small business loans of $5,000 is that the applicant use a credit card, an extremely expensive form of credit. Many of these loan programmes have low default rates, suggesting that lending to the poor is not the inherently risky proposition which is suggested sometimes by conventional wisdom. The Grameen Bank has a repayment rate of 98 per cent.[19] These programmes have potential as alternative institutional models of lending and saving. They may provide greater empowerment to individuals while also tapping into ideas of community. There have been many criticisms, particularly by feminist groups of both the intrusive and disempowering institutions of welfare state administration and of discrimination by mainstream lenders. Over 90 per cent of the Grameen Bank loans have been made to women. It is possible therefore that these institutions may form a small part of a new model of 'positive welfare'[20] where the objective is not solely economic redistribution but rather the amelioration of cultural exclusion and marginalization and an increase in autonomy and self-reliance. There are much higher levels of political involvement measured by voter turn out, among the borrowers from the Grameen Bank so that there is a connection between access to credit and citizenship. Indeed, Muhammed Yunus, the founder of the bank, argues that credit is such a basic need that it should be regarded as a human right. 'It is the beginning of economic life.'[21]

6.   CONCLUSION

This discussion of aspects of inequality in markets for consumer services illustrates the extent to which ideologies such as 'freedom of contract' act as constraints on challenging the existing institutional structure of lending. Too little attention has been paid to the shaping effects of the institutional structures of markets because of a belief that existing structures represent the natural development of market practices. If such a belief were ever sustainable, it seems difficult to maintain in the present international economy. On the one hand comparative research is increasingly identifying the

---

19.   See 'Great Hopes from Little Loans Grow', *Financial Times,* 14 August 1998 at p. 10.
20.   See A. Giddens, *Beyond Right and Left* (Polity Press, 1994) where he discusses the concept of positive welfare.
21.   Op. cit., n. 19.

variety of institutional alternatives, as exemplified by the different possibilities in the transition from communism to capitalism in Eastern Europe. At
the same time the first world, with its growth of an underclass, seems to
face similar problems to those which stimulated the development of the
Grameen Bank. In the area of financial services there is the need for much
greater experimentation in the provision of financial services if they are to
meet the needs of all consumers.

INDEX

International Banking, Finance and Economic Law

1. J. J. Norton, Chia-Jui Cheng and I. Fletcher (eds.): *International Banking Regulation and Supervision: Change and Transformation in the 1990s*. 1994
ISBN 1-85333-998-9

2. J. J. Norton, Chia-Jui Cheng and I. Fletcher (eds.): *International Banking Operations and Practices: Current Developments*. 1994
ISBN 1-85333-997-0

3. J. J. Norton: *Devising International Bank Supervisory Standards*. 1995.
ISBN 1-85966-1858

4. Sir Joseph Gold: *Interpretation: The IMF and International Law*. 1996
ISBN 90-411-0887-4

5. R. Smits: *The European Central Bank: Institutional Aspects*. 1997.
ISBN 90-411-0686-3

6. M. Andenas, L. Gormley, C. Hadjiemmanuil, I. Harden (eds.): *European Economic and Monetary Union: The Institutional Framework*. 1997
ISBN 90-411-0687-1

7. T. Wan: *Development of Banking Law in the Greater China Area: PRC and Taiwan*. 1999
ISBN 90-411-0948-X

8. R. P. Buckley: *Emerging Markets Debt: An Analysis of the Secondary Market*. 1999.
ISBN 90-411-9716-8

KLUWER LAW INTERNATIONAL – THE HAGUE / LONDON / BOSTON